D0061655

Chicken Soup for the Soul: The Cat Really Did That?
101 Stories of Miracles, Mischief, and Magical Moments
Amy Newmark. Foreword by Dr. Robin Ganzert

Published by Chicken Soup for the Soul, LLC www.chickensoup.com
Copyright ©2017 by Chicken Soup for the Soul, LLC. All Rights Reserved.

The publisher gratefully acknowledges the many publishers and individuals who
granted Chicken Soup for the Soul permission to reprint the cited material.

Front cover photo courtesy of iStockphoto.com/Maravic (©Maravic)
Back cover photo of cat with toy courtesy of iStockphoto.com/gabes1976 (©gabes1976)
Back cover photo of cat with yarn courtesy of iStockphoto.com/heatheralvis
(©heatheralvis)
Interior photo artwork courtesy of iStockphoto.com/heatheralvis (©heatheralvis)
Photo of Amy Newmark courtesy of Susan Morrow at SwickPix
Photo of Robin Ganzert courtesy of Michael Price

Cover and Interior by Daniel Zaccari

Distributed to the booktrade by Simon & Schuster. SAN: 200-2442

Publisher's Cataloging-In-Publication Data
(Prepared by The Donohue Group, Inc.)

Names: Newmark, Amy, compiler. | Ganzert, Robin, writer of supplementary
    textual content.
Title: Chicken soup for the soul : the cat really did that? : 101 stories
    of miracles, mischief, and magical moments / [compiled by] Amy
    Newmark ; foreword by Dr. Robin Ganzert, President and CEO, American
    Humane.
Other Titles: Cat really did that? : 101 stories of miracles, mischief,
    and magical moments
Description: [Cos Cob, Connecticut] : Chicken Soup for the Soul, LLC,
    [2017]
Identifiers: LCCN 2017942298 | ISBN 978-1-61159-970-1 (print) | ISBN
    978-1-61159-270-2 (ebook)
Subjects: LCSH: Cats--Behavior--Literary collections. | Cats--Behavior--
    Anecdotes. | Cat owners--Literary collections. | Cat owners--Anecdotes.
    | Human-animal relationships--Literary collections. | Human-animal
    relationships--Anecdotes. | LCGFT: Anecdotes.
Classification: LCC SF445.5 .C453 2017 (print) | LCC SF445.5 (ebook) | DDC
    636.8/002--dc23

PRINTED IN THE UNITED STATES OF AMERICA
on acid∞free paper

25 24 23 22 21 20 19 18 17   01 02 03 04 05 06 07 08 09 10 11

101 Stories of Miracles, Mischief, and Magical Moments

Amy Newmark

Foreword by Dr. Robin Ganzert
President and CEO, American Humane

CSS

Chicken Soup for the Soul, LLC
Cos Cob, CT

Chicken Soup for the Soul

Changing lives one story at a time®
www.chickensoup.com

Table of Contents

❸
~Who Me?~

❹
~Learning What's Important~

❺
~A Purrfect Life~

❻
~My Heroic Cat~

❼
~Four-Legged Therapists~

❽

~Eight Lives and Counting~

❾

~My Goofy Cat~

❿
~Meant to Be~

Foreword

Cats are the most amazing creatures. They are fascinating, independent, goofy, brave, hilarious, and beautiful. They entertain us, inspire us, and make us feel loved. For those of us who know and love cats, every day is *Caturday*!

As I am writing this, my own feline, Rosebud, wants me to be sure to let you know that she is a rescue and has her own amazing journey to share. Rosebud was found several years ago in a storm drain and placed in a foster home with other cats, dogs, and even a few parrots.

Rosebud doesn't get along well with others and she has a strong independent streak we refer to as cat-titude, so Rosebud's foster mom needed to find the purr-fect home for her. She called me and said this cat was destined for me.

With two cats and three dogs already living in a house with my three children, I was wondering how Rosebud would adapt to our home. But she quickly found herself a new Best Friend Forever in my daughter Aidan. Rosebud ignored the other cats and dogs, and focused her attention on Aidan. Several years have passed, and now Aidan is moving into her first apartment after graduate school. Rosebud will be joining her in Atlanta soon. I look at the beautiful bond between Aidan and Rosebud and it warms my heart.

That bond is the underlying theme of all the heartwarming stories that fill *Chicken Soup for the Soul: The Cat Really Did That?* There are tales of amazing rescues, where the cats display such amazing tenacity and resilience that you'll be inspired to overcome whatever challenges you have in your own life. There are stories of rascals and goofballs that will help you gain perspective on what really matters in life and teach you to relax and go with the flow. You'll probably tear up when you read the stories about cats changing human lives and acting like four-legged therapists. And then there are the hero cats, the ones that save their humans from fires and crime and perform other miracles.

You'll find yourself laughing a lot, too, as you read about some truly crazy cats. I laughed out loud reading the story "Fashion Diva," about a male kitty who loves wearing costumes and wins contests. What the diva doesn't know is that he's wearing dog costumes, because he's a rather large kitty and can't fit into the cat outfits!

When you read "The Pair," in which an introverted, autistic girl picks out a shy, frightened cat at the shelter, you'll be amazed by how the two of them blossom once they are put together. There truly is a special cat for everyone, with every need, at your local shelter.

And being an animal rescuer, I just loved the story "One of a Kind," in which the family rescued the feral kitten, and the kitten ends up saving the family from a fire and a burglar! As animal rescuers often say, who rescued whom?

And as a proud parent of several senior pets, I cried over the story "Kindred Spirits," where an elderly lady visits a shelter for weeks and finally adopts the senior cat she has fallen for as her new BFF. It's such a powerful reminder of the value of adopting senior cats.

If you love cat-titude, humorous antics, and heartwarming adventures, be prepared to fall in love with these stories and these precious cats. I am so grateful that Chicken Soup for the Soul has brought us yet another series of stories that will melt your heart and hopefully encourage you to open your home to a new cat.

Cats make purr-fect pets for some people, but it's important to remember that although they appear to be very independent, they are actually dependent on us humans for their needs. We provide the food, water, medical attention, shelter, and companionship, and they provide us with years of unconditional love and devotion that far outweigh the daily responsibilities.

If you wish to have a feline join your family (and I hope you do!), remember to consider the following:

- Do you want a kitten or an adult cat? Kittens need a lot of attention and will have to be house-trained. On the plus side, they do adapt well to their new home and surroundings. But for many people, especially those who work outside the home, an adult cat is a wiser choice.
- Do you want a long or shorthaired cat? Longhaired cats require daily brushing to keep their fur from matting, so be prepared to spend time grooming your new feline best friend.
- Do you want a male or female? Both male and female felines can be equally playful and affectionate! Gender is purely a personal preference.

You may be the purr-fect cat owner if you…

- Believe caring for a pet for fifteen to eighteen years does not seem like a lifetime.
- Look forward to having your ankles rubbed by an affectionate, loving creature.
- Don't mind sharing your house with someone who sheds.
- Don't mind sharing your house with someone who will never clean up after herself.
- Love a housemate who will randomly and regularly entertain you with outrageous and silly antics, at his whim, not yours!

Set the stage for a life filled with love and companionship by adopting a cat from your local shelter. American Humane created Adopt A Cat Month® in 1983, and every year since, during the month of June, we have encouraged adoptions from local animal shelters. But those of us who know how much fun it is to have cats in our lives know that *every* day is *Caturday*, and *every* month should be "Adopt a Cat" month!

Once you adopt a feline friend, be sure to care for your cat by remembering the following:

- Twice is nice. Visit your veterinarian twice a year to keep your kitty healthy and happy.
- No tubby tabbies! Lower the risk of obesity by feeding your cat the right food and providing exercise. Ask your veterinarian about the right diet for your cat based on his age and activity.
- Don't bug me. It's easy to prevent parasites with year-round protection.
- Lost and found. Be sure to get your feline micro-chipped!
- Cleanliness counts. Use proper sized litter boxes for better cleanliness.
- Play for prey. Cats need exercise and play, so be sure to provide toys and activities.
- The More the Merrier! Cats are social, and adopting two or more provides for a loving home.

So if inspiration strikes after enjoying these purr-fect stories, please visit your local shelter to adopt a new best friend. Remember, there is no greater love than that of a cat. And thank goodness they have nine lives, since they have so much love to give!

And while you are enjoying this collection, know that Chicken Soup for the Soul is generously donating part of the proceeds from your purchase of this book to American Humane, allowing us to save more lives of our animal friends. Thank you for making a difference and for helping us to build a more humane world!

~Dr. Robin Ganzert
President and CEO, American Humane

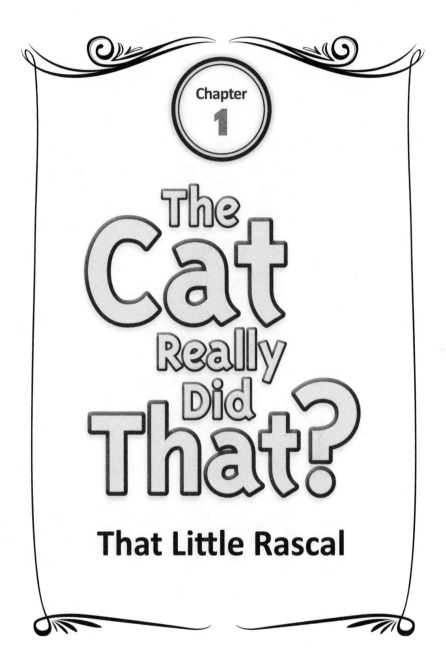

Chapter
1

The Cat Really Did That?

That Little Rascal

A Cat Named Icky

My relationship with cats has saved me
from a deadly, pervasive ignorance.
~William S. Burroughs

One morning in early spring a scruffy-looking, shorthaired, gray-and-white cat showed up on my front porch. I really didn't want to adopt a pet, so even though the cat was friendly and way too thin, I did not feed, pet, or encourage him in any way.

Regrettably, the cat didn't take the hint. After he hung around for a few days, I broke down and scratched him between the ears. I put food and water bowls on the porch. Evidently, that convinced the cat he was home, and he never left.

The next week, after a visit to the vet, I allowed him to move into the house. I named him Ichabod, because for some reason he reminded me of Ichabod Crane from *The Legend of Sleepy Hollow* — so the named seemed appropriate.

Unfortunately, my three-year-old niece couldn't pronounce Ichabod, so she shortened the cat's name to Icky — and that's the moniker that stuck.

A cat named Icky.

It was mid-May by the time winter finally released its frozen grasp that year, and I started working on preparing the flower and vegetable gardens every afternoon when I got home from work. Icky was my constant companion in the garden, following me around as I weeded, hoed, and pruned. Every day, after a short while outside, Icky would fall asleep in the warm sunshine and continue to nap until I called him inside for his dinner.

That spring the garden was invaded by snails. Well, maybe "invaded" is the wrong word considering the speed at which snails move, but the newly forming vegetation was besieged by the slimy critters. They nibbled the nasturtiums, bit the begonias, gobbled the gladioli, and devoured the daisies, all while sluggishly slithering along at, well, at a snail's pace.

It was frustrating that I couldn't stop the slowly creeping creatures. I plucked snails off the pansies, flicked them off the forsythia, rinsed them off the rutabagas, and even squashed a few on the squash. It did no good; every morning, there were more snails.

I called a local gardening center and asked for an environmentally friendly way to alleviate the infestation. They suggested placing shallow bowls of beer around the garden. Supposedly, the odor of the beer would attract the snails. They would sip the liquid, become inebriated, and slide into the bowls, leading to their demise. I felt a little guilty but I was desperate enough to give the idea a try.

The next afternoon, I stopped at the market to buy a six-pack of cheap beer and some shallow bowls. As soon as I got home, I put out my defensive weapons.

That evening, like always, I called for Icky to come in and eat. Usually he hurried in the door, but not that evening. I stood on the front porch and called a few more times. When Icky did not appear, I slipped on my shoes and went out to search for him.

As I was wandering around the garden, Icky suddenly stumbled out from between two rosebushes with his tail drooping. He shook his head, turned in a circle, and fell forward onto the ground. He meowed loudly as he got back up on wobbly legs. Something was obviously very wrong, and I rushed to Icky, scooping him up in my arms. He purred loudly as he cuddled against me and attempted to lick my cheek.

One whiff of the cat's breath and I knew.

"Oh, no," I groaned. "Icky, you're drunk!"

A quick inspection showed what had occurred. Most of the beer-filled bowls I had left out for snail traps were empty. I didn't know a lot about cats, but I assumed this was not good.

Should I administer some aspirin? Make a pot of strong, black coffee? Perhaps a cold shower? What was the best remedy for a blotto feline? I had no idea, so I called the vet.

"Oh, dear," said the vet. "Beer can be toxic to cats. How much did he drink?"

"At least half a bottle," I explained. "He's really plastered."

"Well, just try to keep him calm. Hopefully, he'll sleep it off in a few hours. Just watch for vomiting or diarrhea."

"He's already sound asleep on the couch," I said. "He had no interest in food when I brought him in, so I'll just let him snooze and keep an eye on him."

Icky didn't move from his spot on the couch all night. Luckily, after a good night's rest, he recovered in time to join me in the garden the following afternoon. As far as I know, he has never imbibed again.

Icky continues to wander in the yard with me while I garden, and I continue my battle against the snails. Needless to say, I never attempted the beer-baited traps again.

Nowadays, I use bowls filled with a sugar-water-and-yeast mixture that works similarly to the beer to help control the snails — but doesn't intoxicate my cat.

~David Hull

One Click

Way down deep, we're all motivated by the same
urges. Cats have the courage to live by them.
~Jim Davis

annah, a college girl who fostered strays, walked out of her apartment one day to discover a tiny orange kitten lurking at her door. She thought he was feral because he quickly ran away. The next day, the kitty returned. This time, he scratched at the door, so Hannah assumed he was hungry. He even rolled over, revealing his fluffy, white belly, and produced a purr so loud it was almost an exaggeration. Next came a pitiful, manipulative meow, as if pleading for a meal. Of course, kindhearted Hannah fell for it and fed him.

Eventually, Hannah took the two-month-old tabby to be placed for adoption at the Humane Society of Dallas County Dog & Kitty City. They named him Cheeto.

That's where I came in, broken-hearted from the loss of our beloved Squeaky, a cat who had graced our lives for seventeen years. I was getting older, so I was looking for a maintenance-free kitty, if there was such a thing.

A gray kitten in a cage reached out to me, scratching my hand slightly and producing a few drops of blood. Simultaneously, a veterinary nurse was vaccinating Cheeto.

"Here. Hold him," she said to me. I grabbed the fidgety little creature as he bled from his shot onto my bleeding hand. Our blood got co-mingled. That clinched it.

"It's destiny! We were meant for each other," I said.

I took him home and changed his name to Ollie.

Have you noticed that regardless of their humble beginnings, some cats develop an entitlement attitude from the get-go?

Ollie had nothing but the fur on his back when he came into our lives. His story could be "From Rags to Riches," because he soon had toys, mechanical mice, strings, feathers, and balls. He had a different cat bed in each of three rooms, yet he slept with us in our bed. He received a scratching post as a "Welcome to Your New Home" gift from a friend. He had a cat condo with three levels. Before long, however, he turned his nose up at any toy or gift more than a few days old.

And he was even in our will. If anything were to happen to us, we bequeathed Ollie to our granddaughter, Lindsey.

One day, my husband and I decided to buy a new bed. I did an online search while Ollie was comfortably curled up in a designer shoebox by my keyboard. He was always by my side when I surfed the Internet, basking in the light and heat of the computer. Sometimes, I'd go to a cat site, and together we would peruse the latest craze in cat toys. He might give a high-five to the screen, indicating which item pleased him.

But back to the Internet search. I remembered sleeping on a wonderfully relaxing mattress at a hotel. It was the Westin Hotel Heavenly Bed. I was so pleased to find it on Amazon. I clicked to place it in my shopping cart but once it was there, I saw the very high shipping charge, so I didn't go through with the purchase.

"See what you can find locally," suggested my husband. "You could always go back online if you don't find it in a store."

The next day, I found the perfect mattress at a local mall. Free delivery. It arrived a couple of days later.

Soon after we were happily sleeping on our new bed I received a somewhat garbled message on our answering machine: "Here to deliver your (unintelligible). What's (unintelligible) address?"

He left a number that I couldn't understand, so I ignored it. I figured it was a wrong number or a telemarketer.

The next day came another message: "I'm in Dallas and have your mattress on my truck. Where do you want it delivered?"

The man left a number, and I called him right back. "There must be some mistake. They've already delivered our bed. We've been sleeping on it for several days now," I told him.

"Lady, all I know is I have a Heavenly Bed on my truck, and I drove all the way to Dallas to bring it to you, as ordered."

Once I heard "Heavenly Bed," I realized what must have happened. I knew I had put the bed in my cart, but I also knew I had never completed the transaction. No one had access to my computer but me... and *Ollie*!

Maybe it was my fault for leaving my computer unattended, but who would have dreamed a cat would walk on my keyboard and hit just the right, or wrong, keys? I guess all it took was one step, literally, to enable the 1-Click feature and complete the order.

Amazon was so understanding. They referred me to the mattress vendor, saying, "If it's fraud, they will work with you."

I tried to explain it wasn't fraud. My privileged cat, who has three beds of his own, but prefers ours, was the perp. I'm not sure the vendor believed that my cat placed the order, but they eventually agreed to cancel it.

That's how Ollie became "the cat who *almost* purchased a Heavenly Bed on Amazon."

Since then, I sign off my computer when I leave it unattended. With Ollie's taste for fine things, there's no telling what that cat will order next!

~Eva Carter

Hide and Seek

I have studied many philosophers and many cats.
The wisdom of cats is infinitely superior.
~Hippolyte Taine

He had been found wandering, weak and hungry, when he was rescued. Given his penchant for drinking from the water faucet, I suspect that's how he managed to survive. The vet estimated that this beautiful, mink-colored Siamese was just shy of a year old.

The staff of the Humane Society that took him in named him DC, short for "Darn Cat." I met DC when I took my two Cockapoos to be groomed at the Humane Society, an event they always dreaded, as evidenced by their trembling and crying. When I picked them up that afternoon, the groomer pointed to DC and told me how the cat had jumped onto the groomer's table and sat calmly with each dog as it was groomed, easing its fears and forming a heartwarming bond. Since DC was about to be put up for adoption, I jumped at the chance. My dogs obviously loved him, and his personality stole my heart. He quickly bonded with me and my husband, acting as though he had known us all his life.

Often we would find him hiding under a throw rug or cuddled into the back of a recliner. If not playing hide-and-seek, he and the dogs would take turns chasing each other through the house, up and down the stairs, and in a circle from the kitchen to the living room, to the dining room and back to the kitchen. They loved to cuddle together for naps and they became inseparable friends.

One day became forever etched in my memory. It was especially hectic as I tried to get the house straightened up, furniture dusted, supper planned, dishes put away, and laundry done. I transferred the first load of wash into the dryer and placed a second load in the washer. The family room was in need of a good vacuuming, so I lugged the vacuum out of the hall closet and down to the family room, plugged it in and moved some items out of the way. Just as I was about to turn it on, I heard a strange soft thump, then several more muted thumps, evenly spaced, several seconds apart. I knew I hadn't put any sneakers in the dryer, so what might it be?

Suddenly, I knew. I raced to the dryer and frantically started pulling out wet towels. As I had feared, there was DC, buried in towels. He was hot, dizzy, and smelled of wet fur. Apparently, he thought the dryer would be a great hiding place, and he had jumped in unnoticed.

I carried him to the next room and carefully placed him on the floor. He rested on his side, panting heavily. The dogs rushed to his side, licking him and whining softly. He seemed to feel the love and responded meekly with a little meow. No doubt he was sore from the tumbling he had endured, but apparently the towels had cushioned him, protecting him against broken bones and internal injuries.

The dogs and I sat next to him, gently soothing him with soft touches and encouraging words. After about ten minutes, his breathing slowed, and he sat up cautiously. He tried to take a few staggering steps, but vertigo got the better of him. He lay back down and willingly drank some water from a syringe.

As he relaxed, I folded some laundry and carried it up to my bedroom. I debated with myself about taking him to the vet or giving him a while longer to recuperate. After a few minutes, DC climbed the stairs, joined me in the bedroom, and jumped up on the bed as though nothing had happened. With a sigh of relief, I knew he was going to be okay. The dogs followed behind him and settled down on the floor next to the bed as though vowing never to let him out of their sight.

Thankfully, DC never used the dryer as a hiding place again, but I never turned it on after that without checking first to be sure he was safe.

We enjoyed twelve more years with DC until he passed quietly in his sleep. Our lives were made much richer for the love and antics of this little character. That adorable "Darn Cat" will live forever in our hearts.

~Marti Robards

The Rescue

If you're curious, you'll probably be a good journalist
because we follow our curiosity like cats.
~Diane Sawyer

is glowing eyes gave him away. I spotted him hiding under our porch—a tiny thing with scaly, bald patches where there should have been black fur. So I did the only rational thing—I grabbed an empty box, laid my trap, and scooped him up. Bringing him inside, I wondered how I'd explain this to my husband. We are both very allergic to cats, so convincing him to let me help this tiny kitten would take all of my persuasive powers.

Opening the box in the light of my kitchen, I discovered the situation was worse than I had thought. He was malnourished and missing large amounts of fur all over his shaking body. I could feel his tiny bones and his swollen belly. I determined he couldn't be more than four weeks old—so young to have suffered so much already.

Luckily for me, my husband is as much of a sap as I am. So, we loaded up on allergy medicine and settled in to nourish our rescued kitten back to health. Most of his ailments were cured with lots of food and attention. The bald patches were easy enough to fix after a trip to the vet.

Before we knew it, he was running around the house at full speed and causing all sorts of mischief. He liked to hide in the most random places and wait for us to pass by. Once we were close enough, he would pounce out on our feet, scare the daylights out of us, and bound off before the screams were fully out of our mouths. For some reason, he only played this game when we had been home for hours. If we left the house, he would come running to the door to greet us when we returned.

So, imagine my surprise when we came home from the gym, and there wasn't a cat winding his way around our feet. It seemed very odd, but I wasn't too worried at first. I called his name, expecting him to come running, but he didn't appear. My husband and I checked his usual spots, but he was nowhere to be found. So we checked again. And again. We grew more frantic as time passed. After an hour of calling his name and checking every room, we grew worried that he had somehow escaped. But a quick check of the windows and doors proved they were all locked and secured. After another hour, I became convinced that some criminal had literally "cat-burgled" us. I just knew that someone had broken in, seen how awesome our cat was, and stolen him!

I tried to remember what people do when a cat goes missing. Did they put up signs? Offer a reward? I had never had a missing pet, and I felt as lost as I thought he was. My husband figured we had done everything we could for the night, so he set out dinner and tossed a load of laundry in the washing machine. As soon as the washing machine hit the spin cycle, we heard it: a loud, wailing *meoooooow*!

Jumping up, we ran to the washing machine, opening the lid to find nothing but wet, sudsy laundry. We stared at each other, trying to determine where the sound had come from, when we heard it again. *Meoooooow.*

It had definitely come from the washing machine, but it was clear he wasn't inside the machine. So where was he? I looked on the sides and between the washer and dryer, but there was no sign of him. Climbing on top of the washing machine, I peeked over the back.

Again, his glowing eyes gave him away. He was upside-down with his arms and legs spread as far as they could go, stuck between the wall and the washing machine. His eyes were open incredibly wide with a look of pure panic, and he let out another screeching *meoooooow*. I reached down and rescued him from his precarious position, laughing with relief. Later, we determined he had climbed on top of the washing machine, slipped and fell behind it, and then somehow grabbed onto the small vents in the back of the machine on his way down.

Needless to say, that was the very last day he climbed on anything again. All of his surprise attacks now come from much closer to the ground!

~Jessica Edwards

My Musical Cat

*There are two means of refuge from the
misery of life: music and cats.*
~Albert Schweitzer

t was that kind of a day. I looked forward to coming home to my cat. "Boo!" I called. But, as usual, he didn't come to me. Weren't pets supposed to comfort a person? Was I chopped liver? Apparently, I wasn't because if I were actually chopped liver, Boo would not be ignoring me.

I found him in the kitchen. He was swishing his tail as he gobbled his food. "There you are," I said, petting him. "Why didn't you come to me?"

Boo stopped eating for a second and gazed up at me with his green eyes. "Meow?" he said, with an inquisitive look.

I knew Boo was smart. So, why was he ignoring me when I called him? It seemed the only time he came running was when I opened a can of cat food.

"You know you are supposed to come to me when I call you," I scolded. "Don't you know you're reinforcing all the negative stereotypes about cats?"

I petted him for a while and then left the kitchen. I strolled over to the piano and started playing. Next thing I knew, Boo had raced into the room and leapt up on the piano bench. He was rubbing his face against my arm, purring, as I tried to play the song.

"Hey, move out of the way. I'm trying to reach for a chord." That didn't stop him. He kept head-butting my arm in a state of bliss.

I rolled my eyes. "Just like a male. When I want you, you won't come, and when I don't call you, you're all over me."

A few weeks later, a friend was visiting. "Play something on the piano," she said.

I launched into song. Within a few minutes, Boo had jumped on the bench beside me, purring.

My friend laughed. "Wow, your cat really likes the way you play."

"Yeah, he does," I said. That's when it dawned on me. Boo always jumped up on the piano bench when I was playing. My cat loved the piano!

One night after that, I was awakened from a sound sleep when I heard piano notes tinkling. Trembling, I sneaked down the stairs, flashlight in hand.

My flashlight panned the room as I clutched the banister and shook in my slippers. There was something on the piano. It was moving. My flashlight beam fell upon it. Boo was walking on the piano keys.

"Really, Boo? At two o'clock in the morning?"

It became our routine. Every time I played the piano, Boo leapt up on the bench. Obviously, he loved the piano more than me. I went on with my life.

When another friend came over with his guitar, Boo rubbed against his ankles as he strummed the chords.

"Strange. Your cat isn't like other cats. He's so friendly," said my friend, who was a dog person.

"He likes the way you play."

A few days later, I was sitting on the couch singing my favorite song. As I sang, a dark, plump blur dashed across the room and dived into my lap. It was Boo. He kneaded my lap and kissed my face as I sang.

Wow, I thought. *Boo loves the way I sing.*

And then, I had a horrible thought. *What if he hates the way I sing, and he's trying to shut me up?* I banished the thought immediately.

Boo did not act like a cat who hated my singing. He was purring, happily rubbing his whiskers against my chin in bliss. He kneaded my lap. And right in the middle of the song, he snuggled in my lap, purring like a kitten, and drifted off to sleep.

It happened again and again. Every time I sang that song, if Boo was in earshot, he would stop everything he was doing and come running. I never saw anything like it. I never knew a plump cat could move so fast and defy the laws of gravity while soaring in the air to reach my lap. It was now obvious that he truly loved all music, not just the piano.

Yet when I came home from work, he was nowhere to be found when I called out his name. "Boo, where are you?" My voice echoed through the house.

This is ridiculous, I thought. *He only comes running when he hears the sound of a can opening. Or… when he hears music.*

I decided to put him to the test. I launched into his favorite song. There was a loud clatter from upstairs, and then thumping as his heavy body dashed down the stairs. He skidded into the room in front of me.

"Meow?" he said.

I was delighted.

I kept singing. He purred some more.

I don't bother to call Boo anymore. If I want Boo to come to me, I launch into his favorite song, and he will move heaven and earth to find me.

Sometimes, when he is in the middle of joyous rapture, purring to the sound of a piano, guitar, or singing, I wonder if he's really a frustrated musician trapped in a cat's body. No, that couldn't be possible, could it?

~L.A. Strucke

Our Marmalade Safecracker

All I do is eat and sleep. Eat and sleep. Eat and
sleep. There must be more to a cat's life
than that. But I hope not.
~Garfield

R ansom's mind revolved around two things — naps and food. The rescue shelter's staff had warned us. Whether it was dry kibble or juicy live critters, Ransom didn't care as long as food was readily available. This became a problem since this hulk of an orange marmalade cat never knew when to stop.

Through the years, we tried several devices to slow his gluttony. For a while, a bowl with upright prongs regulated his intake — until he learned to flip the dish and spill out the food. Never satisfied with twice-a-day feedings, he'd shadow us, yowling, "I'm huu-n-gry," until we caved. In between the caterwauling, he'd sleep off the meal on the back of my favorite chair, only to wake ready to beg again.

When we switched to feeding him small, frequent, grazing portions, Ransom's attention switched to a more paws-on approach for acquiring kibble. Plastic or paper, he chewed through every package after prying open any cabinet door we hid it behind. The result of his scarf-and-barf behavior often left my dear husband calling for "cleanup in hallway five."

We resorted to locking his food within Tupperware. The Cereal

Keeper turned into great entertainment for two bored, empty nesters like us. First Ransom would crash the Tupperware to the floor. We would high-five each other, believing we'd finally outfoxed the thief. He would paw at the airtight seal tirelessly.

Then, one day, Ransom managed to work it open. My husband soon resembled the comic-strip character Jon, waging war over food with Garfield. Always hungry, that cat, like our own, resorts to clever and conniving ways to get food. Perhaps this is a common characteristic amongst ego-driven, marmalade cats.

My husband, not a great lover of felines, would promptly reset the container and cinch down the lid. Garfield—I mean Ransom—waited until my husband settled into the recliner before head-butting the container. Then the cat worked his paw around and around the lid. We expected him to grow frustrated, but with practice, Ransom became deft at peeling the seal off with one smooth move.

My husband continually relocated the container higher and higher, only to have Ransom scale greater elevations while we were away. The alpha males' contest ended when a souvenir lay shattered on the floor. That night, the cat's food was secured within an empty, plastic cat-litter container with a theft-proof, screw-top lid. That wasn't a big problem for Ransom, though. We heard him in the wee hours of the morning, sliding his stash steadfastly across the living-room hardwood floor, determined to crack this lock.

One Sunday afternoon while we watched television, Ransom, after licking the crumbs from his bowl, waited expectantly for us to notice him sitting beside his food jug. To gain our attention, he ran his claws politely down the container's ribbed side. The sound he made seemed to please him.

He strummed away at his improvised washboard musical instrument while defiantly glaring at us. And then it happened. He put his two front paws around that screw-top lid, and somehow he managed to twist it in the right direction. Apparently, that day, I'd barely tightened the thing. With only two swipes—pay dirt! Food spilled across the floor. Ransom choked down mouthfuls of kibble before my husband jumped from the recliner and confiscated the loot.

Maybe a marmalade cat's larger head holds a few more brain cells, allowing the cat more reasoning to achieve its goals. Where my other cats had been content to lounge in patches of sunlight and wait for their meals to appear, this cat did not. We'd find our cat staring down the container as if he possessed some telekinetic power to move objects with his mind.

He began stalking the container, checking if the lid was fastened down tight. He'd stand with one front leg around the container's shoulder. Then he'd brush his other paw along the lid's side as if to spin it.

One evening, the elements of the universe aligned. A claw caught against the textured surface. The lid loosened a bit. Encouraged, he clawed the cap again and again, hooking the lid occasionally until it started turning with each advancing swipe. Finally, it clattered to the floor. With one shoulder, the big cat toppled the jug and then crouched down to gorge on his prize.

Soon this skilled safecracker could spin that lid using both his paws with the speed of a Rubik's cube champion. Not to be outwitted, and because we, too, still needed to open the container — though my husband had considered gluing it shut — we wedged the container between two heavy planters so the thing couldn't tip over. Though this made it much harder for me to feed the cat, neither my husband nor Ransom seemed to mind. By now, safecracking was second nature to our feline.

One could almost hear him thinking as he turned that lid: *And now, what shall I choose? A gray kibble morsel or a red one?*

Settling himself onto his haunches, the maestro went to work. Holding up one paw before his face, splaying it out wide, he cleaned it thoroughly — or so I thought. Instead, he'd discovered that a wet paw sliding through the open slot brought up pay dirt every time, with bits of food sticking both between the pads of his toes and onto his fur.

It didn't matter what we tried, our cat burglar could open any container. Finally, we settled on leaving good enough alone. By keeping the liter container less than half full, we found a solution we could all live with. The challenge of hoisting food out with his wet paw gave him some exercise and slowed down his eating.

The whole thing never ceases to amuse us. My husband likes to tease me, too, pointing out that our cat's figured out the righty-tighty, lefty-loosey rule, and yet I still struggle to hook up a garden hose.

~Susan A. Hoffert

The Power of Purr-sistence

*A cat's eyes are windows enabling us
to see into another world.*
~Irish Saying

I browsed the cages at the adoption event, looking for the perfect cat to take home. Meows and purrs abounded as sweet, furry faces peered at me. After walking to the end of a long row, I felt a firm tap on my shoulder. Turning, I saw a gray tiger-striped tabby had reached out a paw to get my attention. Charmed at his bravado, I rubbed his ears. He closed his eyes and purred as loudly as my neighbor's noisy pickup truck. This cat wasn't the least bit shy, and I decided on the spot he would be mine.

From the first moment Bogey sauntered into his new home, it was obvious he would take command. First, he explored the area by sniffing every corner. Then he quickly discovered the best hiding places, flirting with potential attractions such as my new curtains. By the time he curled up on the bed and purred his approval, I wasn't quite sure what I'd gotten myself into.

Before long, Bogey gained several new skills. He figured out how to open cabinet doors to climb inside. He discovered that the bathroom contained plenty of toilet paper for him to unfurl. He even learned how to open the sliding glass door and let himself into the yard. No matter how much I corrected his behavior, he'd only rub against my legs and purr loudly.

I learned to secure every door.

If I dared to set an item on a counter or a table, Bogey would leap up and paw all but the heaviest items straight to the floor — whether they were breakable or not. Assuming a look of innocence, he'd then purr helpfully while I cleaned up the mess.

I learned to put things away.

While I was at the computer trying to work, Bogey would push himself to recline half on my lap and half on the keyboard, preventing me from typing. I would lift him off, and he'd immediately return to his position on my lap, stretching himself as long as he could to cover the maximum area. This routine would go on indefinitely if I didn't relent and let him stay where he wanted. Bogey cemented his victory with closed eyes and ecstatic purrs of contentment.

I learned to push my arms and elbows out wide and work around him.

Any time I sat down to read, Bogey was right by my side. He pushed his head against the book and within seconds insinuated his entire body between the page and me. Then he'd reach both front paws across my chest as though to hold me down. Redirecting him only made him more determined. He returned to the same position, more like a boomerang than a cat. When I finally sighed and gave in to his wishes, he again rewarded me with deafening purrs.

I learned to put my book off to the side. I can still see it, and I am not interfering with His Majesty's desired position.

The cats I knew before were reserved and aloof. Bogey has never been anything but bold and brassy. But as the years have passed, I've learned to admire Bogey's tenacity. He never gives up, and it has paid off.

We've formed a relationship based on mutual respect: He lets me know what he wants, and I do it.

But there's another lesson I have learned from Bogey. Trying to stay one step ahead of a cat has enhanced some admirable qualities in me. I've become a little more patient, much more observant, and I've developed the flexibility of a yoga master.

~Pat Wahler

The Charmer

You can keep a dog; but it is the cat who keeps people,
because cats find humans useful domestic animals.
~George Mikes

He was dark black, furry, yellow-eyed and a troublemaker. He would "run away" and my grandma would always say: "Don't worry, he'll be back." And return he did. However, he always came with "baggage."

Midnight wasn't an average cat. He was a player. After each excursion he brought back a female. And she would be pregnant. So not only did we have to feed Mr. Midnight, but we also had to make sure his pregnant girlfriend was fed, too.

He made a habit of going missing so much that it became normal to us. "Has anyone seen Midnight? No? Okay, he'll be back sooner or later."

Midnight moved like a human and reminded me so much of my granddad — confident, outgoing, and charming. I could only imagine how he seduced those female cats. I wondered what kind of pickup lines he used; on second thought, he was so smooth he probably never needed them.

There was one female cat in particular that I remember. She was a beauty: with dark-gray and white fur and mesmerizing green eyes. I felt as if Midnight really loved her because he kept her around for a while. Even after she had kittens he wanted to be in her presence.

The "Green-Eyed Beauty," as I liked to call her, had a mystique about her. Like Midnight, she was confident and sure of herself. I'd watch them lie together by the front steps for hours, enjoying each other's company. I always felt like they were the feline version of my grandma and grandpa. Their love was genuine and real.

On the rare occasions that Midnight was around solo, he was a dream. It was the equivalent of sunshine after a rainy day. He filled our lives with such joy. His personality was unmatched. He had spunk and an air about himself, borderline arrogant and narcissistic.

To this day, I have no idea where Midnight came from. He could have been a rescue, stray, or someone else's, but he clung to us. He trusted us, and he reciprocated the love we gave to him. I've yet to meet another animal like him. He had so many human character traits and such a great spirit.

One day, Midnight disappeared and never returned. I don't know what happened to him, but I am grateful to have spent some of my best early years with him. Just the thought of him makes me smile. He may never know what joy he brought to our lives, but I can only hope that wherever he is now, he's spreading to others the same love he gave to our family.

~Candis Y. McDow

Timeshare Kitty

It is in the nature of cats to do a certain
amount of unescorted roaming.
~Adlai Stevenson II

Amid the hustle and bustle of friends and family transporting their dinner plates from the kitchen to the dining room, who should appear but our newest kitty, John Smith? Surprisingly unafraid of the strangers, he scurried through the legs of our guests directly to my husband, Larry, who was carving the turkey on the kitchen island. John Smith stretched his tiny frame so long that his paws almost reached the top of the counter.

"Look at him!" and "Oh, how cute" were the delighted comments of our Thanksgiving guests.

Suddenly, our next-door neighbor, Betsy, rushed to the hungry kitty, scooped him up and clutched him protectively to her chest.

"Stevie! Baby! Where have you been? What are you doing here?" she exclaimed in joyful surprise.

"What? His name is John Smith," I declared. "He's my new cat."

"It's Stevie!" insisted Betsy. "Surely I know my *own* cat."

She explained he'd been missing for weeks, and continued to cuddle him and kiss him.

"But he's our John Smith," my nine-year-old granddaughter piped up. "I named him myself."

"Didn't you see the sign with his photo that I posted on the street corner?" Betsy inquired.

I hadn't seen any sign.

"I've had him three months," I asserted.

"I've had him five," was Betsy's retort.

"Actually, we've had him eleven months," interjected my granddaughter.

Everyone laughed because the kitty was obviously nowhere near that old.

I wasn't sure how long we'd had John Smith. All I knew is one day he walked through the front door and straight into my heart.

One of the guests suggested we let the kitty decide who the rightful owner was. Betsy put him down gently on the kitchen floor, and everyone stood back to see what would happen next.

"Come here, John Smith," I softly cooed.

"Come to Mama, Stevie," coaxed Betsy.

To the amusement of the observers, the cat turned up his nose at both of us and returned to Larry, stretching up against him as far up as his little legs could reach. After all, Larry was The Magnificent Turkey Carver.

Then I placed a couple of pieces of turkey into the cat dish. Of course, it was not an attempt to bribe the cat...

"No, no, no! We don't eat people food!" Betsy spoke up, shaking her finger at me. "It's not healthy."

Betsy was one of those health nuts — I mean *enthusiasts*.

"I don't usually give him people food, but it is Thanksgiving," I replied, feeling a little miffed. "Next you're going to tell me the cat should be gluten-free," I added sarcastically.

Our guests found this interaction between Betsy and me amusing, but I didn't want to give up *my* John Smith, with his quirky personality, exquisite white fur, and two different color eyes.

John Smith enjoyed his turkey, and then, when someone opened the patio door a little later, he let himself out.

That night, as I lay in bed recalling the events of the evening, I could hear Betsy in her back yard calling, "Stevie! Here, Stevie!"

In the darkness next to my sleeping husband, no one could see the satisfied grin on my face except maybe John Smith, who was peacefully purring on my belly.

But some nights I'd hear Betsy calling his name when he wasn't with me. I'd call him, too, and when I looked out the window I would see him casually meandering in the opposite direction. I knew he could hear me. Was he in search of yet another loving family?

Sometimes, he would disappear for days.

Still assuming the primary caretaker role, I kept the appointment I had previously made to have John Smith vaccinated. I felt it was probably time to get him neutered, too, since he appeared to be about five or six months old.

As the vet examined John Smith, I asked if he was old enough to neuter. The vet's response was unexpected.

"Yes, he is old enough, but it's not a good idea," she said, smiling.

"Why not?" I asked.

"Because he has already been neutered," she laughed. Checking her files, she added, "I did it myself last month."

Then she spoke directly to him. "How are you doing, Stevie?"

So maybe Betsy had been right. Maybe he had been *her* cat in the beginning, but by now he was also *mine*.

We never did resolve whose cat he was originally. Eventually, Betsy and I reached an amicable agreement that he would be our timeshare kitty.

We made sure that he received the proper vaccinations. Betsy fed him his morning meal, and I was the dinner chef. Treats came from both sides of the fence, but we took care that he stayed slim and healthy. We agreed that having two moms was better than one.

In the coming years, John Smith (aka Stevie) strolled through the hole in the fence from our yard to Betsy's whenever he wanted. He was a cat, after all, and therefore The Boss.

~Eva Carter

10

Where's Baby Cinder?

When I play with my cat, who knows whether she is
not amusing herself with me more than I with her.
~Michel de Montaigne

Cinder was always an extremely playful cat. As her name suggests, she was a black cat, with long fur and gorgeous, big, round blue eyes. She had been the runt of the litter and was sized more like a kitten than a cat. She never weighed over seven pounds. What she lacked in size, however, she made up for in determination and playfulness. She was very special, and I often called her my "Baby Cinder."

One day, I came home from work exhausted after a long day, very slow rush-hour traffic, and a couple of errands I had to do on the way home. Normally, Cinder would run out to greet me when I arrived home, but this time… no Cinder.

I called out, "Cinder, Mommy's home."

"Baby Cinder, where are you?"

"Cinder, please come to Mommy!"

No Cinder. I was perplexed. *Could she have gotten out somehow?* I didn't think so, but she was so quick. *Maybe she ran out the door when I left this morning.* I told myself to calm down. Cats are known to hide and not come when called, although Cinder did not usually do that. I needed to do a thorough search of the house.

First, I searched all over the living room. I grabbed a flashlight and looked behind and underneath the couch, which was a favorite hiding place for her. No Cinder. I searched behind and underneath all the furniture, behind the draperies, on the bookshelves, and under the recliner where she loved to hide and sleep. It was Christmas season, so I looked in and under the Christmas tree. After all, she had climbed the tree and tipped it over when she was younger. Still no Cinder.

Next, I searched the kitchen. She had been known to open the cupboard doors with her paws, so I looked in all the lower cupboards, beneath the mobile island, beneath the baker's rack, and underneath the table and chairs in the dining area. Then I searched the utility room. *Could she be behind the washer, dryer, or furnace?* No. Still no sign of Cinder. My heart was pounding now. *Where did my Cinder go?*

The two bedrooms were next. I crawled underneath the beds, looked behind the nightstands, behind and underneath my desk and bookshelves, behind my desktop computer stand, and on the windowsills. I even pulled my heavy dresser and chest of drawers out a few inches to see if she somehow squeezed into those areas. Still no Cinder. There weren't many places she could hide in the two bathrooms, but I gave them a thorough inspection. All I could think was, *My Baby Cinder is gone. She must have gotten out somehow.* My heart was so heavy. Every cat is special, but Cinder was extra special. She was like my child.

In my frantic mind, I thought: *If she got outside, is it likely that she would stay around the neighborhood? She has only been outside a few times on a leash. She is so playful that she would probably take off and explore.* So, I went outside and started calling her. I asked the neighbors if they had seen her. No one had. Surely, her black fur would show up against the white snow. I was also looking for cat footprints. I walked through all the streets in our townhouse complex, which was several blocks long. I even searched in the bushes. I kept calling, "Cinder... where are you?" I wandered through all the cul-de-sacs calling for her. No luck.

I decided to expand my search. I jumped into my car and drove up and down all the streets of my suburb for over an hour with the heater on and the window down while calling her name. She knew her name. Surely, she would come if she heard me calling it... or would she? After all, she was a cat and didn't always answer when called. Again, no luck finding her. I could only hope that someone found her and took her in.

Back home, I decided on my next strategy. I would make signs with her picture and post them everywhere. I would go to all the animal shelters and all the veterinarians in the area the next day to see if someone had brought her in. I would also post an ad in the community newspaper and online. Fortunately, she wore a collar and a nametag imprinted with her name and my phone number.

I was too depressed to cook, so I tossed a frozen dinner in the microwave. I really wasn't hungry anyway. As most single people do, I put the cooked dinner on a tray and took my simple supper into the living room to eat in front of the TV. My heart was broken. I desperately missed her.

It was totally dark outside, which made me even more depressed. My little Cinder was out in the frigid weather… declawed, defenseless, alone, and so tiny compared to most adult cats and other animals.

Needing some cheer, I decided to plug in the Christmas tree. My tree was so beautiful, but I missed my cat lying on her back underneath the tree, batting at the ornaments on the lower branches. Next, I plugged in the lights for the Nativity scene and stood back to admire it. I was puzzled. *Why were Mary, Joseph, Baby Jesus, the Wise Men, and all the animals lying on the table in front of the Nativity scene?* I picked up Baby Jesus to put Him back in the stable, and there lay my little Cinder… all curled up and content in the manger. She had taken all the figurines out and decided the manger was her new hiding place. It was just the right size for her. I had not seen her black fur in there. *Away in a manger, no crib for her bed, my little Baby Cinder lay down her sweet head.*

My heart melted as I looked into her big blue eyes.

~Diane P. Morey

11

My Plastic Nemesis

All of the animals except for man know that the
principal business of life is to enjoy it.
~Samuel Butler

T he continuous *thump, thump, thump* piqued my curiosity. I peeked my head into the bathroom where I saw my black-and-white feline sprawled on the floor. "What are you doing, Grenoble?"

His right paw stretched up into the cat feeder I had placed there eight hours earlier. Catching sight of me, he grinned slyly while continuing to *tap, tap, tap* at the mouth of the feeder to make it drop food one piece at a time.

"Stop it," I demanded.

He darted for the door, but stopped just outside where he sat undaunted, daintily licking the crumbs from his paw. Meanwhile, I stewed in the bathroom, staring at the "cat-proof" feeder that was anything but cat-proof. The inventor clearly had not owned an aggressively hungry cat.

I had joyfully invested fifty dollars in the gadget because it was supposed to relieve me of the twice-daily feedings I'd resorted to since Grenoble was eating himself into diabetes territory. He consistently scarfed all but a few pieces of the food before my other cat, Mykonos, could set foot in the bathroom. The most annoying part, though, was Grenoble anxiously trailing behind me all day while he cried for more food.

Staring at my plastic nemesis, I decided I needed help overcoming its flaws. I strode onto my balcony where my parents, who were visiting, sipped coffee.

"Hey, Dad, are you up for helping me fix something?"

"Sure. What is it?"

"The cat feeder. Grenoble can get it to drop food, so he's still eating too much."

"What do you have in mind?"

"We need to strap something across the opening so he can't reach up inside."

Five minutes later, we were driving to a hardware store. We brainstormed ways to use the items hanging before us. Deciding to try a ruler, we sawed the item to fit across the opening and screwed it onto the bowl. Dad and I admired our clever design.

We returned to the balcony where we discussed how different cats are from dogs. Having grown up with dogs, I was still learning about my cats' demeanor, needs, and quirks. I had even purchased a book on the topic, but it neglected to discuss what to do if a cat is a mastermind of cat feeders.

Then I heard it. *Thump, thump, thump.*

"No way!" I yelled, as I ran to the bathroom where Grenoble had resumed his position, right paw extended into the feeder. He was uninhibited by the ruler. I scooped him off the floor and closed the door.

"I'm heading back to the store," I announced to my parents as I grabbed my purse and keys.

I returned with a second ruler, which my dad installed below the first one. I carried Grenoble to the feeder and sat on the toilet to watch his reaction to the twice-altered contraption. Sensing a new challenge, he tried his prior tactic. It failed. Then he attempted to lift the bowl off the feeder with his right paw. Unsuccessful again. Victory!

Thinking the feeder issues were resolved, I was perplexed when I awoke the next morning to a loud *snap*. Curious, I stepped into my slippers and padded down to the bathroom to investigate. I was greeted by Grenoble happily eating from the top of the feeder. The screw-on lid lay to the side where he had carelessly abandoned it.

"You have got to be kidding me," I growled. "Why can't you just eat less?"

I returned the lid to its position, set Grenoble outside the door again as I closed it, got dressed and headed for my car. When I returned, I resolutely set a brick on top of the feeder.

I looked at Grenoble, who sat casually beside me, inspecting my handiwork.

"Good luck getting the food now. I think I've finally thwarted your efforts."

He smiled and looked at the feeder. I saw the wheels turning as he schemed new ways to get his precious food.

I settled on the sofa so I could call my parents to inform them of the latest developments in the feeder saga. As I shared my brilliance with them, I heard a loud *thump*.

"Gotta go," I said. I darted to the bathroom.

Grenoble was body slamming the feeder into the wall. Each time he hit it, food cascaded into the bowl.

"I give up," I said. "You win." I shuffled back to the sofa, plopped down, and sulked.

After a few more thumps, Grenoble sauntered across the floor. He leaped onto my lap and rubbed his pale pink nose against my hand. I stroked his head while mulling over his weight problem.

"I was trying to get you healthy, big guy, but you're too stubborn."

He responded with a rumbling purr. I gazed into his hazel eyes that exuded love. I realized Grenoble was happy and still adored me despite my efforts to limit his food intake. So what was I stressing about? I no longer had to feed the cats twice per day, and when I thought about it, his cat-feeder antics were actually hilarious.

Smiling at my feisty feline, I said, "So, Grenoble, the body slamming was pretty creative, but I think you can do better than that."

I carried him back to the bathroom and placed him in front of the feeder as I sat on the toilet to observe.

~Heather Harshman

Chapter

2

The Cat Really Did That?

Learning to Love the Cat

The First Time My Cat Died

The cat could very well be man's best friend
but would never stoop to admitting it.
~Doug Larson

I wasn't a cat person before I met Marcel. Marcel was Jennifer's cat, and I was in love with Jennifer, so it behooved me to fall in love with Marcel. But Marcel was hard to love. He was a shorthaired black-and-white tabby with a long body and deep, almost human, brown eyes. He liked to climb into Jennifer's lap, burrow his head into the crook of her elbow, and let her scratch him on the neck and jaw for hours. But with me, he was aloof, skittish, and quick to claw.

"He'll come around," Jennifer said, pressing her forehead against his and rubbing his ears. "When I adopted him, the Rescue said he'd been a stray. Someone found him in the engine of their car trying to keep warm. He's been through a lot."

"He puts me through a lot," I groaned, showing her the scratches Marcel had made on my forearms when I sat in a chair he'd decided was his.

"You just have to be patient. When I first got him, he stayed behind the refrigerator for two weeks," she said. "He wouldn't let me touch him, and he refused to eat. But eventually, he came out, and now look at us. Just give it time."

I did, but Marcel and I never quite warmed up to each other, and I had the scars to prove it.

Eventually, Jennifer and I got married. Marcel and I came to realize that since neither of us was going anywhere, we would have to form an uneasy truce. I fed him at night and stayed out of his favorite spot on the couch, and he'd occasionally rest his head on my lap when I watched TV or rub his chin on my leg when I was eating lunch.

"He loves you," Jennifer insisted one night, grinning as we sat up in bed. Marcel was lying on my stomach, purring a low, powerful rumble.

"No way," I protested. Almost immediately, he jumped up, clamped his teeth on my hand, and fled the room. "He loves *you*. He only tolerates *me*."

Then, late one night, there was a knock on the door of our apartment. I answered it and was greeted by our retired neighbor, Lois, fighting tears in her nightgown and curlers.

"Marcel's been hit by a car," she said.

Marcel had always been an indoor/outdoor cat. In the fall, he spent most of his time walking the grounds of our complex, eyeing the birds and climbing a tall tree that reached over our building to sun himself on the roof. I'd never seen him cross the street, but apparently, this evening, he had.

I thanked Lois and went back inside to tell Jennifer the news. She broke down crying.

"It's okay," I said, feeling my own emotions rise but immediately tamping them down. "I'll take care of everything."

I walked downstairs, hoping to find nothing — a false alarm, an over-reacting neighbor — but instead found a sobbing college student standing by a black sedan, and a twisted pile of fur in the street.

It didn't look like Marcel. It wasn't meowing for dinner or batting at flies. It wasn't twisted into impossibly comfortable positions in the shafts of sunlight beneath the windowsill. It wasn't Marcel, not anymore.

I sent the college student away, insisting it was only an accident, and asked Lois to go back inside so I could take care of my wife's cat. I wrapped his body in an old blanket and put him in a box that had contained a collection of 1950s detective novels that Jennifer had gotten me for my birthday — one of those gifts you get from a loved one that proves they know you better than you know yourself.

I carried Marcel back toward the apartment, but then I stopped. I didn't know what to do. I couldn't take him inside because I didn't want to traumatize Jennifer. I thought about leaving him outside or in my car, but that just seemed impossibly cruel.

As I stood at the bottom of our stairs, pondering this, Jennifer appeared, crying and clutching a Kleenex. I put the box at our feet, took her in my arms, and cried. We cried for her loss — the loss of her cat and the loss of her friend. I thought about the times they sat together and the times he let her scratch him and the times we all snuggled on lazy Sunday mornings. I realized I wasn't only crying for her loss, but for mine as well.

And then I heard him. His purr. Deep and soothing.

I looked around, confused, and there he was — standing at our feet, rubbing his face on the box and looking up at me like, "What's everyone crying about?"

We laughed — it was all we could do — and then raised Marcel into our arms, despite how much he loathed being carried, and laughed some more.

"It wasn't Marcel," I said.

"No." Jennifer laughed through her tears. Marcel struggled to get out of her arms, pressing his paws against her chest and whining, but she wouldn't let go.

"He's alive," she said. Finally, after she'd received a few scratches, she lowered him to the ground. He ran upstairs and returned to his spot beneath the windowsill.

In the morning, I took the box to the Humane Society and handed it to a teenage volunteer. I waited until she confirmed that the cat had no microchip and had not been reported missing.

"He's most definitely a stray," she said, "but we'll keep him here for a bit just in case someone comes in looking for him."

"If they do," I replied, "tell them I'm sorry for their loss."

"They get under your skin, huh?" she said, catching me.

"What?"

"Cats. Some of them can be real terrors, but I can tell by how you brought in this one, and how you stuck around to see if it had an owner, you've got one you care about pretty deeply."

"Yeah," I said, smiling to myself. "I guess I do."

I paused to watch her take away the cat that was not Marcel, the cat that was not my cat, and I realized for the first time just how much Marcel meant to me. Losing him for those few minutes made me see just how big a space he filled in my life, in our lives. I didn't think about the times he scratched me, but the moments before, when he let me pet him, even though he was scared. How we formed a truce that led to acceptance, and an acceptance that turned to love. He didn't have to try, but he did. He didn't have to take me in, but he did. He showed me how giving my wife could be, to take in a troubled animal and never give up on it. And he showed me how brave he was to open his heart to me, even when it was hard.

I realized in that moment the gift Marcel had given us: He made us a family.

And I realized that I was a cat person.

~Josh Burnell

A Cat of My Own

My cat came out of nowhere and
became my everything.
~Author Unknown

When I was a kid, my house was a cat magnet. My parents were both well known in the community and so were their passions, one of which was animal rescue. They were always adopting animals from the local shelter. At one point, we had six dogs, thirteen cats, an aquarium filled with lab rats saved from euthanasia, wild birds whose wings had broken (separated from the cat community in their own room), lizards, turtles, mice, two horses, and even a goat.

This might have been fine if we lived on a farm, but we didn't. We had a large house — a grand 19th-century home that over time had served as a general store, a doctor's office, a post office, and a feed depot — but even a house that large could feel small with the ever-growing menagerie of animals. Whenever someone in the neighborhood — or even the wider community — found a stray cat or dog, they knew it would find a home if they just dropped it off on the front porch of Raphael and Frances Mark.

I tell my daughter Emily these stories, and she thinks it sounds like a wonderful paradise, but it wasn't always fun. I actually came to hate the cats because they were the most persistent presence. I'd open a kitchen cabinet in the morning for a bowl or plate, and there was a cat in there looking down at me. Going to sit down at the dining room table, I'd have to remove a cat from the chair — sometimes two. Cats on top of the TV, on the couches, on top of the refrigerator, on the stairs, under the coat rack, on the radiators — they were everywhere, like some awful vermin. My friend Betsy Jacobs, who loved cats, told me my problem wasn't the number of cats, but that I hadn't found my own. I had no idea what she meant.

One New Year's Eve, we all came back from dinner to find the latest surprise on the front porch — a large black cat with enormous golden eyes and a red ribbon tied around his neck. He was in pretty poor shape. His coat was worn and dirty, and his tail was broken, twitching back and forth at an odd angle. Of course, there was no question what would happen next. My mother went to pick him up and bring him inside, but he wasn't having it. He backed away, hissing and growling, into a corner of the porch.

The last thing I wanted was another cat, but I did want to help Ma, so I got down on the cat's level and talked to him until he walked toward me. I picked him up and carried him inside. I got him some food, and he calmed down a bit until my brother Jason sat down near him. Then he attacked. He grabbed at Jace's hand, scratched furiously, and then shot under a bureau in the dining room where he glowered and hissed at us. Jace said, "That thing's like an assassin. You ought to name him Carlos," referring to a villain in a novel that was popular at the time. The name stuck, and the cat stuck to me.

Since I was the only one who could handle him without being mauled, he wound up in my room and became *my* cat. He wasn't like the other cats in the house. He would entertain me by leaping from the top of my bookshelf to the top of my open door and do a little tightrope walk across it, back and forth, before hopping down. He was a great nuzzler and loved to sit on my lap while I read. Every night, he'd jump up on the bed when it was time to sleep and, if I stayed too long at my desk working on something, he'd hop up and knock my pen away to let me know it was getting late.

He was also an uncanny judge of people. He finally warmed up to Jace, but I learned to trust his judgment about new friends I'd have over. If Carlos liked them, they were worth the time. If he didn't, they usually wound up being a huge mistake. He liked most of my friends, but was especially fond of Betsy. Carlos lived a life of luxury in my room and wasn't inclined to exert himself very often, but he always got up when Betsy visited, hopped onto the little table at the end of my bed for her to pet, and sometimes even climbed up on her shoulder. I knew I liked Betsy even without Carlos's approval, but it was still nice to have it.

Carlos liked Betsy so much that, when I got a letter from her, he would purr and sit in my lap while I read it. If I got a letter from anyone else, he either wouldn't come near or, sometimes, would slap at it. If he didn't like someone, he wasn't at all shy about showing it by allowing them to come near and then latching himself onto their hand, biting and scratching. But when someone met with his approval, he was the sweetest gentleman and most caring friend. When I was sick with mono, he wouldn't leave me, not even to eat or drink. And when I'd come home from school at the end of the day, he'd jump off the bed and trot over to greet me at the door. He liked it even better when I'd come home with Betsy, and he'd climb up on her shoulder and nuzzle her ear.

One day Betsy said, "See? I told you. You just had to find your own cat." She was right. Without even knowing I was doing it, I became kinder and more affectionate with the brood of cats around the house. Getting to know Carlos allowed me to recognize the personalities of the other cats. They weren't just obstacles to sitting, walking, or eating anymore. Sam favored the top of the refrigerator because it was warm. Dwarfy liked sitting in laps because she was a people-cat. Mama liked the radiator in the downstairs hall because no one bothered her there.

Carlos was especially pleased when Betsy and I started dating and she spent even more time at the house. If I tried playing a board game with anyone else in my room, the cat would walk all over it and actually kick the pieces. When Betsy came, though, he just curled up between us and watched until he became bored and fell asleep. Carlos opened the world of cats up to me and showed me how fascinating, warm, and wonderful they can be. He was long gone by the time Betsy and I got married, but he lived on in the first gift I gave her in our first apartment: a small, black kitten.

~Joshua J. Mark

14

Pansy, the Two-Timing Cat

The cat is domestic only as far
as suits its own ends.
~Saki

I live with a crazy cat lady. My girlfriend, Diana, has adopted more than a dozen carnivorous felines. They sprawl in every nook and cranny of the house, lounging about like gods. I think we have far too many cats. Diana wants even more.

As a kid, I once watched my neighbor's German Shepherd corner a tom. The cat leaped on the dog and raked its nose with his claws. The pooch scampered off, howling. From that day on, I interpreted a cat's display of affection as a personal nightmare of clawing and flashing sharp teeth.

It took me a while to warm up to cats after that. I was the guy who rolled his eyes when friends went on about their tabbies. I didn't understand their undying devotion. Nor could I comprehend the cutesy names they assigned to their animals, like Fluffy, Boots, Mr. MooMoo, Pookums and Socks. Yuck!

After a couple years in residence, I've finally been accepted by Diana's cats. By "accepted" I mean they've learned how to work me to get what they want, which is usually another can of food or a large dollop of whipped cream from the fridge.

I've become a personal servant to Diana's herd. I'm alert to their slightest request. They constantly come and go. I act as their doorman. At mealtime, they rush us like hyenas piling on for a kill. They sit in our laps, sleep on our bed, and keep us awake with their late-night antics. I've learned to grin and bear it.

Cats are a lot like the people you meet on dating sites — never quite what they appear to be. When a dog is hungry and you feed him, he shows gratitude. When a cat is hungry and you're late with his food, he throws your cell phone in the garbage disposal. The smarter ones then hit the switch.

I only recently grasped how remarkable and intelligent cats are. The ones around here are like automobiles. Some are full-time hunters (4-wheel drive), others only go outside in good weather (sedans), and a few never leave the house (luxury models). Some meow softly like a Prius hybrid. Others yowl at full volume like a Mack truck hitting the brakes.

Diana's most amazing cat was a bandit-faced female named Pansy. Pansy was a slayer of rodents. She did not like to be held and preferred to live outside. On the rare occasions she wanted a caress, she let us know by flopping down in our path. Diana invested a huge amount of emotion in her relationship with Pansy. What she got in return was cold-shouldered rejection.

Pansy had it made: complete reign of the house, plenty of food, and a warm bed. Then she began secretly visiting a neighbor down the street, close to a field where she hunted mice. A week later, she stopped coming home. Diana would call for her. No answer. She would set out bowls of kitty chow and saucers of milk. But the little two-timer never came back. Did Pansy abandon us for a wealthy family with a private groomer and a veterinarian who made house calls? Was it simply a shorter commute to her hunting grounds? Who knows? Whatever the reason, it broke Diana's heart.

Late one evening after yet another fruitless search, I told Diana that her cat would probably never return. She needed to accept the fact that Pansy was a two-timing mouser who was born to wander. Diana had to learn to accept Pansy's affection in the cold and aloof form it was given.

I explained that there were many cats like Pansy. When they rub against us, it isn't a sign of love; it's how they spread their scent. These same cats only purr because they know humans will reward them. They barf up hairballs and use our furniture for scratching posts because they believe it's their cat-given right.

Afterwards, Diana nodded and said she understood. The poor woman wasn't crying, but she was close to it.

But the next morning, she was down at the field, calling for Pansy, hoping to entice her home with a fresh can of whipped cream. "I wish I could catch her," she lamented. "I'd like to put flea medicine on her." Oh Diana, still wanting to care for that unfaithful cat.

~Timothy Martin

Gizmo and Boots

*You cannot share your life with a dog, as I had
done in Bournemouth, or a cat, and not
know perfectly well that animals have
personalities and minds and feelings.*
~Jane Goodall

Gizmo was born on a muggy August afternoon in the stall of a horse named Lucky at an equine adoption farm where my family briefly volunteered. The owner's oldest son, who was about ten at the time, came running out of the barn, beaming from ear to ear and carrying a newborn kitten to show me and my girls. We all fussed over the tiny ball of fur. The boy then led us to Lucky's stall, where a pretty, little, tortoiseshell cat lay peacefully feeding her new arrivals.

We were somewhat concerned about the welfare of the kittens since they were sharing a stall with a horse, but each day we'd check on them and see they were doing just fine.

On the tenth day, the mother had moved the kittens. I could hear them crying and went on a mission to find them. It didn't take me long to follow their little cries. Their mother had moved them to a bale of hay across from Lucky's stall but she was nowhere to be found.

We set about our chores for the afternoon. Then I took my children home for dinner and then headed out to the local pet store to get some supplies in case there was a problem.

The mother cat still had not returned by the time I got back.

We searched around the farm and could only assume the worst, so I brought the kittens into the house along with the little feeding bottles and other supplies I had purchased. They were ravenous; we had no trouble at all getting them to feed. Once their little tummies were satisfied, we introduced them to a cat living in the home who had recently lost her own two kittens.

The foster mother took to them right away, and began cleaning and stimulating them to do their bathroom business — something I also didn't know needed to be done! She lovingly washed them all and curled up with them, happy to have a little family again.

I went back the next morning to see how things were going. It appeared the kittens' new mom didn't have any milk left. The kittens were desperately kneading at her belly and crying. I took them away one at a time and fed them before returning them to her. The farm owner became very aggravated about the whole situation. She didn't want to be stuck feeding a bunch of kittens every few hours, so I offered to take two of them home with me. A little beige one didn't seem to be doing well, so I took that one along with a ginger-and-white one.

I fed them frequently, but the little beige one was not responding. Sometime in the night, the poor little mite passed away curled up next to his sibling — whom we had christened "Gizmo" due to his big ears and little face. He was a polydactyl kitten (meaning extra digits on each paw), also known as a "mitten kitten." Thankfully, he was still alive and screaming for his breakfast, so I set about feeding him.

Gizmo's will to live was strong, and he grew in size, strength, and attitude each day. He was only the size of my palm when he first came home, but the slightest meow from the little carrier he slept in would send our dog, Boots, running upstairs to hide. We had rescued Boots himself as a puppy when his mother passed away.

One afternoon, I carefully placed the kitten on the kitchen floor, and Boots stood there paralyzed with fear. Eventually, he got up the courage to sniff Gizmo, who was trying to walk a few steps. He was quite awkward at first with his extra toes. Once Boots realized Gizmo wasn't going to tear him to shreds, he lay down and cautiously watched him. Within several minutes, he was gently licking Gizmo, and from that point forward they were great friends!

We'd all sit and watch as Gizmo would climb on Boots and bat at his ears. Boots would let him bite and attack those big ears. A bond had formed between a kitten and a dog who had both lost their mothers. Boots had been raised by people, yet here he was, being a parent to this tiny kitten.

They had seven years together before Boots passed away in October 2016 at age fourteen. We consider ourselves very lucky to have witnessed the love that developed between those two orphans — born of different species, but good friends.

~Karen Reeves

16

The Guest Cats

As we all know, cats now rule the world.
~*John R. F. Breen,* Who's Who of Cats

n 2005, I retired. Such a wonderful word. I moved to a small house with a large yard. At the same time, my daughter-in-law's grandmother was moved to an assisted living facility. She had two indoor cats that she couldn't take with her.

My son called to ask if I would mind housing two cats for a short while. No one could justify taking the cats to the pound. It certainly wasn't their fault Grandma Fisher couldn't care for them.

I hesitated. I'd never had a cat, let alone an indoor cat. Everyone made me feel guilty, though, so I agreed to "babysit" the two cats until a suitable home could be found. Everyone thought it would be a short time, perhaps a month or so.

The cats were declawed, neutered, and not quite three years old. They were beautiful, longhaired white cats. The larger of the two cats was more curious than friendly; the second cat wanted no part of me. I didn't actually see him for the first two weeks. He came out of hiding at night to eat, drink, and play with his brother. Occasionally, I would see a white streak as he scurried away when I surprised him.

When I did finally see the whole cat, unmoving at the water bowl, I was surprised. He was beautiful. I picked him up; he went limp and sort of dangled over my arm. After scratching between his ears, I put the cat back on the floor. I wasn't sure, but I thought I might have broken him in two. I was unaware some cats go limp when they're picked up.

However, after that single encounter, he followed me everywhere. If I took a book to read on the front porch, he would sit on a table in front of the window and watch me until I came in.

It took some time, but he is no longer the shy cat. His name is Harry, and he greets everyone at the front door. His brother, Louis, is the strong, silent type. Louis doesn't follow me around. Instead, he joins me to read the morning newspapers. Somehow, he curls under my left elbow and appears to be scanning the newsprint in front of him. Louis also likes to watch baseball on TV.

Harry, on the other hand, prefers quiz shows and *Dancing with the Stars*. Regardless, if I'm watching TV, reading or knitting, one or both of the cats are within arm's reach. They sleep right outside my bedroom door... like sentries. They remind me of the lions outside the New York Public Library. Both can be very stately in posture when they choose.

Over time, we have become good friends. Both like to be brushed, and it has become our evening ritual.

Periodically, I remind someone that Grandma Fisher's cats are still in residence. I get smiles and nods, but nothing is ever said. I expect someone to at least say, "Yes, we're working on that." But... nothing.

Years have passed. Both the cats and I are getting older. At this point in time, I suppose it would be cruel to suggest that different arrangements be made. We have established a routine of daily living. It is Louis's (self-imposed) job to guide me through the house. When I get up from the table, sofa, or computer, he is sure he knows where I should be going and is two feet in front of me the entire way. If I don't go where he leads, he pouts. It is Harry's job to be sure they are fed on time... and to ask for treats.

This was supposed to be a short cat-sitting stint. Evidently, everyone but me has forgotten that. There are days I want to call my son and remind him that ten-plus years is not a short period, but I know I won't ever do it. They seem to love me, and I certainly have developed affection for both Louis and Harry—my guest cats.

~Charlotte A. Lewis

17

Until I Met Kittery

Cats are absolute individuals, with their own ideas
about everything, including the people they own.
~John Dingman

ntil I met Kittery, I never knew that a cat could be a nurse-maid, babysitter, and toddler's best friend — all wrapped up in a furry, brown-and-white bundle.

Kittery entered our lives during my summer internship after my junior year of college, when my wife Jennifer and I were living on the coast of Southern Maine. We'd rented an apartment about four miles from the ocean. It was close enough to smell the clam-flats through our open windows each evening as we lounged on our futon, watching the news.

On one of those evenings, a tiny kitten trotted through our open apartment door with the bow-legged gait of a cowboy, walked across the living-room carpet, and entered the kitchen where we'd set up a bowl of cat food for our cat, Gypsy.

As this little, fuzzy kitten started munching away on our cat's food, my wife and I watched in amazement. Where had it come from? Why was it so hungry? Could we keep it?

We soon discovered from the downstairs neighbors that the kitten had been born only a few months earlier. While all of the other kittens were given away, this little male kitten and his sister remained unwanted because of their congenital defects. That explained his cowboy walk.

Adopting him was a no-brainer. We named him Kittery, after the

Southern Maine town where we hoped to live one day.

Over the next few years, Kittery became part of our family. We graduated from college and moved to Connecticut, where we rented a cottage by a lake in a small town called Coventry. Kittery was a fine cat, but it was when my wife got pregnant with our first child that he started showing his true colors.

One morning, as I was getting ready for work, I heard my poor wife inside the bathroom, losing her entire breakfast. It had become a morning ritual not long after we learned she was pregnant. However, this particular morning I heard another retching sound, and it wasn't coming from inside the bathroom. It was coming from just outside the bathroom door.

As I poked my head out of our bedroom door and looked across the hall, I spotted Kittery tossing his own breakfast onto the floor — a sympathetic gesture, apparently.

Kittery loved Jennifer so much that when she got sick, he got sick.

This morning ritual between Jennifer and Kittery went on for months. It was the first real clue that something about this cat was very special.

When Kayla was born, we weren't sure how Kittery would respond to her, seeing as he always seemed to act like he was our own baby. Would he dislike her? Would having cats around a baby be dangerous? As new parents, we didn't know what to expect.

Our concerns were put to the test one evening when my wife lay Kayla down on the couch so that she could get a drink from the kitchen. No sooner had she left the living room than Kittery jumped right up onto the opposite end of the couch.

I was sitting on a chair beside the couch, watching both Kittery and the baby closely. At any sign of trouble, I was prepared to whisk away the cat.

Kittery gingerly walked closer to Kayla and put his moist, pink nose up next to her little feet. He sniffed, and then walked closer. As he walked beside her, I thought to myself, *This is it. He's going to lie on top of her face and try to smother her!*

Just as I was about to push the cat aside, he slowly stretched out along the edge of the couch next to Kayla, his malformed hips causing his back legs to sprawl out like that of a frog. He placed his head down on his front paws and closed his eyes.

It dawned on me that he wasn't trying to hurt her; he was trying to protect her! He'd placed his own body as a shield so that she wouldn't roll off the couch. When my wife returned, I put a hand up to gesture to her to look at the couch. When she spotted Kittery playing nursemaid to the baby, a look of amazement spread over her face, and she broke into a smile.

From that point forward, every time we placed our little baby girl on the sofa, Kittery would immediately jump up onto the couch and stretch out alongside her, protecting her from harm.

The relationship between Kittery and Kayla blossomed over the next few years. One day when I came home from work, I saw three-year-old Kayla following Kittery around the house. I'm not sure if they were playing follow-the-leader, but it sure looked like it.

Then, suddenly, Kittery flopped himself down on the floor, spreading out into his signature frog-legged sprawl. To my amazement, little Kayla stood over Kittery like he was a horse and lowered herself onto his back.

My first reaction was to run across the kitchen to remove her from the poor cat's back, but then I stopped when, to my amazement, he let out what I could only describe as a "happy meow." As she bounced her legs up and down, Kittery closed his eyes and purred, his tail flowing happily back and forth across the floor.

I realized that Kayla wasn't quite "sitting" on him — she was bouncing her legs, pretending that he was a horse, and he was more than happy to play along. It was a moment I'll never forget.

Many years later, when Kayla turned twelve, Kittery fell ill and passed away. He had been such an important part of the family that we couldn't bring ourselves to bury him in some random plot in the woods behind the house. Instead, we paid to have his ashes placed inside a small oak box with his picture pasted on the front.

To this day, Kayla often looks at the oak box with the old picture on the front and reminisces about her old friend, Kittery. Some kids have imaginary friends, but our daughter was lucky enough to have a childhood friend who was quite real, even though he wasn't quite human!

~Ryan Dube

The Cat That Couldn't Meow

I love cats because I enjoy my home; and little
by little, they become its visible soul.
~Jean Cocteau

knew something was up the minute our dog let out a short bark. Coming out of the barn, I watched a silver-grey blur streak off the back porch and across the drive. Someone had dropped off another cat. A kitten to be exact. I guessed her to be about six months old.

I felt anger well up against the person who would send a kitten off into the unknown just before the winter snows. Pushing aside my feelings, I went back into the barn and added a scoop of cat food to the barn cat dish. I figured it was just a matter of time before the kitten figured out where safety and food could be found — if it didn't get hit on the busy highway first. My three barn cats were already munching when the kitten found the lighted doorway and shivered her way into the barn.

Her first few weeks were spent skulking — getting her bearings — deciding how safe I was. After all, the last human in her life hadn't been all that trustworthy. It didn't take long for her to recognize who was feeding her, and I was greeted at the barn door each morning to a good leg rubbing and a healthy purr. Unlike her barn mates though, the kitten never meowed. Her mouth opened but no sound came out. Her vocal expressions were only audible when the dog came near, eliciting a throaty growl or a squeak; when she was deeply content she would purr. But there was never a meow.

I named her Dusty. It was either that or Blue to go with her unique silver-blue fur with subtle stripes. Those were combined with her startling yellow-green eyes.

The following spring Dusty had a litter of four kittens. Normally, I would find new homes for each one, but the winter had been hard on my cat population. My oldest had died of old age. Another simply vanished, as transient creatures do in a neighbourhood full of dairy barns where spilled milk is more appealing than dry cat food. The third became a victim of the resident eagle, leaving me with Dusty and her four little ones.

Dusty was smart. She steered clear of the highway traffic, ducked for cover when the eagle's shadow fell across the lawn, and knew exactly when mealtime arrived.

When my daughter talked about getting a cat for her children, I thought of Dusty and her warm heart. She always looked for the children when their van pulled into the drive. She wrapped herself around their skinny legs and purred constantly. Maybe Dusty would be in a better place with this cat-loving family, so I offered her to them, knowing that I would see her often, and she would receive all the petting she deserved.

She settled into her new home like a queen settles onto a throne. It didn't take her long to notice that children don't always close doors, and soon Dusty learned that she had a place on the arm of the couch when she wanted it. Another litter of kittens surprised the family — four again — and Dusty taught them well. They learned the art of mousing and how to slip through an open door on the heels of busy children. They found their voices — high-pitched yowls and purrs. They mastered the leg wrap so as to offer affection without tripping the recipients.

But as the kittens grew, Dusty became surly. She wanted her space. New homes were found for two of the kittens, but the other two had wedged their way into this young family's hearts. My daughter commiserated that three cats were one too many, and I offered to take

Dusty home.

Again, she settled in, and I assumed she would be content to return to her barn life. Dusty had other ideas. She had mastered the art of ducking and weaving. Her third day home brought with it the realization that the dog loved her mat by the door more than she loved her vigilance against cats. As I entered the kitchen after morning chores, a silver-blue torpedo shot past me. The next half-hour was spent chasing Dusty down and returning her to the outdoors. My husband came home for lunch and again the cat found her chance.

It didn't take us long to realize we were fighting a losing battle. A trip to the store provided the necessary cat accouterments, and a trip to the vet put an end to Dusty's kitten bearing years. As Dusty has settled in to our house, I've discovered things that make her an asset as an inside cat. The mouse population in our old farmhouse has dwindled. Also, Dusty's feline impulse to massage is a huge benefit. Often I find myself winding down at the end of a day, with Dusty parked on my lap and kneading my leg muscles or perched on the back of the couch and working at a shoulder. When she's finished with me, our little masseuse moves on to my husband. And what can be more adorable than a cat that looks up at you with devoted, yellow-green eyes, opens her mouth and offers a silent, heartfelt meow?

~Donna Fawcett

19

Casper

*I believe cats to be spirits come to earth. A cat, I am
sure, could walk on a cloud without coming through.*
~Jules Verne

I am not a cat person. Yeah, sure, when I was younger, I would
love going to the pet shop and seeing the kittens play. They were
so cute when they were chasing balls of string. But then I picked
one up, and it clawed at me and screeched like something out of
a horror movie. I was definitely not a cat person.

Instead, I got a beautiful mini-Schnauzer named Charlie, and
of course, I walk him regularly. If it weren't for that, the other thing
wouldn't have happened.

One day, I took Charlie out for a quick walk right after a rainstorm. I heard a strange sound as we walked under a tree. I thought
it was some kind of bird crying out. But when I looked up, I saw it:
a tiny white kitten, clinging to a branch and crying. When our eyes
connected, it was like he knew. Even though he was at least twelve
feet up, he jumped.

I ran to the little guy, Charlie by my side, and grabbed him off
the ground. One of his eyes was closed, his nose was bleeding, and
he was skin and bones. I didn't know what to do at first. I held him
in my arms, looking around as he clawed at me with his tiny nails. I
thought someone had to own him, but no one came out to thank me
for saving their kitten.

So I ran home, with Charlie trying to jump up and see what was in my arms and making that horrible noise.

I called my husband. "Come home! I'm standing here with a kitten in my arms."

"I'm sorry, a what?"

"A kitten. It's hurt. You need to come help me."

My husband came home, and we put the kitten in a shoebox and drove to our vet. She had explained over the phone that if we brought in the kitten and they treated it, we would have to pay for it. If we put the kitten outside their door, they were not allowed to take it in.

So, despite the fact that I was not a cat person, I thought to myself, *I picked him up and brought him home, so he is my responsibility now. We will pay for whatever is wrong with him and find him a good home.*

Turns out, he hurt his nose, but it would be fine. He was skin and bones because he had left his mother and was probably eating out of the trash. His eye was irritated, and he was so flea-infested that the poor thing probably would have been dead in a week if I hadn't found him.

We treated him and asked stupid questions that cat people know but dog people don't. We thought he would have to drink milk. News flash: Cats drink water.

He had worms, so we had to go back to the vet a few weeks later for more shots.

He snuggled with me and purred when I petted him. He curled up next to Charlie, who had never seen a cat before, but was more than happy to have a new friend.

We bought litter, cat trees, bowls and cat food, all the while thinking, *We are both sort of allergic to cats, so once he's healthy, we will find him a good home.*

But that didn't happen because we fell in love with him.

Casper is what we named him. An all-white domestic shorthair with a slightly smaller left eye than right, he became Casper the friendly cat. It was the week of Halloween when I found him, and to be frank he scared the heck out of me when he jumped at me from the tree.

Casper now eats the best food I can provide, is showered with toys, enjoys snuggling up in Charlie's old bed, and enjoys lying in the sun or slapping Charlie's feet as he walks by. Casper is part of my family now. Sometimes I catch myself looking at him, wondering why someone didn't take care of him the moment he was born, imagining how scared he must have been in the storm that day, or what would have happened if I hadn't found him. But I did, and I'm happy I did.

So no, I wasn't a cat person, but I am now.

~Jessica L. Moran

20

Oliver Twist, the Original Grumpy Cat

To err is human, to purr is feline.
~Robert Byrne

When my wife Diana and I first started dating, she said, "Love me, love my cat." There were two obstacles to this, however. First, I was a dog person. Second, Oliver Twist was an excessively grumpy cat and rather possessive of his "mom." This wasn't going to be easy for either of us.

My first extended encounter with Oliver was coming home from visiting Diana's mother. I had taken the train from Springfield, Illinois, to northwest Ohio to meet her family for the first time. Diana had driven out earlier in her tiny Toyota RAV4 and had taken Oliver along, as was their custom. I rode back with them on the seven-hour drive to Diana's house in Decatur, Illinois.

Since I didn't speak Feline, I wasn't aware that Oliver had called shotgun. He was less than ecstatic that I was in his place, so he spent most of the trip sulking in his kitty carrier in the back seat.

Along the route, I did learn some cat language while being introduced to a couple of his travel quirks. He would yowl in annoyance when we hit the rumble strips on the turnpike that warned of the approaching tollbooth. He would also let out a comparable yowl, the difference perceptible only to Diana's trained ear, when we got close enough to smell Decatur. To me, it was the stench of processed soybeans, but to

Oliver, it smelled like "almost home."

Once in Decatur, he climbed up into my lap, which had nothing to do with me and everything to do with the fact that he wanted to be in the front seat for the final stretch of the trip. My lap just happened to be occupying that space.

Suddenly, Diana had to swerve around somebody who had stopped short in front of her. Oliver did what comes naturally to cats. His claws came out, and he grabbed on tight to keep himself stable. Except that he was on my lap at the time.

Unaccustomed as I was to being stabbed in the legs with sixteen curved needles, I yelled in pain. Oliver turned and barked at me. Yes, barked. Like a dog. I had never heard a sound like that come out of a cat before, but even with my limited experience with cats, I could tell it was not a happy sound.

We arrived at Diana's house a few minutes later. She went inside for a moment to replace Oliver's travel litter box and left me in the car with him. The instant she was out the door, Oliver jumped into her seat, turned back to me with a look of deepest loathing, and gave a loud, theatrical hiss in my direction.

Being unloved by an animal was new territory for me. Dogs are easy. All you have to do is be there and they think you're awesome. Cats, I was learning, take some work. Particularly this cat, who I later learned had been found abandoned in the woods when he was just a tiny kitten. Nevertheless, I believed that this half-feral ball of gray fur and attitude had a soft spot somewhere, and I was determined to find it.

The ice between Oliver and me ended up breaking in a rather unexpected way. Diana had bought some coffee to keep at her place for visitors. One day, I was brewing a pot when I heard an inquisitive meow behind me. There was Oliver, looking at me for the first time with an expression other than one that suggested a desire to kill me in my sleep. He hopped up onto the counter and began sniffing at the coffee pot. When it finished brewing, and I poured myself a cup, he kept following me around, meowing insistently, and trying to get at my cup. At first, I thought, *What a pest!* Then I had an idea.

I went back to the kitchen and found an old dishrag. I poured some coffee on it and dropped it onto the tile floor. Immediately, Oliver began to roll around the floor with the rag, purring delightedly. Apparently, coffee was his catnip!

I wouldn't say that we immediately became besties, but Oliver did tolerate my presence after this incident. I referred to him as my "stepcat." He was always really Diana's cat, but he gradually became more cordial to me. When I would greet him after work with a "Hey, Oliver," he would nod in my direction and give me a short meow. I always had the feeling that he knew exactly what I was saying at any given time.

Then one night several years later, as I sat in the recliner, Oliver hopped up on my lap, stretched out diagonally across my chest, and laid his head on my shoulder. He stayed for several minutes, letting me pet him and purring in my ear. That was when I knew I had finally won him over.

Not long after that, Oliver became very sick. After a few days of vomiting, we took him to the vet and learned that poisoned gluten from China in his cat food had caused his kidneys to fail. We took him to the animal hospital to flush out his kidneys to see if they would rebound. However, our vet had already put two cats down that week for the same problem, so he was not optimistic. He left some time open for Oliver's final appointment and waited for us to call.

We didn't make that call, though. After about a day and a half, the animal hospital called and said to come get Oliver because he was doing better. This did not mean, however, that he was in a better mood.

Upon arriving at the hospital, we heard him before we saw him. You could hear that howl from the lobby. His eyes were huge, and he was not letting anyone get near him. But he was alive, and to us, that was worth the hassle and the vet bills.

Oliver lived another seven years after this incident. In his old age, he developed diabetes, and had to take insulin injections, which he allowed me to administer without complaint.

His body finally wore out at the age of fifteen. When we finally did take him to the vet to have him put to sleep, he was still growling, being fractious to the very end. Even so, that crabby, old kitty did manage to do something I never thought possible: He turned me into a cat person.

~M. Scott Coffman

21

Mad Max

*Cat people are different, to the extent that they
generally are not conformists. How could
they be, with a cat running their lives?*
~Louis J. Camuti

It had been three years since my husband Ed and I had pets. Our Sheltie, Casey, had been with us for almost fifteen years. He was the last of a long list of four-legged family members. When he passed away, we said, "That's it. No more pets."

In 2008, we experienced our first tropical storm as new residents of south Florida's east coast. That got me focused on how I wanted to live, and after the storm, I said to Ed, "We need a pet. The house is too quiet, and I have gone too long without one."

"Are you sure?" he asked. "It would tie us down again."

"I'm sure."

Ed had his reservations, but I was determined to get a cat from the Humane Society of the Treasure Coast. The storm had reminded me that a dog would still have to be walked, no matter what the weather was like.

We agreed to get just one cat. One Sunday afternoon, while Ed was working, I drove to Petco in Stuart, where the Humane Society had dogs and cats for adoption. On the drive there, I pictured a sweet, female, shorthaired cat. I would name her Lily. Ed would instantly fall in love with my sweet Lily. Just the thought of it made my heart warm.

I entered the store and started scanning the cages that the shelter had brought, looking for my Lily. As I surveyed the kittens and cats, I locked eyes with a young cat with brilliant blue eyes. It was love at first sight!

The nice lady from the shelter came up to me. "Looks like Ol' Blue Eyes likes you. Would you like to hold him?"

"Him?" I wanted a *her*. But I couldn't take my eyes off this handsome, little guy with his beige-and-brown long hair and the dark mask on his face that surrounded his blueberry eyes. *Forget Lily, this little guy is definitely coming home with me.* "Yes, I would love to hold him," I said as I smiled.

He and I bonded instantly. After the paperwork was completed, I shopped for necessary supplies. Finally, we were on our way home. I learned that my new cat was a Snowshoe/Ragdoll mix, and he was a year old. Realizing he had some Siamese in him, I understood his chattiness as we conversed on our ride back to Port St. Lucie. The first thing I told him was that a name change was in order. I wanted one to match his personality, but it might take an adjustment period before the right name came to me.

Ed loved our new addition to the family as soon as he met him. "He is definitely unique with that mask on his face," he commented. "It makes his eyes so blue."

In the days and weeks to come, our blue-eyed boy settled in. You could say he took over the house. Cat toys were scattered everywhere, and I became his new playmate and wrestling partner. His abundance of energy never ceased and his quirky personality became more and more evident. We finally found a name to match his antics... Max. Mad Max to be exact. Max was funny, loving and exhausting.

By springtime, I noticed Max could not bear to see me leave the house. He would come after me, ready to pounce, claws and all. He also had to have my undivided attention whenever he was awake. Max helped with everything I did around the house. On laundry day, Max was fascinated by watching the washing machine fill up with soapy water. He sat on the dryer watching me drop the dirty clothes in one by one. Each shopping day, he would sit on the kitchen counter with his head in each grocery bag to see what I had bought. He was constantly getting into mischief—until the day came when I had had enough. We needed to make some changes.

When Ed came home from work, I sat him down. "Max needs a playmate," I stated emphatically.

"He has one… *you*."

"I need him to have a playmate other than me. Let's go back to the shelter and find him one."

Ed looked at me as though I had lost my mind. "What?"

The next morning, we drove to the Humane Society of the Treasure Coast on a quest for a female about the same size and age as Max. This time, it was Ed's choice, and he picked a sweet, longhaired, black-and-gray girl. We named her Mandy. Lily was long forgotten.

It took a few days for Max to adjust to this new intrusion and for Mandy to acclimate herself to her new surroundings. Then one night, around four o'clock in the morning, we heard what sounded like a herd of elephants racing through the house. We both woke up at the same time. Ed whispered, "I guess the adjustment period has officially ended." We laughed and went back to sleep.

Max and Mandy became attached to each other and to us. Max favored me, and Mandy attached herself to Ed. I believe they knew who chose them. Either way, they have been a blessing to our home.

Last year, we lost Ed to cancer. Mandy looked for him for weeks. I would often find her sitting on the arm of his recliner, waiting for him to come and sit with her. Slowly, Mandy became my lap cat. We sit together every afternoon and evening while I read or watch television. Max still owns me, but he has been gracious enough to share my lap with Mandy several times a day. I always knew deep down that "Ol' Blue Eyes" would one day grow into a fine gentleman despite his quirky personality.

~Catherine Ancewicz

Chapter 3

The Cat Really Did That?

Who Me?

22

Happy Hour

People who love cats have some of the
biggest hearts around.
~Susan Easterly

had just lost my second cat in a few months and I knew I needed time to grieve. On the other hand, I hated coming home to an empty house. When I saw the shelter's ad in the Sunday newspaper and its picture of a beautiful, tortoiseshell cat available for adoption, I told myself it was too soon. And yet, over the next couple of days, I kept looking at that ad: "Sweet as a lump of sugar, Ellen DeGeneres is available for adoption." *Ellen DeGeneres, the cat?*

When I couldn't resist any longer, I called the shelter to see if Ellen was still available. She was, and off I went to get her.

Sharon, the owner of the shelter, had named all the furry residents after famous people. There was a tall gray male named Einstein, as well as Lance Armstrong, Tom Hanks, and a peach-and-gray calico named Oprah. And there among the many cats was the lovely, little tortie named Ellen DeGeneres.

After an interview with Sharon and a pile of paperwork, I headed home with Ellen. Sharon had suggested that I put her in a small room and let her adapt to the house slowly, but as soon as I opened the cage, the small cat stretched and walked straight into the living room, confidently taking ownership of her new home.

A few minutes after I got home with the feline Ellen, the real Ellen DeGeneres called the shelter live from her show to ask how she could help get the cat adopted. Her assistant had seen the newspaper ad. Sharon tried to reach me, but I was busy telling my mom about my new cat and didn't hang up until about five minutes before the show's taping was scheduled to end. As soon as I ended the call with my mom, Sharon called and told me to call in to *Ellen* immediately.

I was patched through to talk with Ellen (the human) about bringing Ellen (the tortie) home. She thanked me for adopting a shelter cat and asked how things were going. She also warned me that Ellen the cat would no doubt be very interested in happy hour. And she is indeed, only of course cats are nocturnal creatures, and so Ellen's happy hour with her catnip socks generally occurs around five in the morning.

Sharon wasn't kidding about Ellen's sweet nature. I call her the Buddha cat because she has absolutely no hunting instinct, and I'm one of the very rare human cat owners without scratches on her hands or arms. I can play with string, catnip toys, and crunchy balls with no fear that my hand will become a target. And all creatures, creepy and otherwise, are safe in our house. Spiders, ants, and even a mouse that shared our home for about a week have remained unharmed by Ellen.

Although my cat Ellen's famous connection to the wonderful comedian was written up by the local paper, I didn't think much about it as we settled into our lives — at least until I was at a professional meeting with a colleague who mentioned the story about my famous cat. One of the other scientists at the dinner brightened and said that she'd seen the show on which Ellen DeGeneres had featured Ellen the cat.

It has been almost twelve wonderful years since I adopted Ellen from the shelter. In the intervening years, she's flown on a plane for our move to Boston and been driven three thousand miles across the country when we moved to California. My sister came along to help me on that trip, which I called "Two and a Half Girls Hit the Road." Besides her occasional attempts to lie across the dashboard, Ellen spent most of her time during the long drive in my sister's lap or sitting on top of her carrier in the back seat, watching the country roll past.

After several years in California, Ellen and I finally returned to Portland, Oregon, where we started our journey together so long ago. Ellen is almost fifteen now. I'm hoping she'll be one of those twenty-something-year-old record breakers. I've become very spoiled by the companionship of a sweet-natured cat with the famous namesake and a rather early-morning, "happy hour" habit of playing with her catnip toys.

~Laurel Standley

23

One Clever Kitty

There is no more intrepid explorer than a kitten.
~Jules Champfleury

The abandoned kitten lay stretched out across my husband's hands. Paul fed the newborn — her eyes not yet open — with a tiny bottle from our veterinarian. Our children named her Stripes after the dark, symmetrical lines that ran from her face down to the tip of her tail. Despite the lavish attention the kids paid to our little kitty, she selected Paul as her special person.

Paul was an early riser, and Stripes kept him company each morning while he ate breakfast. When he returned home from work at night, Stripes ran to him and demanded attention. Paul would caress her as she lay on her back, stretched out the same way she'd done as a newborn.

When Stripes was three years old, we moved to a new home near a Dairy Mart. The convenience store was just across the street — kitty-corner from us, so to speak — and Paul walked there for milk twice a week. Paul began to notice Stripes trailing him to the store — always at a distance. He worried about her crossing the busy street, but when he tried to catch her, she always remained just out of reach. The kids were never able to snag her, either. Whenever Paul left for the store, Stripes slipped out the kitty door or hid in the bushes, waiting to follow him.

Stripes would sit outside the Dairy Mart and wait for Paul. Other shoppers noticed the kitty waiting patiently beside the doors. They would laugh at the sight of a cat sitting by the entrance of a milk store.

The clerks began asking Paul, "Did you bring your kitty cat with you today?"

"I don't bring her," he'd say. "She follows me!"

Whenever Paul returned from the store, Stripes jumped up on the bench beside our refrigerator, sniffing at the milk jugs as he set them inside.

One day, Stripes grew even bolder. When Paul came out of the store carrying two gallons of milk, she trotted in front of him in a zigzag pattern. Stripes pawed at his legs, even snagging his jeans. He tried to ignore her and walk faster, but she thumped against him and meowed noisily. Then she plopped onto the sidewalk, right in his path, almost making Paul trip. She seemed to be demanding a ride home.

Finally, Paul relented. He rearranged the jugs and picked up Stripes. He must have been quite the sight, balancing a kitty draped over his shoulder, as well as two gallons of milk.

The next time Paul walked to the store, the kids and I sat on the porch to watch. As soon as he crossed the street, Stripes shot out of the bushes beside our house. She galloped along the sidewalk and across the road. Once Paul was inside the store, she trotted over to the large glass doors, sat down, and daintily licked her paws.

We waited to see what would happen. Sure enough, when Paul emerged with the milk jugs, we saw Stripes dance in front of him. She even rolled onto her back, reaching for his legs. Surrendering, Paul set down one jug and picked up his furry friend. She cuddled his neck as he picked up the milk, steadied his load, and carried her home.

We all ran to greet Paul as he walked up the driveway, Stripes riding contentedly on his shoulder.

"I can't imagine why this kitty is so obsessed with your milk runs," I said to Paul. "I never feed her milk. It's not supposed to be good for cats."

A guilty expression crossed my husband's face. "Actually," he said, "I feed her the little bit of leftover milk from my cereal every morning."

I pulled the cat gently off his shoulder. "You are one clever kitty," I cooed to her. "I think you figured out that Papa goes to the store to buy you milk!"

"Mama!" one of the kids cried. "She needs a treat for being so smart!"

And from then on, every time Paul and Stripes returned from the Dairy Mart together, our milk-loving kitty was rewarded with a spoonful of her own.

~Janny J. Johnson

24

Who's Your Mama?

Cats know how to obtain food without labor, shelter
without confinement, and love without penalties.
~W.L. George

When I was growing up, we always had pets — mostly dogs, but an occasional cat. I happen to adore cats, but I married a dog lover who was dead set against getting a cat. So, we had no pets.

That situation continued… officially. But one hot St. Louis morning, while I was outside watering the plants, I made friends with a stray black female cat. As a teacher, I was off for the summer, so when my husband would leave for work in the morning, I would invite the cat into our apartment. She would spend the day with me. In the afternoons, I would lie on the couch and read, and she would sleep on my belly. Before my husband came home from work, she would go back outside.

One day, as we were reading and sleeping, I felt movement in her belly and realized she was pregnant. From then on, I called her Mama Kitty. Each day, I felt more and more movement. One morning, she was nowhere to be found, and I figured she had given birth. I knew she would have hidden the kittens and herself in a safe place, so I searched all of the areas close to the apartment.

I found missing bricks in a wall between apartments and saw there was an opening. When I called to her, she answered, but would not leave her babies to come to me. So, every day for the next six weeks, I left food and water for her. My husband knew nothing about any of this.

One evening, as I was lying on the couch reading, I heard the glass storm door rattle as though someone was shaking it. There stood Mama Kitty with a kitten in her mouth. I opened the door. She brought in the kitten, set it down, and went back to the door. She brought me a total of five kittens, and when she went back to the door, I assumed she was going to fetch kitten number six. Wrong! She took off. I guess she figured since I had taken care of her, I would take care of her kittens.

Of course, my husband was home, and I had to admit what I had been doing all summer. It goes without saying that he was not pleased. We lived the rest of the summer with five adorable kittens scampering through the apartment, getting themselves into all sorts of mischief. I promised my husband that I would find homes for all of them once school started, and when school began I put out the word on the school grapevine and found homes for all five within a week. I tried to talk him into keeping one, but no such luck, although later on in our marriage we adopted two strays.

Periodically, I would see Mama Kitty outside, but she would no longer come to me, no matter how much I sweet-talked her. I had fulfilled my purpose to her satisfaction, and she valued her independence more than she wanted a home.

~Sandy A. Reid

25

Hide and Don't Seek

Some people say that cats are sneaky, evil, and cruel.
True, and they have many other fine qualities as well.
~Missy Dizick

t had sounded so easy, and at first it was: cat-sitting for friends on vacation. Not housesitting... cat-sitting. With a nice home, neighborhood watch, police patrol, and the latest in alarm systems, my friends certainly didn't need me to watch the house. I was there for one purpose only — to keep Tony company while his humans were away on vacation.

It was easy. The first three days, whenever Tony woke from a nap, he and I would play with his favorite toys, especially the "birdie" on the string swinging from a stick. Tony was a regular guy: regular in using his litter box, regular in eating and drinking, regular in sleeping and playing.

In fact, he was so regular and on schedule that I felt concern on the morning of day four, when his litter box was still as clean as I'd left it at bedtime, his fresh water and food were undisturbed, and his toys were untouched. He'd not only failed to show himself, he'd not even made a sound.

"Oh, no," I worried aloud. "Something's happened to him!"

I began my search with the usual "Here, Tony. Here kitty, kitty, kitty."

Nothing.

He couldn't get out, so he had to be in the house. But where?

I crawled on tops of cabinets and looked down behind. I lay on the floor under furniture and looked up. I pulled curtains aside and looked around.

Still nothing.

I'm usually calm, but I could feel my heart racing.

I walked through the house shaking the container of treats that usually brought Tony running.

Nothing.

I walked through the house with an open can of cat food — his favorite kind, salmon.

Nothing.

I walked through the house, jiggling the birdie on the string.

Nothing.

Then it hit me: Get on the Internet!

Grabbing my laptop, I typed in, "How to find a hiding cat?"

Presto! An answer.

But wait, hundreds of people before me had asked the same question, and hundreds more had answered. One brought a measure of solace by saying they'd had their cat three years and still couldn't find her hiding place.

Every minute counted, but I read enough to see the top three answers were:

1. Rattle the jar of favorite treats.
2. Open a can of favorite food.
3. Shake a favorite toy.

All things I'd already done!

Hours passed, and I was nervous beyond belief. My blood pressure was rising, and I didn't even have a blood-pressure problem.

By now, my hands were shaking, and my knees were weak.

In desperation, I prayed, "Lord, I've done all I know to do. These folks will die if they come home next week and something has happened to their beloved Tony. Please, help me find this stupid cat."

Then it dawned on me: Cats like to be alone and prowl. I would pretend I had left!

After turning off the TV, I opened and shut the outside door, but quietly remained inside, hiding.

It wasn't thirty seconds before I heard a "thunk" when Tony came out of hiding, jumping onto a metal filing cabinet before landing on the floor and prancing in smugly to his food, water and litter box! I declare he was grinning.

A few days later, when my friends came home and I related my adventure (without saying it had surely shortened my life), they said unconcerned, "Oh, he does that all the time. Guess we should have told you."

~Kathryn J. Martin

26

The Alpha Mouse

*Cat: a pygmy lion who loves mice, hates
dogs, and patronizes human beings.*
~Oliver Herford

We had a visitor. There were holes in the items in our cupboard. Plus, there were telltale droppings in the cabinets adjacent to the kitchen sink.

This had never happened in the history of our household before. The feral cats in the neighborhood were our first line of defense, and I assumed that our six house cats were catching any mice that actually made it inside.

But the evidence was there.

I tossed out everything the mice had touched and put everything else in large, sealed cans or glass jars. Then I scrubbed down the insides of the cupboards and drawers. After that, I laid down new, clean shelf paper.

After all that work, I was dismayed to find droppings on the clean paper the next morning. This mouse obviously had no fear of my dogs and six cats! It was going to be up to me to catch the little guy and let him go outside.

I bought the best "critter-friendly" trap I could find and set it up under the sink, filled with mouse-tempting munchies. The mouse enjoyed the buffet without ever setting off the trap.

Next, I called my friend who lived in a more rural area and asked her what she did. She said she used a type of flypaper trap for mice. She told me that she had a lot of mice around, even with her cats and dogs, and these traps were a humane way to catch the little critters. When they became stuck on the paper, she put on garden gloves, picked them up, and carried them out to the field, where she turned them loose.

I bought flypaper and put it in all the areas the mouse had visited. The next morning, all the sticky paper traps had been turned upside-down, but no mouse was glued to any of them. I had met my match.

I would have to get someone to come in and catch the little bugger. I hated to do that because I knew the exterminator would kill him, but I was now between a rock and a hard place. I couldn't have a mouse inside our cupboards, and my cats didn't seem to be a deterrent.

I was going to call the exterminator the next day. But early that morning, the dogs and I rushed to the kitchen when we heard loud noises coming from there. All six cats were meowing, hissing, and growling. They were in a semi-circle under the kitchen table, facing the corner of the back wall. In that corner, standing barely three inches tall on its hind feet, with its front paws waving and its teeth bared, was a very ticked-off mouse. He was ready to take on the world. The cats all faced him, but remained a good six to twelve inches away from the fearsome creature.

I finally gave up on my eight ineffectual pets, grabbed a dishtowel, and threw it over the mouse. Then I picked him up in the towel, put him in a mason jar, and released him far from the house in the field.

When I got home, the cats all surrounded me, rubbing against my legs and purring. Then they dashed to the kitchen and sat looking expectantly at the cabinet where I kept the kitty treats — as if they had done something amazing by holding the horrible monster at bay until I could grab him.

Even though they didn't do what cats are supposed to do, I had to admit that they did outdo the mouse trap and the sticky paper, so

I guess they did do something right—even if it took six of them to corner one tiny field mouse. I gave them a handful of kitty treats—and accepted our new reality. The alpha animal of the pack was the mouse.

~Joyce Laird

27

This Is Who I Am

A cat has absolute emotional honesty: human beings,
for one reason or another may hide their
feelings, but a cat does not.
~Ernest Hemingway

The first time he did it, we thought it was a one-time thing. My husband and I were cooking dinner, and we heard this guttural screaming coming from the bathroom. We ran to see if Boo Boo Kitty was okay, only to find him dragging a towel he had taken off the rack. He had it in his mouth and was tripping over it as he carried it through the kitchen. He was howling like a fire alarm.

Boo Boo was a crazy cat that we adopted from our local shelter. Every animal we've had came with its own bit of kookiness, but Boo Boo was by far the most unusual. He didn't pay much attention to us at first, apparently because he had this obsession with dragging anything fabric through the house. He would get into our closets and pull shirts, pants, and sweaters from the hangers. He would grab blankets off our beds and run through the house screaming, as if to say, "I'll save you. Come with me!"

Boo Boo didn't care who saw him do it, and I knew it could happen at any time. That's what made him so lovable. One afternoon, I was lying on the couch watching a movie with him curled up on my chest when the doorbell rang. Boo Boo took off because the doorbell always scared him. It was my day off, and I hadn't cleaned the house yet, but at least I was dressed and looked decent enough to answer the door.

My neighbor had a big smile on her face as she handed me a plate of her gorgeous cookies. "Are you busy?" she asked.

"Hi, Anna! No, of course not. How sweet of you to bake for me!" I motioned for her to come in while saying a silent prayer, "Please, God, help Boo Boo Kitty be on his best behavior."

Anna, a lovely older woman, lived across the street. She would often invite me over for tea and some of her homemade Italian cookies. Her teacups looked like they should have been in a museum, as did everything else in her house. On the other hand, I liked to think of my house as having that "lived-in" look — comfortable, like an old pair of sneakers.

Anna never had a pet, so her house didn't have scratched-up furniture or fur balls hiding in all the nooks and crannies like ours did. She did everything with grace and perfection, so I was always a little hesitant to have her in *my* house.

I saw Boo Boo Kitty run into the bedroom as I invited Anna to sit down. Unfortunately, the bedroom was where he got into the most trouble.

We were having a delightful conversation at the kitchen table when I heard the howling begin. I tried to ignore it even though I knew what was coming.

"How's your garden doing this summer?" I asked Anna. Boo Boo's howling was getting louder and closer to us.

"My tomatoes are bigger than last year," she said, trying to hide her obvious concern over what she was hearing.

"Oh, nothing better than homegrown tomatoes," I said. I could feel the sweat beading up on my forehead.

Boo Boo was now emitting his primal scream as he dragged a pair of my husband's pajama bottoms into the kitchen. He must have grabbed them off a shelf. This particular day, of all days, he had the pajamas I had given my husband for Valentine's Day — with Cupids and hearts all over them.

I still tried to act like nothing out of the ordinary was happening even though I felt like I was having an out-of-body experience. I kept babbling, "Boy, you'll have to give me the recipe for these cookies, Anna. They're fabulous!" She was, of course, ever the polite lady and thanked me for the compliment while shifting her eyes toward the cat. Boo Boo dropped the pajamas at her feet as if to say, "Here is a wonderful gift for you, Anna!" He looked so pleased with himself. Meanwhile, I was trying to figure out how to explain this situation to a woman who seemed perfect in every way.

We continued to chat as I tried to hide my embarrassment. I snatched up the pajamas and was pretty sure my face was redder than the hearts that covered them. I explained that Boo Boo was a shelter cat, and we had saved his life by adopting him. I went on to say, "I really love pets, but sometimes they can be kind of quirky." I just kept chattering, and I think I even told her about all my childhood pets. I couldn't stop talking. At this point, Boo Boo was rubbing on Anna's leg, leaving a large patch of gray fur on her crisply ironed, navy slacks.

While I was embarrassed, Boo Boo was just the opposite. He was unabashedly sharing himself, with all his quirkiness. He didn't care that he was dragging pajamas around the house and screaming. It was as if he wanted to say, "This is who I am, and I want you to know me."

I thought later to myself, *What a great way to be.* Boo Boo taught me a lesson about not trying to be someone you aren't. I shouldn't have been embarrassed just because I had a weird cat.

My neighbor stayed for quite a while that day, and I thought she would never come over again, but she did several more times. I'm assuming she liked coming over because she could let her hair down and relax a bit in our way less than perfect home. She seemed to enjoy Boo Boo's crazy antics. I know he liked her, too. He wouldn't have given heart-covered pajamas to just anyone.

~Marijo Herndon

28

When Dad's Away, the Cat Will Play

Time spent with a cat is never wasted.
~Author Unknown

remember that warm summer evening when it all began. "Look, Mom, there's a kitty!" My younger daughter pointed toward the empty lot next door. An orange cat crouched down, spying through the grass. Madison jumped up.

"Wait a minute." I held my finger to my lips. "We don't want to scare him."

I inched toward the cat. "Hey, kitty-kitty." Big green eyes stared back at me. "It's okay, kitty."

The cat straightened and meowed. Slowly, I reached for him. His body arched as I slid my hand across his back. He was friendly. I scooped him up and carried him back to the girls. He purred every step of the way.

"Don't let him go! I'll get him a piece of ham," Taylor said as she ran to the house. But this cat had no desire to go anywhere. He was quite content with all the attention.

"Can we keep him, Mom? Please?" Madison clasped her hands together as if in prayer.

"You know Dad is allergic. There's just no way." The cat rubbed his forehead against my leg. Surely, this sweet kitty belonged to someone. "His family is probably looking for him," I said. "We don't want to get too attached."

But the girls ignored that advice. By the end of the night, they had named him Toby.

It wasn't long before Toby became a regular visitor at our house. Every day, I spotted him sitting in the sunshine on the front steps with at least one of my girls. Someone always fed him, played with him, and showered him with attention.

We checked with neighbors, hoping to find his owner. Everyone knew about the "friendly, orange cat," but no one knew where he came from.

By the end of summer, our next-door neighbors decided to adopt him. It was the perfect arrangement. Each day, he came by for a visit. Every night, the neighbors brought him inside. They even called him Toby.

While Toby charmed his way into our hearts, he also wanted to make his way into our home, especially on cold, dreary days.

"I think we have a stalker." I smiled at Madison and pointed to the window. Toby propped his paws up against the glass and gazed into the house.

"It's freezing out there," Madison said. "Can't we bring him inside?"

Toby peered in hopefully. I shrugged. "I suppose," I said. "Just keep him on the rug—and be sure to vacuum when you put him back out."

Madison arranged a blanket on the rug and made him a bed. Toby snuggled in, his paws pushing in and out with a slow and steady rhythm. "See," Madison whispered, "he's not hurting anyone."

"If Dad sneezes during supper, this is the last time Toby comes in."

Dad didn't sneeze, so as the temperature turned colder, we became bolder.

"Can we take Toby downstairs while we watch a movie? I'll keep him on a blanket. I'll even vacuum later." Madison held Toby next to her cheek and gave me an exaggerated grin. Outside, the wind howled.

"I suppose," I said, crossing my arms. She and Toby disappeared downstairs. I followed later.

About halfway through the movie, Madison jumped up and pressed the mute button. "Is that the garage door?"

My middle daughter gasped. "Dad's home! Put Toby out!"

Rather than boot the cat outside, Madison scooted him into a closet just as we heard footsteps coming down the stairs.

"Hey, I'm home," Curt called out. I pictured Toby, confused and stuck in a dark closet.

Please don't meow. Please don't meow.

Curt walked across the room, stopped by the closet, and leaned against the door. "What's for supper?"

"Um… chili," I said. "It's ready. Let's eat." As Curt turned toward the stairs, a little white paw reached out from under the door. But Curt hadn't seen it. Madison and I looked at each other and exhaled in relief.

Then one night, the girls and I went to a school program. Just as the sixth-graders kicked off their version of "Hot Cross Buns," my phone vibrated. I glanced at the text message on the screen: "Why is this cat running into our house?"

Uh-oh.

My phone buzzed again. "Obviously, someone has been letting it in the house. It acts like it owns the place."

I leaned over to Taylor. "We've been busted. Dad knows we brought Toby into the house."

"What? How?"

I shoved the phone into my purse. "Let's just say that Toby let the cat of the bag."

My girls and I had done a good job keeping that little family secret. The only problem was, we forgot to tell Toby. In the end, we learned a valuable lesson: Tell the truth — or someone will tell it for you. Even if that someone is a friendly, orange cat.

~Sheri Zeck

29

The Cat That Wouldn't Hunt

While the cat's away, the mice will play.
~Author Unknown

When we moved from Delaware to Florida in the late 1970s, our first order of business was to search for a building lot and get started on our house. The thin walls of apartment living added pressure, and we quickly found a lot in a subdivision not far away. It was within a bicycle ride of our apartment, and I enjoyed the exercise and visiting my husband Jim daily at the building site. However, after we moved into our new home, we found the neighbors a little too close. Within two years, we were again looking for a lot a little farther out in the country.

We fell in love with rolling hills and fields of corn. Soon, we found our perfect building site in a small, new subdivision among maize and horses. Within nine months, we were moving again. Farmland abounds in Delaware, and we felt right at home almost immediately. We loved the country atmosphere, and the closeness to shopping and all the other perks our new town had to offer.

Even a kitty found us—a stray someone must have dropped off—so now we were a family with an animal living in the country. Perfect. We named our kitty Fetcher, because Jim taught him to fetch pecans when he rolled them across the floor. Fetcher would pick them up in his mouth and bring them back every time.

One night, I was awakened by the tinkle of piano keys, and I attributed the ghostly music to Fetcher. I rolled over and went back to sleep, only to be awakened again a short while later. I got up to investigate and was surprised to see Fetcher sleeping at the foot of the bed. Now I was wide-awake and tiptoeing toward the piano. Fetcher slept on.

I saw and heard nothing, so I went back to bed, hearing no more music the rest of the night. I figured Fetcher, being the smart cat we knew him to be, was playing tricks on me.

Over breakfast the next morning, I heard the keys tinkle again. This time, I was looking at Fetcher and knew it couldn't be him. Jim said, "Mouse." Yes, it was harvest time, and we had a visitor. Unfortunately, he had found our piano, a spinet. Jim got busy removing the top and looking down into the inner workings, but he couldn't find a mouse. Next, he removed the front above the pedals, but all the work was for nothing. And where was Fetcher all this time? Sleeping.

So we resorted to the old standby mousetrap — baiting it with bacon and peanut butter. Not wanting Fetcher to be caught in the trap, we placed it under the top lid of the piano and waited. Fetcher never realized he was the cat side of the cat-and-mouse team. He remained disinterested. After all, his food was lovingly prepared by staff every day and placed in his dish.

Several nights passed with more eerie music, and twice we rushed to look under the lid after hearing the pop of the spring, only to find the bacon gone and a lonely smear of peanut butter left on the trap. Fetcher found this mildly interesting, but soon he went back to sleep while I lay bug-eyed staring into the darkness, waiting for the next snap.

It got to the point that we considered adopting another cat — one that could earn its keep. Or maybe we could borrow one from a neighbor. Should we post a sign at the front of our development?

Feline mouse catcher wanted for the night. Must be well trained with a high success rate. Urgent. Reply to this number as soon as possible.

Or maybe, I thought, I should post an ad on Craigslist. Nothing would appear weird there.

Finally, the mouse did succumb to the trap, and fortunately we found no damage inside the piano. Fetcher never showed any interest in the rodent and wouldn't even get near it when we tried to show it to him. Later, we learned that female cats are the better mousers. Instead, Fetcher was a retriever extraordinaire. He always ran after sliding pecans — and the grinding sound of the can opener. That cat sure had it good.

~Connie Biddle Morrison

Ringo's Own Rescue

Prowling his own quiet backyard or asleep by the fire,
he is still only a whisker away from the wild.
~Jean Burden, *Celebration of Cats*

My best friend and I worked with a rescue group called the Mercy Crusade, which was very active in the 1960s and '70s. I believe the group is still around as a spay-and-neuter facility, but back then it was a group of people who fostered animals of all types in their homes until they could be permanently placed on ranches or air-lifted back into the wild, depending on their needs and the type of animal. The Crusade provided all the food and any needed veterinary care for the refugees until they were settled.

We had sheltered dogs, cats, reptiles, foxes, birds, and even a bobcat at one time. They would be welcomed by our permanent residents: our three girls, three dogs, multiple cats, one pigeon, and one iguana.

One rainy night, I had left the window open for our cat, Ringo, who liked to come and go from outside. As my husband and I slept, well bundled up in our blankets, I felt a vague thump on the bed. Thinking it was just one of the cats hopping up to snuggle down in the blankets, I rolled over and pulled the comforter up around my neck.

Then something suddenly dropped on my chest and touched my neck. There was something small and round scratching my face! Ringo was an accomplished hunter, so I screamed and brushed it onto the floor, thinking it was a rat. In a panic, my husband jumped up and turned on the light.

"It's Ringo!" I said. "Another one of his hunting trophies."

Ringo was renowned in the neighborhood for clearing our gardens of mice, rats, and gophers.

My husband looked around, but saw nothing by our bed. "Either a bad dream, or he took it back out the window," he said. "Go back to sleep."

He turned out the light, and I pulled the blanket back up around my neck, making sure there were no foreign objects in the folds. Then I heard it: a small "thump, thump, thump," as if something was hopping around under the bed.

I reached across the bed and turned the light back on. Then I spotted Ringo sitting next to the bed, intently watching something. I looked over and saw it — a very tiny, totally black bunny was hopping around his feet. And Ringo the great hunter was just looking at it. Then he jumped on the bed and, purring, curled up at my feet.

My husband and I looked at the bunny in amazement. Ringo was now sound asleep and had forgotten the whole thing.

We got up, took out one of the large carrier cages, and made the bunny a home in the bedroom. The next day, the girls were overjoyed with Ringo's gift and named him Spunky.

Spunky grew into a healthy, medium-sized rabbit. He became close friends with all the animals in the house, but particularly my iguana Freddy, who loved to sleep curled around the rabbit, with his head resting on the warm, soft fur of his back.

Ringo did not stop being an avid hunter, but he was fiercely protective of his rabbit friend. I don't know what made Ringo decide to rescue this tiny bunny instead of eat him. Only he knew that. But they remained close friends for years. It was just one of those strange and beautiful miracles that animals can bring into our lives.

~Joyce Laird

Finding Dexter

Dogs have owners; cats have staff.
~Author Unknown

Dexter never missed a meal, which was followed by a nap on the sofa. During his non-nap hours, he played at being wild on our three acres. But when it came to comfort, he knew that *inside* was the place to be. Dexter was an elegant cat who liked his outdoor adventures in small doses.

One day, Dexter did not show up for breakfast. That was okay, but given his preference for staying indoors, I got really worried when he did not return by the evening. In rural Mississippi, there were all kinds of terrifying possibilities, so I spent hours calling for him outside.

Before I went to bed I had to try one more thing. I leashed up Timber, our brilliant Jack Russell Terrier. Timber loved to play the "find him" game with our son. Maybe he could find the cat. They had been buddies for six years, ever since we brought Dexter home as a kitten.

"Outside"

Miraculously, Timber sniffed the air and headed off. "Good boy, Tim. Find Dexter!" I had no idea what the dog was smelling, but he was definitely following a scent. I hoped it was not a raccoon, or worse… a skunk.

Timber stopped at the corner of our property where the fence was supported by a thick, round fence post, perfect for a cat to scale. "Did he go up here, Tim? Find Dexter!"

The dog turned and looked at me like I was nuts. There was no way he could scale the post, but placating me, he walked back and forth along the fence, each time stopping and sniffing at the corner post.

It was not a good idea to wander through my neighbors' pastures in the dark, so I planned to go out first thing in the morning. I prayed that Dexter would be okay for the night.

I barely slept at all that night, and I got up several times to see if Dexter was back. He was not. I forced myself to wait until good light at seven o'clock in the morning, and then I grabbed Timber, hopped in the car, and drove to the closest outside access to that corner post.

"Find Dexter!" Timber took off with his nose to the ground. A couple of hundred feet later, we were stopped by another fence.

My only hope was that Timber was truly onto Dexter's scent. The dog was intent on a cat-sized hole in the fence. If he really was following Dexter, the cat was headed into the hayfield directly behind our property. Three abandoned silos stood there in the field, beckoning to all forms of small, wild animals and enticing an energetic explorer like Dexter. Timber kept air-scenting toward the silos.

Across the fence, I bellowed loudly enough to wake any still-sleeping neighbors. "DEXTER!"

"MEEEEOOOOOWWW" came the almost equally loud yowl echoing from inside one of the old silos.

"Timber! You are wonderful!" I exclaimed. "Good dog! You found Dex. Good, good dog!"

The next task was to remove the cat from the twelve-foot-high crossbeam inside the silo. He had gotten up there but, in classic cat fashion, could not get down. I retrieved a six-foot ladder and my six-foot-four-inch son. It would be a stretch, but a rescue was initiated.

Successfully extricated and back in the house, Dexter chowed down and napped stretched out, taking up the major part of our sofa. As he snoozed, I wished I could read his kitty mind. Was he dreaming about his night on the silo beam? Was he planning a new adventure for us? Was he grateful or humiliated that he was rescued by a dog? Did he even care?

Most likely, he simply felt that his rescue crew barely met his expectations, and that they were awfully slow in doing so.

~Gretchen Allen

32

Cats with Benefits

*Looking at cats, like looking at clouds, stars or the
ocean, makes it difficult to believe there is
nothing miraculous in this world.*
~Leonard Michaels

After my wife died, I found myself suddenly homeless, along with our two cats. My wife's house was in a trust and had to be sold as part of settling her estate. This was no problem for me... I was mobile. I planned to travel anyway, because I no longer wanted to live in our home without her. However, I could not take the two cats on the road, so I had to find homes for them.

Several friends asked for Sweetie, the small, gray longhair who was an appealing lap cat. I chose Eva's close girlfriend whose household had just lost their cat. One weekend, I drove Sweetie up the Pacific Coast from San Francisco to her new home in Eugene, Oregon. During the drive, Sweetie roamed free in my car, mewing nervously at first while I cooed, "It's okay, it's okay," and played classical music to soothe her.

Soon, she stretched to look out the window at the passing countryside, which my wife had enjoyed during her long illness. Finally, Sweetie curled up in my lap. Her new home in Oregon turned out to be ideal for her — after I was allowed to install a cat door so Sweetie could roam a wooded cemetery behind the house.

Back in San Francisco, I faced the big problem. No one had volunteered to take grumpy Occie. Friends knew this fat, brown tabby would flop on her back to invite a belly rub, and then nip your fingers if you petted her the "wrong" way. From one day to the next, we never knew what mood Occie would be in, whether she wanted us to pet her or was luring us into a trap. Even my cat-loving sister said she would only take Occie as a last resort, if no other home was found.

So I was truly surprised, even shocked, when an ex-girlfriend of mine named Janice told me over the phone, "Sure, I'll take Occie." She offered, despite never meeting the cat, and after I warned her about Occie's strange temper. Janice lived an easy hour's drive north of San Francisco, and Occie seemed happy with the house and its big back yard right away. Years later Janice confided she had taken Occie in hopes I would drive up to visit her more often, which did happen while I was in California.

The real surprise for the cats' new moms came several months later when Eva's estate settled. Each of them received a $5,000 check to cover cat care.

Our friends said, "You should have told us! Anyone would have taken Occie!"

But I had kept those bequests secret. I wanted homes where people really wanted the cats. Now, I tell this story to encourage people to volunteer when they hear of homeless cats, because in addition to the obvious joy of sharing a home with a cat, you never know what other benefits might be attached!

~Sam Moorman

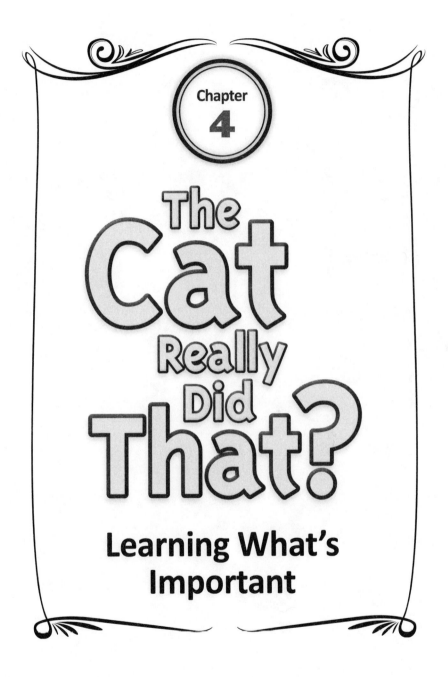

Chapter 4

The Cat Really Did That?

Learning What's Important

33

It Takes a Village

Kittens can happen to anyone.
~Paul Gallico

T he box meowed. My colleague struggled to get the heavy cardboard box in the door of the veterinary hospital without spilling its precious cargo onto the busy street outside. The box containing two adult cats had been left there during the night. Overnight they had lost their former identity.

These one-year-old females were attached to each other, so we kept them together in a large cage. One was a gray-and-white tabby, obviously pregnant. We named her Bethany. She had a sweet face and demeanor, gentle eyes, and an aura of softness about her. The other was a spirited brown-and-black-striped tabby we called Jasmine. Since we couldn't vaccinate Bethany — this would cause irreparable harm to the kittens — we made her comfortable. She was in her third trimester.

Instead, we vaccinated Jasmine and decided to spay her soon. "Soon" meant a lot of things at our clinic. We were always busy, and the orphans often got bumped from the overbooked surgery schedule. "Soon" meant more like sometime in this lifetime when the stars align kindly, or something like that. But within a week, it became painfully apparent that Jasmine was also pregnant. Because of the vaccination, we would have to spay her and abort the defective fetuses. We all felt sorry for Jasmine, but the surgery was done more quickly than "soon." Jasmine recovered smoothly and was reunited with her feline buddy.

When Bethany went into labor, I separated the two cats and

hung curtains over Beth's cage doors so she could deliver her six kittens in safety and privacy. It was a large litter — three males and three females — and they were a colorful lot, all shorthaired, tiny, and perfect. There wasn't a runt among them.

The only one put out by the whole scenario was Jasmine. She watched Bethany's closed-off cage from across the room and howled pitifully. Apparently, she still had enough hormones in her system to make her long for kittens herself. Jasmine had been deprived of something her body was preparing for. She was miserable, and I cringed when I heard her plaintive cries.

Three days later, as I cleaned Bethany's cage and examined the kittens, I let Jasmine out to get some exercise. All she wanted to do was sit outside Bethany's nest and nudge me relentlessly. I decided to try something that felt a little bit crazy at the time. I let Jasmine in to see her friend.

The two girls sniffed noses. There were no growls or hisses or protective postures on Bethany's part. Suddenly, Jasmine began nurturing the kittens, cleaning them and nestling up with them. She assumed full motherly chores with the exception of nursing. Keeping a cautious eye out for this unusual pairing, I allowed them to stay together for the day. The mama and wanna-be mama made an excellent duo in tending to all the kittens. The babies got the best of both worlds.

At the end of my shift, I separated the two mothers. Needless to say, Jasmine was angry. "Wait," said the vet. "Bethany and Jasmine are bonded. The kittens are safe."

I blinked. "But won't she eat her young or something?" I asked.

"She hasn't yet, has she?" This wise veterinarian had seen more than I had as a new vet tech. I reunited Jasmine with her adopted family.

By the time the kittens opened their eyes, they had already accepted both adults as their parents. While Bethany rested or nursed, Jasmine cleaned them, played with them, and kept them from bothering their exhausted mom. Both adult cats were young, but together they muddled through their first litter with grace and ease. For a little comic relief, the staff would let the family out of their cage to explore the surrounding room. The kittens got into holes and cracks, so we quickly became adept at kitten-proofing this room of the hospital.

Cats are purported to be solitary hunters of small prey, but I dispute that premise. I've seen enough cats display pack behaviors to wonder just how solitary they really are. I think we underestimate their ability to bond. In the fifty or so rescued cats that have come through my home at various times over several decades, I've observed strong attachments, and also, grieving behavior when one of the pair dies. Perhaps we deny their sociability. Jasmine and Bethany were a family, raising those kittens together.

The kittens were eventually weaned and placed in new homes. Bethany was spayed to prevent future litters. The sweetest part is that the two mamas were later adopted together into a permanent home. They retired from their mothering chores and, last I heard, were happy, chubby housecats, living an idyllic life in the Hollywood Hills.

~Terilynn Mitchell

34

Lion-Sized Courage

Are we really sure the purring is coming from the
kitty and not from our very own hearts?
~Emme Woodhull-Bäche

"Look at this one, he's gorgeous." Orange and white markings adorned the kitten from the tip of his tail to the top of his head. I stuck my finger through the bars and scratched him as best I could, and then asked if I could hold him.

"Sure," the young girl said. "He's only been here a couple of days. Cute, huh?" She plopped the plump kitten into my arms. He was heavier than he looked.

"How old is he?"

"Not real sure. He was dropped off without any information," the girl replied. "Maybe six months?"

"He's really pretty," my husband Roger said, which sounded funny coming from a guy, but I had to agree. "He looks strong, like one of those cartoon cats with a football helmet on its head. He's probably healthy as a horse."

"Looks like it," I said, and told the young girl we'd give this marmalade cat a new home. She was very happy to write up another adoption. We named him Red for his coloring, but we should have called him Smasher or Offensive Tackle. He smacked his head into anything he could, then rubbed back and forth. We soon learned it was to mark his scent on us and also to get his head scratched. He loved that part. We happily obliged.

The best part came when I'd return home from getting color and a weave at the hair salon. Plopping myself on the couch after almost four hours in the beautician's chair, I'd let out an exasperated sigh. That's when Red would come running. He would jump up to the top cushion and proceed to head-butt me over and over. "Red, what's gotten into you?" I'd say, but he'd keep going.

"Why don't you move," my husband said with a smile, "or get off the couch?"

"Nah, let him have his fun. I don't mind." After a few minutes, Red would sink into the pillow top and nestle his full-bellied body right up against my head. "What is it, the smell you think?" I asked Roger, not turning my head to talk to him but inquiring while sitting very still.

"I don't know, but he's happy as a clam."

"And probably falling asleep, right?"

Roger laughed. "Yeah, he is."

What we didn't know about this outgoing, playful, growing-like-a-weed cat was that his size and strength belied a hidden condition. And even if we'd known about it upon adopting him, we still would have taken him in.

Red's robust size of twelve pounds never gave him any trouble—a big but healthy cat. His meows and constant clamoring for attention were part of his charm, and we never tired of talking to him. Having orange and white cat hair stuck to the back of our pants was okay with us, too. It was a small price to pay for a cat who loved us.

Then, when Red was almost ten, he began to lose weight. He never stopped doing his head-butts, and he still loved to be petted, squashed right next to one of us on the sofa. But he was losing weight rapidly, and his visits to the litter box became more and more frequent. I took him to the vet. "Diabetic," Dr. Love pronounced. "No way you could have known or could have stopped it." The kind vet looked me straight in the eyes. "Cats get it more often than you'd think. It can be managed."

"Great," I said while rubbing Red's neck. "What do we have to do?"

After hearing all about the twice-a-day insulin shots and the diabetic-management cat food, we were armed for battle.

"Okay, who's going to give him the shot?" Roger asked the first morning. "The vet showed you how to do it, right?"

"Yup, and it's super easy. Call Red up here."

Roger stood at the kitchen counter. "Come on, Red. Get on up here." Red jumped up on a chair, onto the table, and then onto the counter, and then immediately head-butted Roger's hand and let out a huge meow. He stood stock still as I pinched his fur, inserted the short needle, and injected the insulin.

"Done. Good boy, Red." I turned to Roger. "Your turn tonight."

And that's the way it went for five years. Red jumped up every morning and every evening, head-butted our hands, and then stood still for his insulin injection. There wasn't a cowardly bone in his body. We came to call him our Courageous Lion because of his size and coloring, but also his courage. He seemed to know those shots kept him well, and after adjustments to the dosage to get it right for his size, Red regained all of his weight.

In the sixth year after he was diagnosed, a trip to the vet revealed that he no longer needed the insulin or the diabetic-management cat food. We would have continued his regimen for as long as he needed it, but the tests didn't lie. Maybe his Courageous Lion attitude had head-butted that nasty diabetes to the curb.

During those years of twice-a-day insulin shots, I gradually began to see that Red's fearlessness was teaching me something. Whenever I faced a challenge of my own, I'd think of him. If Red had the strength and courage to meet his disease head-on, then I could meet my own situations head-on, too. My cowardly lion style was replaced by the same fearlessness that Red exhibited. What a great role model that little cat turned out to be.

~B.J. Taylor

35

Unexpected Visitors

A kitten is, in the animal world, what
a rosebud is in the garden.
~Robert Southey

The phone rang while I was preparing dinner. "Hi, Mom, we're heading home now." It was my son Chris. He and his friend Jenn had been out of town the day before.

"Great," I replied. "We'll expect you in a couple of hours."

"Wait, Mom, I have something to tell you." Just then, my oven timer dinged.

"Tell me when you get here," I said. "Pie's ready. Got to go."

As I started to hang up, I heard Chris say, "We're bringing some extra company."

Extra company? Yikes! Would there be enough food to go around?

"How many?" I asked.

"Four," said Chris.

"Four? Chris, I can't feed four extra people on such short notice!"

"Good news, Mom," he replied cheerfully. "You don't have to feed people. The company I'm bringing home is four abandoned kittens."

"Kittens? Chris…"

"We're stopping at Sandra's on the way. She's getting formula for them." Our animal-loving daughter had a summer job at the local veterinary clinic. "They'll have to be fed every four hours. Don't worry, she'll explain it all to you."

"Explain? Explain what?" Too late. Chris had hung up.

The timer dinged again. My pie! I yanked open the oven door to a burned-apple smell. Too late for the pie, too.

I made a cup of tea to calm my nerves and phoned Sandra.

"What's up?" she asked.

"Four newborn kittens," I replied.

"Not to worry," she said. "I got the formula and bottles. The vet said they'll have to be fed every four hours. I'll come and show you what to do."

Show me what to do? "Sandra, I don't know anything about caring for newborn kittens."

"I'll help," she said. "But I work all day, so I can't look after them full-time."

And I don't work all day? I'm a writer. Writers work day and night. Well, sometimes.

"I have to go," Sandra broke in. "Chris and Jenn just arrived. See you soon."

I love animals passionately, but being caregiver to four newborn kittens was more than I could handle. I resolved then and there to follow that sage advice, "Just say no."

I was working on it when the front door opened. "Mom? Come see the kittens," Chris called from the vestibule.

I went downstairs, silently repeating the "just say no" mantra.

Four tiny kittens lay snuggled together in a basket in Jenn's arms.

"Where did you find them?" I asked.

"We heard cries coming from the roof of our motel," Jenn said.

"The guy in the office said a pregnant cat had been hanging around," Chris jumped in. "He kept chasing her away, but he thought she'd had her kittens on the roof."

"He said he hadn't seen her for several days, so he figured she'd been killed on the highway, and now he was stuck dealing with them. We knew what he meant by 'dealing with them,'" Jenn said ominously.

"I told him we'd look after them," Chris said. "I borrowed his ladder and got up on the roof. Somehow, the mother cat got inside the air-conditioning unit and had her kittens there. She must have been desperate and thought it was a safe place."

I blocked out the thought of what might have happened to the kittens if Chris and Jenn hadn't come along.

At that moment, the smallest kitten gave a faint squeal. Before I knew what I was doing, I reached in and picked it up.

"He's the runt of the litter," Jenn said. "He may not survive."

"Unless he has the best care possible," Chris added. "Care only a mother can give."

"I am not a mother cat," I reminded my son as I wrapped my sweater gently around the unbelievably tiny bit of life in my hands.

The door opened, and Sandra came in. Her eyes went to the sweater-wrapped bundle in my arms. I saw the knowing smiles she, Chris, and Jenn exchanged.

"I brought everything you'll need for the kittens — formula, feeding bottles, wipes," Sandra explained. "We'll work out a schedule, and we'll all help. Mom, look at them." She picked up the white one with orange and black markings. The kitten obligingly wobbled her head and managed to look sweet and pathetic at the same time. "How can you resist?"

The bottom line was, I couldn't.

In no time, the kittens were awake, filling the house with their hungry chorus. My "just say no" mantra vanished in the twitch of a whisker.

That afternoon, Sandra walked me through the steps of kitten care. "They have to be fed every four hours. Then there's the toileting." I won't go into details, but suffice it to say disposable diapers do not work on kittens.

And so I became a kitty mama. If I thought my children had been messy eaters, the kittens outdid them hands... er... paws down. And bathing a kitten is no easy job. Imagine a body so small that it fits into the palm of your hand, with twig-like limbs and paws the size of a dime. Imagine toweling them dry, taking care not to get tiny claws snagged in the cloth.

When I was on my own that night for the ten o'clock feeding, reality hit. There were *four* of them and only *one* of me. When one kitten woke up, its hungry cries woke the others. Suddenly, I had four little, pink mouths emitting heart-rending pleas. Begging the one I was feeding to hurry so the others could have their turn fell on deaf ears. Last but not least, every towel and blanket that lined their basket had to be washed because no one was toilet-trained.

Fortunately, as the days went by, I did have help. On alternate days, Sandra took the kittens to the veterinary clinic where the staff argued over who would get to look after the adorable quartet. Strangely, no one offered to do the night shifts, though.

As well as feeding the kittens on schedule, we had to keep track of every gram of formula they drank. I couldn't bear to list them as Kitten 1, 2, 3 and 4 so I named them — Bailey, Zoli, Chloe, and for the littlest one, the biggest name of all — Leo the Lion-Hearted.

Once named, the kittens developed individual personalities over-night. Leo certainly lived up to his name. His heart stopped twice, thankfully when he was in my daughter's care. Using two fingers — for that was all that would fit on his tiny chest — Sandra managed to massage his heart back into action.

Good news! They all survived and thrived. Zoli and Bailey were adopted by Sandra's mother-in-law, and they are living a life of leisure. Chloe went to live with a friend of Chris's, and wee Leo was adopted by a client at the veterinary clinic.

Fourteen years have passed since those four unexpected visitors arrived. Looking back, I am thankful beyond measure that I had the opportunity to play a part in ensuring their survival. It was an up close look at the miracle of new life.

~Marilyn Helmer

36

My Annie-versary Kitty

A cat lover and his cat have a master/slave
relationship. The cat is the master.
~Arthur R. Kassin

'm going to be late for work today," my friend Michelle
called to tell me. "My cat decided to have her babies this
morning. In a basket of clean laundry."

I laughed. "I'm guessing the laundry is no longer clean."

"You guessed right. You're going to take a kitten, aren't you? I
can't keep them all, but I hate to take them to a shelter."

"Yes, we'll take one. I don't want them at a shelter either."

My husband and I already had one cat, a male named Tigger. He
loved to cuddle, and he'd never met a stranger. Any time I sat down, he
crawled into my lap for a snuggle. I just assumed all cats were that way.

Boy, was I wrong.

Several weeks later, Michelle told me that I could pick out my
kitten. "I already know which one you're going to want," she said. "The
runt is a female, and she's so tiny and cute. You can have whichever
one you want, but I predict you'll fall in love with her."

I smiled. The thought of a tiny, cuddly kitten had that effect on
me. "We'll come over tomorrow. Today is our first wedding anniversary,
so I'm sure we'll be too busy celebrating."

But that night, after we'd had dinner at our favorite restaurant,
my husband offered to take me to Michelle's house. "I can tell you
don't want to wait," he said with a smile.

He knew me well, as did Michelle. Her prediction was right. That tiny female kitten tugged on my heartstrings, and I knew immediately that she was the one I wanted.

We named her Annie, in honor of our anniversary. Our Annie-versary.

When we got home, I watched as Tigger inspected this new creature in his space. I was concerned that he might not like her, but I worried for nothing. Within moments, the two were snuggled together under our bed.

The next evening, Annie was still there.

"I can't coax her out," I told my husband.

"Just give her some space," he said. "She's still adjusting to a new place and new people."

I took his advice and tried not to worry about her. But it soon became obvious that Annie wanted nothing to do with us.

"What's wrong with her, Tigger?" I murmured into his fur during a snuggle session. "Can't you tell her we're nice people, and she doesn't need to be afraid of us?"

If Tigger told her, Annie didn't listen. She found every hiding place in our small apartment and used each one to her advantage. I would occasionally see a tiny black streak run by, but most days, I didn't see her at all.

"How's Annie?" Michelle asked after a few weeks.

"She hates us, and I don't know why," I answered. "She hides, and when I try to coax her out with food, she does whatever she can to get away from me. She avoids all contact with us."

Michelle sighed. "Maybe she just needs more time to adjust."

But weeks later, the problem had gotten worse, not better.

"She acts like she's been abused or something," I told Michelle. "She hisses at me any time I try to touch her."

"I had a cat like this once," she said. "They can be socialized, but it takes a lot of time and effort. It's a big commitment. And if it doesn't work…"

I shook my head and pictured that sweet, little face. "Tell me what to do."

"You've got to make it impossible for her to hide from you," she said. "Choose a room in your house and block off all of the hiding places in that room. Put Annie in there and visit her every day. Don't try to touch her. Just let her get used to being in the same room with you."

Our one-bedroom apartment had a small den that would be perfect as Annie's new room. I blocked off the hiding places and moved Annie's food and litter box into the room. It took nearly two hours, but eventually we were able to chase her into her new room.

The visitations started the next day.

When I walked in that first time, I could see Annie frantically looking around for somewhere to hide from me. When she realized there was nowhere to go, she backed herself into a corner and just stared at me.

I spent hours sitting in that room, staring at a cat who wanted nothing to do with me. Oftentimes, I would bring Tigger in with me, hoping that his friendliness toward me would influence Annie's behavior.

No such luck.

Michelle said Step Two was to bribe her with food. "Put a tablespoon of tuna on a plate and set it a few feet away from you," she instructed. "Still don't try to touch her, but talk to her in a soothing voice while she eats it. If she doesn't eat it with you in the room, take the treat with you when you leave. She'll wait you out if you let her, so you need to teach her that she only gets the food if she comes close to you."

It took two weeks before Annie ventured out of her corner to eat the tuna. And even then, she'd eat one bite, run back into the corner, and then venture out again for another taste.

It was so frustrating. "Why the mistrust, Annie?" I'd ask her softly. "I'll never hurt you."

Finally, after four months of daily visits, Annie let me touch her. It was the first time since the day we'd gotten her.

Gradually, she came close to me without the plate of tuna between us. She would allow me to pet her, and then one day, she crept into my lap.

It was amazing.

On our second wedding anniversary, I decided to let Annie out of the den, hoping she wouldn't find a hiding place and stay there for the next six months.

Instead, she crept out of the room and slowly explored the apartment. Then she jumped onto the couch and lay down next to Tigger. When I sat down, both cats crawled into my lap.

I nearly cried with relief.

Annie taught me that relationships aren't always easy, but they are always worth the effort. She taught me the fine art of simply sitting with someone, of being available to them when they finally come out of their hiding place and decide to open up and let us in. She taught me to go slowly and be patient, and to occasionally smooth things over with a tasty treat. And, most importantly, she taught me to never, ever give up on someone.

~Diane Stark

37

Sinbad's Sofa

When you're used to hearing purring and suddenly it's
gone, it's hard to silence the blaring sound of sadness.
~Missy Altijd

I f you've wintered in the heartland, you know the kind of blizzard I mean — a gale-whipped snow that burns your skin like
needles. I pumped gas for three cars that night, each appear-
ing suddenly from the whiteness like an apparition. The drivers
huddled behind the wheel while I filled their tanks, paid wordlessly,
and drove off, to be swallowed by the blinding storm.

Just after midnight, a longhaired, black cat appeared, his eyes
glittering in the station lights as he paced outside the glass entry door.
I could see he was yowling, but his voice disappeared in that pitiless
wind.

I let him in. He ate a bit of my hours-old burger, washing it down
with water from a paper cup. All the while, his watchful eyes never
left me. His immediate needs met, he went exploring.

It didn't take him long to find the sofa situated between the rusting
soda cooler and the compressor powering the service-bay lift. The sofa
wasn't much to look at, but it was positioned under our admittedly
inadequate overhead heater.

The cat didn't mind the disgusting state of the sofa. It smelled of
gasoline, engine oil and over-brewed coffee, and it was covered in a
disturbing collage of stains — the origins of which it was best not to
contemplate. I thought the rag bin would be a better place for him. It

certainly smelled better. But would he let me pick him up?

He did. When I set him down in the rag bin, he eyed me with offended dignity before going to work pawing at the rags. He curled up in the resulting indentation, and I congratulated myself on my successful bait-and-switch. Less than an hour later, I settled down for a nap of my own on that sofa.

I slept lightly back then. So when Sinbad's weight hit my chest, it startled me to full consciousness. He shifted around for a moment or two, eventually finding comfort with his nose less than four inches from mine.

I remember wondering if he'd had his shots as he pawed my nose gently, and then nose-butted me. After less than a minute of stroking him behind the ears, his purrs competed with the drone of the soda cooler behind my head. My new companion moved only once that night, momentarily startled by the compressor kicking in to re-pressurize the service lift.

The next morning, the station owner, Jerry, ratified the cat's status as station mascot, dubbing him Sinbad. Jerry's unstated plan seemed to involve underfeeding the cat so that he would keep the rodents in check. I doubt he realized I was feeding Sinbad each night when I arrived for my shift. In less than a month, Sinbad developed a fondness for venison jerky and vanilla milkshakes from the truck stop. He spent part of every night parked in the middle of my chest, purring and kneading me with his paws — occasionally with enough energy to keep me awake. And so it went through the long Plains winter.

By the time the Chinooks blew and the snow melted, Sinbad and I took each other for granted. Warmer weather had him coming and going at will, but never missing his evening snack. When I studied, he treated my open textbooks as his own. His favorites seemed to be *Hansen's History of Art* and *Box* and *Jenkins' Statistics and Forecasting*. Sinbad was not a cat to be ignored. Somewhere along the way, he had perfected the nose-butt, for use when more subtle, attention-getting techniques failed. By May, he ruled the back room and the sofa with the regal hegemony only cats can pull off.

One night when I came in for my shift, Sinbad was nowhere to be found. I asked Jerry about him, but he was as mystified as I was. A week passed, and still no Sinbad. *He's a cat*, I reminded myself each time I worried about him. *Cats do this. He was never yours, so get over it.*

Sinbad had wandered in one night, seeking refuge. I had provided it, along with a comfortable sofa. Neither Sinbad nor the sofa we shared was mine. *He had moved on when it suited him, just as I would move on when I completed the requirements for my degree. And when I moved on, my sofa would be someone else's. That's how it is,* I told myself.

Still, I worried. Had he been snatched by coyotes, mauled by a dog, or hit by a car? Or had he just gone home, now that the snow had melted? The distractions of my senior year gave me other things to think about, gradually driving Sinbad from my thoughts — until Jerry replaced the sofa in the back room.

He was as aware as I was that the old sofa was years past its best. So when he bought a new sofa for his den at home, he brought the old one out to the station. With Midwest pragmatism, he loaded the stain-soaked sofa from the back room into the pickup and hauled it to the dump. In his mind, he was merely replacing an old thing with a newer, more comfortable thing.

But I associated the old sofa with Sinbad, who had not simply curled up with me on it, but had also curled up in my heart. I missed my chance companion and, by association, the sofa we'd shared. Somehow, the new one was never comfortable.

It's been more than forty years since Sinbad wandered into and out of my life with the effortless grace of cats everywhere. I have been through at least half a dozen sofas of my own since then, all nicer and less aromatic than the one in the back room of Jerry's Standard station. I have also come to know countless men and women over those years. Most, like Sinbad, have wandered into and out of my life.

Many etched memories into my story, then moved on, often with little or no explanation. I have come to accept these unexplained disappearances. But some people — and some critters — never truly leave. They hang around, like Sinbad, long after they're gone. Remembering always leaves me with a bittersweet twist in my gut — part regret, part reluctant acceptance, but mostly deep, enduring love. Sinbad, and the people and many creatures I've known, have become a kind of internal clock by which I measure my life and how much of it I have left.

Occasionally, on late nights when sleep eludes me, Sinbad still rubs against my thoughts. When he does, I tell myself his disappearance was just a result of him listening to the mysterious inner wisdom that guided him to me on that bitter winter night — just as it drove him to move on when it was time. But mostly when I think of him, I hope that at some level he remembered the sofa we shared — and that it was a place of deep contentment for him, as it was for me that winter so long ago.

~Dirk B. Sayers

38

Max

Cats ask plainly for what they want.
~Walter Savage Landor

N o one knew where he came from. He just appeared in the hallway of a local rescue's adoption center. Max was a striking gray tabby with a white vest and white paws, not feral but not exactly friendly either. He would most likely adopt out as a barn cat.

The group finally managed to snag him and put him on the schedule for a neuter. Since the spay-neuter veterinarian was out of town, he had to wait several weeks, allowing time to work on his social skills.

Max hated being caged. I visited him daily and explained that life would soon be better. He would have his surgery, try to be friendlier, and find a home of his very own — a nice, warm barn with lots of mice. The day of his neuter finally arrived. While in recovery, they realized that Max had somehow not been tested for feline immunodeficiency virus (FIV). Normal procedure would be to test on intake. The results were discouraging: positive for FIV. As a small rescue group with limited cat isolation, euthanasia would be indicated. On the verge of tears, I realized that I had become attached to this cantankerous little cat. Adopting him seemed out of the question as I already had three cats and no place to isolate an infectious one. *But if not me, who?* It's hard to find a home for a healthy cat, and almost impossible for a sick cat.

I decided to build a cat enclosure. It seemed like a crazy solution, and I didn't really have the time to do it. He would be enclosed by himself and still have his underlying illness. When I suggested my idea, I expected my normally sane friends to discourage me and point out the obvious drawbacks. Instead, the group responded quickly with "We'll help." Planning to get this completed within the week, everybody pitched in to finish in only four days. I think they were afraid I would change my mind, and everyone wanted Max to have his chance. He moved into his new house — a 10x10 chain-link room with climbing perches, a large dog igloo, several cat cubbies, and lots of toys. I still felt bad because living alone in a cage was not my idea of a quality life.

Within a couple of weeks, I received a call from an acquaintance who urgently needed placement for Simon, an FIV-positive cat who was being displaced. It was the perfect solution. Simon and Max were instant friends, and they thrived in each other's company. When the seasons changed, my friends and I winterized the enclosure, making the cats snug in their heated areas. Simon was a very affectionate cat and he and Max frequently groomed each other. Simon loved to be petted and was quick to curl up in my lap when I sat in the chair visiting them. As Max watched intently, his bad habits diminished. He no longer bit or swatted at people. Simon succumbed to his disease after several years, but Max was still going strong. By then, Max was a lovable, friendly cat. Simon had imparted his social skills to Max.

I was now down to two other house cats, both extremely old. The veterinarian felt that exposure to Max would not be a serious threat to such old cats. Thus, the now affable Max moved into my house. He quickly settled in and enjoyed the company of the other cats and even the dogs. He spends most days in the sunroom these days, but he also enjoys roaming my fenced yard and checking out his old digs in the cat enclosure.

Max has shared my life for eight years. With any injury or illness, increased immune-system support is required. Overall, though, he's been fairly healthy. He demands to be petted every day, and he's not above an occasional light nip if I seem to be ignoring him. He rarely meows, but instead gives me a determined stare if he needs something. Food bowl empty? Stare at bowl. Stare at Mom. Stare at bowl. Stare at Mom. His determined stare can even penetrate my sleep.

I wonder about the quirks of fate that brought this special animal into my life and allowed me to help two cats in the process. I wasn't looking to adopt a cat, especially not a sick one. If the blood test had been done in a timely manner, I wouldn't have had the opportunity to get to know him. If I hadn't built the enclosure for Max, Simon wouldn't have had a place to go. If Simon hadn't come, I doubt Max would have ever been a friendly cat. It's amazing how things work together in challenging circumstances and create a terrific outcome!

~Carmen Marlin

39

The Fierce, Bad Cat of Evergreen Farm

*Anyone who claims a cat cannot give a dirty look has
either never kept a cat or is singularly unobservant.*
~Maurice Burton

Many years ago, my precious cat was struck and killed on the road late one evening by the neighbouring farmer. An accident, of course, but he felt horrible about it. I buried her deep in my flowerbed, still wearing her little velvet collar with the brass bell. A few weeks later, I looked down the long driveway of our horse farm and saw my neighbour tromping down the driveway in his rubber boots with a determined hold on a screeching calico kitten. He explained that his mother's cat had had a litter, and this one did not have a home. I wasn't really finished mourning my poor Panther, but who can resist a kitten?

I took her inside and regarded her: tiny but very cute, with brilliant splotches of orange, black, and white. So began my life with Sabu.

She was a hellion right from the start. When people came into my living quarters, Sabu would fly up the back of an easy chair to get closer to their faces and introduce herself with a hiss and a spit. Her early days were spent outside in the company of the farm dog: a one-hundred-pound German Shepherd who thought Sabu was the greatest. For several weeks, I rarely saw her during the day. I would catch glimpses of her bounding after the dog. The Shepherd had one eye on his kitten and the other on the doings of the farm, so I knew Sabu would never be too far away. Occasionally, she would fly through the barn, chasing one of the barn cats.

The humans fared no better. The horse boarders would come to my door to tell me that a wild cat had moved into the stable and was hissing and growling at them. The cat, they said, was sitting on top of their tack lockers and would scratch them if they tried to open their doors. I would go to the tack room, pick up Sabu, apologize, and carry her back to the clubhouse. The blacksmith, who looked after the horses' hooves, complained he could not write his bills at the counter because my cat kept attacking him. I had only one rule for Sabu: She had to come in at night so she never befell the fate of Panther.

Sabu was absolutely fearless and not the least bit nervous. She rode around with me in the farm Jeep, sitting up on the console beside me. She would join me on visits to my parents, who lived several hours away. She showed none of the fear of travel or new surroundings that other cats did. She loved apple pie and turkey and sleeping deep down inside my long, black riding boots.

Although I had to apologize for her a lot, I was secretly proud of my feisty cat. As a professional groom, I lived and breathed horses, but it was often a lonely life. It was a life of pure dedication to the exquisite creatures I cared for, and there were few days off. It was hard to stay in touch with my family, and the farm animals became my friends.

Sabu was my best friend of all. Every night, I would go to the door and call her, and she would come bounding inside. She would jump on my lap, and then crawl up my neck and nestle in my freshly showered hair. She would let out the biggest rumbling purr ever heard and then fall sound asleep. As antisocial as she was with other people, she loved me, and I her.

Years went by. The stable was sold, and Sabu was my companion through thick and thin. My dad would say that I dragged that poor cat "from pillar to post," and I guess I did. At one point, I moved into the bottom half of a house that I shared with my sister. I imagine this was probably Sabu's least favourite home. I was preoccupied with my career as a horse trainer, and she was alone a lot and getting older.

To make matters worse, I had more of a social life now, and to Sabu's horror, I began to bring home dates. It never went well. She would climb up behind them on the couch, and stare and growl and hiss and even spit. Her verbal takedowns were harsh, and her silent stares were withering.

One night, I invited over a fellow I had been dating. We had been set up on a blind date, and I really liked him — even though he was a self-proclaimed "dog person." We settled on the couch to watch a movie, and Sabu silently regarded us from the floor. Then Sabu stood and began to make her way toward us. I knew instantly that her intention was to jump up on the arm of the couch, walk over the lap of my new beau, and settle on my lap.

There was no way this was going to go well unless he sat perfectly still and did not make eye contact.

As predicted, Sabu jumped up, started across my companion's lap, and then did the strangest thing. She looked at him and seemed to do the equivalent of a feline double take. Instead of climbing on me, she turned and put her front paws on his chest and bunted her nose under his chin several times. He stroked her silky fur as if they were old buddies, and she began to purr.

So, I guess Sabu gave us her blessing right then and there. Ron and I continued dating and were married several years later. A major sticking point was Ron's home office. He thought Sabu could be trained to stay out of his home office even when the door was open. That began a battle in which Sabu would play dead and have to be carried from the room and put on the other side of the door. From there, she would lie staring at my husband at his desk, and then extend a defiant paw across the doorway into the room. I swear I could see the steam coming from my husband's ears.

Sabu was with me for nineteen years. And since she had picked him out, my husband was with us on that last sad trip to the vet. I'll always be glad that farmer brought me that unwanted fierce "bad" kitten, way before I thought I was ready for my next cat.

~Joanne M. Copeland

40

One Step at a Time

Always the cat remains a little beyond the limits
we try to set for him in our blind folly.
~Andre Norton

M y mother's words felt like a punch to the stomach. "Figaro's been hit by a car. She's dead." Figaro was a feral cat we'd been feeding in our barn for years. Though she'd never let me pet her, the sight of Figaro's golden eyes watching while I mucked stalls was a familiar comfort. Now, without warning, she was gone.

And that wasn't even the worst part. Barely a week earlier, Figaro had given birth. Now, as Mom and I stared at one another, I knew we were both thinking the same thing: The kittens had just become orphans.

Choking back my tears, I walked out to the barn. I found Figaro's babies in an old cardboard box: three tiny balls of fur — two orange, one black. Their eyes were closed, and their ears were folded up. As I leaned closer, the sightless kittens started hissing, realizing I wasn't their mother.

They had no idea their lives had just changed forever.

My legs were leaden as I carried the box to the house. Mom went to buy milk-replacement formula while I researched how to care for my new "children." At first, my efforts weren't appreciated. The kittens screeched and flailed whenever I tried to feed them, their claws decorating my skin with scratches. I learned how to tell the two orange kittens apart — one had a white stripe down his nose — and established a feeding order. Unfortunately, by the time I finished with the third kitten, it was almost time to start feeding the first one again.

Several sleep-deprived days later, things weren't going well. Though they were thriving physically, the kittens still shrieked every time I touched them. They happily nuzzled the stuffed dog I'd given them, but had no interest in cuddling with their adoptive mom. I was only a source of food and nothing more.

Then one night, as I was holding the stripe-nosed kitten in my hand, gently cleaning him with a washcloth, I realized that he wasn't struggling anymore. Instead, he was staring at me. His calm, blue-gray eyes gazed deep into mine, like he was looking directly into my soul. Our eyes remained locked on each other for several long seconds, and then something amazing happened — a low rumbling noise started to fill the air.

"Are you… purring?" I asked incredulously.

The rumbling grew louder, and I couldn't stop the grin that stretched across my face. Suddenly, all those lost hours of sleep meant nothing.

Over the next week, I managed to "melt the ice" with the other two kittens. As the days passed, blue eyes transformed to amber-gold, and our house became filled with scampering feet. The stripe-nosed kitten, Sputnik, matured into a powerful athlete. He never missed a chance to leap onto the kitchen counter. He loved showing off his cleverness by stealing rubber bands, opening cupboard doors, and flipping light switches. And, like his siblings, Sputnik adored "Cuddle Time." As months turned to years, I forgot what it felt like to watch TV with an empty lap or sleep without three warm balls snuggled beside me.

Then, one morning, everything changed. There was a cat on my pillow and another cat by my feet, but the space by my waist was empty. I noticed Sputnik limping toward the bed.

"What's wrong, buddy?" I asked. "Did you hurt your leg?"

Clearly untroubled, he hopped on the mattress, settled in, and fell asleep. Later that day, though, the limp was worse. Our veterinarian diagnosed Sputnik with a ruptured disc in his back, which was affecting the nerves in his right rear leg. The doctor prescribed some anti-inflammatory medicine and told us it would be a long recovery.

On the way home, we bought a low-sided litter box so Sputnik could climb in without bumping his leg. But by the time we got back to the house, he couldn't even stand up. And by nine o'clock that night, Sputnik had lost the use of his right front leg, too.

Tears streaming down my face, I showed Mom his floppy, useless front leg. We both knew his condition was far more serious than the vet thought. Back at the clinic, a different vet tested Sputnik for diabetes, but the test was negative. X-rays showed nothing, and eventually the doctors could only narrow it down to four possibilities: a ruptured disc in Sputnik's neck, a stroke, an aneurysm, or a brain tumor.

The vets advised us to continue medicating him and hope for the best, but also to prepare for the worst. Back at home, we wrapped towels around all the chair legs so Sputnik wouldn't hurt himself. I could feel his confusion and fear as he tried to walk and failed miserably. The cat who could once easily leap onto the kitchen counter now couldn't even take one step without collapsing. Mom and I took turns helping him get to the food dish and the litter box. We carefully repositioned Sputnik's legs every time they crumpled beneath him and put mats on the hardwood floor to keep him from slipping. We arranged our schedules so he always had supervision, and I even started sleeping on the floor so I could see where he was any time I opened my eyes.

As I watched my cat struggle and suffer, my mind floated back to that moment eleven years earlier when he first started purring in the palm of my hand. And, selfishly, I thought, *Eleven years wasn't enough.*

I needed more time, but it didn't look like I would get it. Sputnik's left pupil became more dilated than his right one — a condition called Horner's Syndrome — and the prognosis was grimmer than ever. Emotions raged within me, my own selfish needs battling with doing what was best for my cat... my baby.

While I was in turmoil, Mom held onto hope. It was Mom who said, "Look!" whenever Sputnik took two successful steps in a row. It was Mom who cheered whenever he picked himself up after falling.

At first, I wouldn't let myself get pulled into her excitement. But soon, the progress was undeniable. One day, he would walk three steps in a row — the next day, four. Despite his dire prognosis, he was getting better. Day by day, Sputnik regained the ability to walk. Eventually, to our very great surprise, he even relearned how to run and jump.

Now thirteen years old and the most spoiled cat imaginable — Mom calls him "The Prince of Everything" — Sputnik is still going strong. He walks, runs, and climbs. We may never know what happened to him, but we do know there's a chance he could relapse. A brain tumor could start growing again; a blood vessel could rupture.

As I learned thirteen years ago, life can change in an instant. In a single rush of oncoming tires, three kittens lost their mother. In a single day, a rowdy, rambunctious cat lost the ability to walk. Somehow, against all odds, he regained it. Anything could happen tomorrow, but for right now, we're happy to take things one day — one step — at a time.

~Gretchen Bassier

41

The Snow Cat

A sense of curiosity is nature's
original school of education.
~Smiley Blanton

A cat adopted in Louisiana and raised in Memphis, Tennessee doesn't have many opportunities to see snow. But a few years ago, my tabby Libby Lou—lovingly referred to as the "worst cat in the world"—finally got her chance to view a winter fairyland.

Surprisingly, Memphis had received a substantial snowfall. And Libby Lou, who loves to look out the windows through our louvered shutters, was very aware that something was up.

I had watched her when she approached the window on that snowy morning. She stopped and stood still. She bobbed her head up and down like someone watching a tennis match in reverse. Her ears twitched back and forth, and her eyes never blinked. She cooed and squeaked. I think she wanted me to know that something very strange had occurred.

She looked at me as if to say, "Is this happening everywhere?" then darted to the next window to find out. She popped open the blinds with her paw, and once again her head followed the movement of the falling flakes.

Of course, she couldn't stop with only two windows. Was our house surrounded by this white stuff? Chattering loudly, she ran from one room to the next, opening the blinds and making her inspection.

I followed her on this epic journey. "What do you see, girl? What's that white stuff falling from the sky?"

She'd meow and chirp to let me know that something of great importance was happening outside of each window.

When was the last time I had gotten so excited about snow? I wondered. During my first years in Memphis, I never let the occasional snowfall pass without pulling on my boots, grabbing my camera, and heading out to take pictures. Memphis doesn't get a lot of snow, but it gets more than south Louisiana, so I was dutifully impressed with the white stuff.

What had changed? When did I start taking the small things for granted and ignoring the many miracles around me? Sure, I was a little older now, but the universe hadn't lost its splendor. Red sunsets that seemingly set the sky on fire were just as beautiful today. The ocean would still smell as clean, and the roaring waves were just as deafening and majestic.

Humans can learn a lot from animals. Animals do not take nature for granted. They appreciate the beauty, stability, and rapture our world provides. I learned a lot that day. A rowdy cat, adopted from a shelter, and a thick snowfall proved to be good teachers.

Today, I enjoy looking up at a starlit sky or crunching through autumn leaves. And the next time Memphis is blessed with snow, I'll be right in the middle of it, bundled up, shivering, and taking pictures. And I'll be sure to bring in a snowball for Libby Lou to chase around the hardwood floor.

~Sharon Rene Dick

42

Bruni

The cat has too much spirit to have no heart.
~Ernest Menaul

walked into my local Humane Society to start my volunteer shift. My co-worker was filling out the paperwork for a new resident in the cage in the corner. "Meet Bruni," she said. "Be careful, though. He's not happy."

That was a huge understatement! Malevolent, yellow eyes stared back at me as I peered into the cage. When I took a slow step toward him, a whirlwind of black-and-white fur, claws and teeth charged toward the front of the cage. Instinctively, I took a step back and looked over at my co-worker.

"Jeez! *Not* happy is right! What's his story?" I asked.

"He was owned by an elderly Italian man who passed away," she said. "Sadly, there is no family member willing to take him."

It's a story that shelter personnel know only too well. Cats make great family pets, and they can also be wonderful pets for elderly people on their own. Unfortunately, most people don't think about the possibility of the cat outliving the elderly person, and many cats, like Bruni, are surrendered to shelters when their owners pass away.

"Let's give him a few days to settle in," I said. "We can re-assess him again after he cools down."

Well, a few days turned into weeks. There was no cool-down in sight. Bruni showed no signs of surrender. He glowered at anyone who dared approach his cage and terrorized the shelter staff. Most new cats that came into the cat shelter cower in the back initially, but then become comfortable with their surroundings and the shelter within a few days. Bruni offered a real challenge. Not only was he angry, but he was very frightened, too. All he had known in the first years of life was a quiet home with his owner. Now, he was caged, surrounded by anxious, stressed cats. He was a sensitive boy who needed help.

That's when my work with Bruni began. I tried all the tricks I had — sitting beside his cage, talking to him, tempting him with treats, attempting to engage him with toys, even bringing in a friend to speak to him in Italian. Nothing worked. He would glare unblinkingly at me, his black ears flattened to his head, daring me to put one finger inside the cage. I sighed. "You are not making it easy, are you, Bruni? You need to be the sweetheart I know you can be." Time was of the essence, too. The longer Bruni stayed at the shelter, the more stressed he became. At this point, Bruni was unadoptable.

I was willing to try anything to get Bruni out of his angry shell. I spoke with other volunteers, veterinarians, and cat experts, and all of them told me the same thing. Patience is what I needed, and I would find the missing key to Bruni's heart eventually.

Then, it happened. I was preparing his food one day, and on a whim, I decided to give him some soft food. There's always a shortage of money at an animal shelter, so soft food is usually given only to kittens and nursing mothers. But I was at the point when I was willing to try anything. I put the soft food in his cage and sat beside him, steadily talking to him. He growled softly at me the whole time he ate. I considered that a victory. At least he wasn't trying to rip me apart!

On day three of my soft-food experiment, I walked into the cat shelter to start my shift, only to hear a soft pinging sound. My co-worker gestured to his cage and said, "Your boyfriend wants you!"

I looked over to see Bruni, solemn eyes blinking at me, his claws gently tugging on the bars of his cage.

I quickly went into the kitchen and prepared more soft food. As I walked toward him with the dish of food, he started to purr and rub against the bars. Joy flooded my heart. He was on his way to being a loving, happy cat!

After our breakthrough, we were inseparable. I would let him out of his cage, and he would follow me around the shelter. I would pick him up, and he would sit on my lap as I did paperwork. If I stopped giving him attention, he would meow and gently bump his head against me as if to say, "Don't stop yet!"

My heart was in dangerous territory. I was falling in love with Bruni, but I knew that as much as I loved him, we couldn't be together. He needed to be the only animal in a household. He really disliked other animals, and at that time, I had three dogs and a cat! I tried not to think about Bruni being adopted, but I knew the day would come when I would have to say goodbye.

Finally, I got a call that I was dreading. "Don't come in today," my co-worker said. "A retired couple is coming in to take a look at Bruni. Jill, they're perfect! He'll have the best home."

My heart sank. I loved him, but I also wanted him to be happy.

"Okay, Jude," I answered. "Make sure they're worthy of him."

When I hung up the phone, I cried. Out of all the cats I cared for at the shelter, he was the one who stole my heart.

When we received a phone call from Bruni's new people, my trepidation about his adoption vanished. "He walked right out of his carrier like he'd been here his whole life," the owner said. "Right now, he's napping with my husband on the sofa. Bruni is a real sweetheart. We love him."

It's been over ten years since Bruni was adopted and I still think about him. He was my toughest assignment and also my greatest teacher. He taught me that patience is indeed a virtue.

~Jill Berni

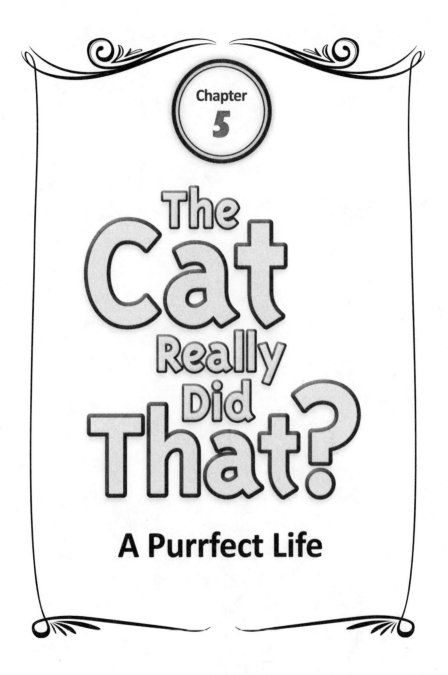

Chapter
5

The Cat Really Did That?

A Purrfect Life

The Turtle Tabby

*You will always be lucky if you know how
to make friends with strange cats.*
~American Proverb

For thirteen years, I worked in a low-cost, no-kill veterinary clinic as a registered veterinary technician. We were located in a poorer area of Hollywood, California, and numerous animals were abandoned at our hospital. We would patch them up and get them adopted. We were pretty good at it, too!

Under rare circumstances, however, an adoption would not work out, and the animal was returned to us. There were many reasons—sometimes valid and sometimes ridiculous. One cat, for example, was returned to us five years after her adoption, because the owner was pregnant and feared the cat "would suck the breath" out of her new baby. Telling her this was a myth didn't faze her.

The returned cat, named Jasper despite being a female, was a healthy, shorthaired black, gold, and white striped tabby, a bit on the chubby side, but with huge emerald green eyes. She was a bit prickly in temperament, and that combined with the fact that she was now six years old, made her difficult to place.

We all set about marketing this new cat. No one seemed interested, and Jasper seemed to get more impatient the longer she languished. I would let her out at night to give her some exercise and a semblance of freedom, hoping she'd settle in to clinic life.

Fat chance of that. She snapped at us when we cleaned her cage.

When we let her out, she would approach other cages and snarl at the poor patients inside. Ever the opportunist, she would reach her arm through the cage doors and steal food from the occupants. She was honestly a bit of a stinker as cats go.

Back then, we had a client who brought in her three hand-sized box turtles regularly for exams. Our vet treated reptiles, and these were very healthy creatures. Marcela always carried her precious charges in a pink plastic tote bag. Each turtle was ensconced in its own little, hand-sewn polar fleece sleeping bag. The bags were different colors: turquoise for Pierre, red for Francois and purple for Nicola. I could never keep them straight. Marcela was an older French woman and slightly eccentric. She spoke with a heavy accent I had difficulty understanding at times.

My co-worker, Leah, was French and fluent in the language. She and Marcela hit it off, so I generally let Leah deal with the quirky woman. I specialized in the cats, and Leah was the reptile expert. At some point, Leah told Marcela about Jasper.

Marcela had recently lost her old cat and was open to getting a new one. She fell in love with testy Jasper. Marcela decided she wanted to adopt Jasper, rename her Bebe, and assign her to be her new turtle guardian.

Leah was enthusiastic about the idea, although I remained skeptical. Leah had mastered the art of placing our "comeback kids," the animals that were returned, but her adoptions rarely worked out. I didn't like the idea of changing Jasper's name, as it was the only thing she had left from her previous life, and besides, the entire concept sounded weird.

"Cats don't care about turtles," I said. "Cats are snuggly, and turtles are — well, what's with the sleeping bags anyway?"

"Marcela has already bought new toys, food and a litter box," Leah countered.

I sighed. "She may be overly optimistic," I said. This adoption would be a disaster once the woman realized what an ornery cat she was getting. I couldn't fathom the green-eyed monster getting excited over turtles in sleeping bags. She could even harm them.

I glanced over to Jasper, who returned a look that seemed to go right through me. "This whole idea is ridiculous. I'm against the adoption," I said. "Besides, does Marcela really want a cat? All she seems to care about are her turtles."

On my next day off, Leah released Jasper to the persistent French woman. I was furious she did this behind my back and waited patiently for the cat to be returned. I only hoped Marcela wouldn't fall ill to cat-scratch fever in the meantime. I also worried if Jasper was getting enough attention in a home that was all about turtles.

Jasper, renamed Bebe, came back two months later. To my surprise, she was merely boarding overnight with her three turtles while their house was being exterminated. Jasper/Bebe hadn't changed a bit in attitude. Only now, she had taken on a new protective streak.

I stood before her cage, trying not to let my mouth hang open. The cat nested atop her turtles like a hen would sit on her eggs. She swatted at me when I tried to reach into her cage. I had to cajole her into letting me feed her turtle babies, which she allowed once she first sniffed the leafy greens. Bebe had become a cat with a job, which is exactly what a cat like her needed. She took it seriously and demanded everyone else do so as well. I found myself swallowing every negative word I'd ever uttered about the adoption.

It was one of those ironic, symbiotic relationships. Reptiles need heat, and by sitting atop them, Bebe provided this, as well as security. At home, she herded her charges and kept them within the boundaries of the yard. She then spent her nights curled up on Marcela's bed.

Jasper and the turtle lady turned out to be a match made in heaven. I learned a valuable lesson from the fuzzy feline. Adoptions will always be a crapshoot, but it's wise not to prejudge too much. You never know what will work. In the end, Jasper/Bebe had found her perfect home.

~Terilynn Mitchell

44

Settling into Siblinghood

*Cats are mysterious folk. There is more passing
in their minds than we are aware of.*
~Sir Walter Scott

I was scrolling through social media when my eyes suddenly grew wide at a photo my friend had posted of a black-and-white kitten. "I found this twelve-week-old cutie pie in a grocery-store parking lot," my friend wrote. "The shelter is overflowing, so I'm fostering her until we can find her a forever home."

I brought the phone closer to my face, squinting to study this tiny tuxedo kitten with big soft ears, long white whiskers, and a mischievous grin that melted my heart. I could practically hear her purring through the screen.

Her right eye was being treated for an infection, but other than that the vet had given her a clean bill of health.

Seeing this lost and lonely kitty reminded me of the first stray I ever encountered. I was six years old, playing in my front yard, when a scruffy, scratched-up, shorthaired tabby limped by. When he saw me, he didn't dart off the way most animals do. Instead, he stopped, dropped, and rolled, stretching out on the grass in front of me. His fur was matted with blood and saliva, and his eye was crusted shut. But his purr was strong, as was his effect on my six-year-old heart. I scooped him up and went running inside.

"Mommy!" I yelled as I cradled the tomcat close to my chest. "This kitty needs us!"

For the next forty-five minutes, Mom played nursemaid, using tweezers to remove claws from the kitten's head, and cleaning his wounds with a warm washcloth and some ointment. As she worked, I thought of names for my new kitty.

"Can we keep him?" I pleaded as I stroked his paw. "I think we should call him Furry."

I spent the remainder of my childhood lugging that cat around like a sack of cherished potatoes. Sometimes, I draped him over my shoulder. Other times, I picked him up under his armpits. His body went limp, his torso slumping over my forearm as his hind quarters swayed back and forth. The epitome of tolerance, Furry let me dress him in doll clothes and push him around in the stroller. Not once did he scratch or squeal. In fact, his face oozed contentment.

This kitten also looked sweet, and I hoped that if we adopted her, my younger son, Trevyn — who was the same age I was when we took in Furry — would build those same kind of wonderful memories with a cherished pet. My older son, Kyler, already had his own memories with our twelve-year-old red tabby, who we adopted when Kyler was two. Just as my parents allowed me to name Furry, I let Kyler choose a name for his kitty. Since he was obsessed at the time with the big, singing purple dinosaur, he picked the name Barney.

Just like Furry and I, Kyler and Barney became great friends. They spent hours together assembling puzzles, playing ball, getting drinks from the sink (well, Barney drank from the faucet as Kyler brushed his teeth), and — my personal favorite — co-napping. Kyler never fussed about taking a nap if his kitty took one with him.

I worried, however, that having been an only pet for the past decade, Barney might not be thrilled with a new, fuzzy addition to the family.

"So," I said to Barney, as he came lumbering into my den like a giant jungle cat, "what would you think if I brought you home a sister?"

He yawned and turned his head to one side, which is the same response I get from my husband when I ask him what he wants for dinner.

When I posed the same question to my sons, they were immediately on board. So, off we went to adopt our kitten, whom we named Daisy.

When we got home, I braced myself for an ugly match of hissing, growling, swatting, and spitting. But none of that happened. Instead, the cats touched noses, and then followed that with lots and lots of butt sniffing (apparently, that's not only a "dog thing"). Mostly, however, Barney sat back and watched as Daisy pranced and pounced around the room, purring after every pounce.

The look on Barney's face said, "That kid has a ton of energy! I really must teach her the power of the nap."

Over the next several days, I watched as the two cats formed a true brother-sister bond — the kind where siblings are simultaneously repulsed by and drawn to each other. Daisy, desperate for a feline playmate, repeatedly batted at Barney's twitching tail each time he ambled by. Unfazed by the fact that her new brother was three times her size, she often hurled her entire body on top of his, wrapping her paws around his torso like a sumo wrestler. Miffed, Barney turned his cheek as if he were brushing off a pesky mosquito, and she slid to the floor.

Although Barney could have easily avoided her by securing a hiding place under a bed or in a closet, he insisted on staying in the same room as this little dynamo. It was as if he was trying to solve the riddle: "What's black and white and bounces all over, but is not a ball?"

Their behavior reminded me of how my children fight like cats and dogs (or, in this case, cats and cats) but still remain fiercely protective of each other. For instance, my sons scuffle on a regular basis, but should one of them ever get bullied, teased, or shoved by an outsider, they declare: "Nobody lays a finger on my brother! Nobody but me!"

The evolution of this feline friendship was fascinating to witness. One second, the cats were side-by-side, munching from their matching food dishes. The next, Daisy was ambushing her bro from behind. Later on, the two were passed out alongside each other on the back of the couch. Moments later, however, Daisy woke up from her snooze and began gnawing on Barney's foot just for the heck of it. Paw whacking and wild wailing ensued.

This type of "hot and cold" behavior went on for several weeks as the new siblings navigated the parameters of their relationship. Then one day, Daisy curled up in Barney's cozy cat bed and fell fast asleep. When Barney happened upon her, I could see the wheels in his head turning.

If there had been a cartoon bubble floating above his orange fluffy noggin, it would have read, "What is this little twit doing in my comfy space?"

Barney then moseyed over to Daisy's food dish and started scarfing up her kitten chow. It was "tit for tat" at its finest.

When Daisy awoke and spotted her brother devouring her meal, she popped right up and ran to her dish. Barney then circled back to his bed and shot her a look that communicated, "You have much to learn, small fry."

As he stretched out in the bed Daisy had warmed for him, her eyes screamed, "Drat! I've been foiled!"

I just chuckled. Clearly, I had worried for nothing. These two had seamlessly settled into siblinghood.

~Christy Heitger-Ewing

45

Doolittle

Until one has loved an animal, a part of
one's soul remains unawakened.
~Anatole France

hree days after moving my daughter cross-country from the warm waters of Florida to the Rocky Mountains of Denver for college, she said, "Mom, I miss my dogs." I understood. Life without a pet is different, and Sofia's beloved yellow Lab, Dino — who had been her friend since kindergarten — had passed away earlier that year. I went online in search of a local place where we could visit pets and possibly adopt one.

While online, I noticed a place called Denver Cat Company. There, people could meet and play with rescue cats available for adoption in the area. Since I would be leaving soon, and my daughter would truly be on her own, we decided to take a taxi and visit the cats.

We were greeted by a lovely young woman whose demeanor reminded me of a friendly librarian. People were mingling with the cats, some of whom were curled up in a window seat, sleeping lazily in the sunshine. Our first official cat greeter was a big, black shorthair named Alata. She reminded me of my first college cat, Beepers, who lived to be twenty-two years old. Beepers saw me through college graduation, my first jobs, my first firing, a marriage, two children, and she coexisted with many other animals who passed through my life, including Sofia's beloved Lab.

Alata was gentle and playful, but we didn't want to separate her and her tabby brother, so we continued to mingle with the other cats. And then we saw him, an orange tabby.

"Doolittle gets his name from the fact that he does little," his card read.

Having had many cats over the years, the ones that did little ranked very high on my favorites list. He was napping, of course. He had curled his large body into a tiny cat bed and was blissfully unaware of who was stroking his downy head. While he remained purring, I called my daughter over to meet him.

He stretched to greet her, but a rather possessive calico that had taken a liking to me began to bat him, despite him being twice her size. His reaction — priceless. Rather than fight back, he just kept his eyes closed and backed slowly into the corner away from her wrath. As she got closer, he lifted himself so that he was standing on two legs, with his eyes still closed, paws up against the corner of the window. When she swung one last time, he simply leapt over her and onto the floor, heading to the food bowl.

Now we could see Doolittle's big copper eyes, too. We were smitten. The kind "librarian" approached and offered Sofia an application for adoption. Doolittle was a house favorite that had been passed up for adoption once before. With his gentle ways and ordinary tabby colors, he was frequently overlooked. As it turned out, though, he did tricks. For treats, he would leap off the stairs in a sort of somersault.

At first, Sofia was hesitant to apply. "What if I don't get accepted as a parent? What if I do? Can we afford him? What if my roommate doesn't like him? What if he's afraid of us?" I realized at that moment that adopting this cat was exactly what she needed to do — to grow her confidence and mature — but I knew the decision had to be hers. Together, we filled out the forms, figuring she could make the final decision if her application was accepted.

We spent a bit more time with Doolittle, taking pictures. Even when a small girl of about four crunched his tail while he was eating, Doolittle never swatted at her. He simply let out a meow and touched her little foot with his paw as if to say, "Excuse me, but that hurts." And then he went back to eating. We left that day with a bit of hope, but also a bit of trepidation about whether or not this adoption would happen.

Two weeks went by, and I had returned to my Florida home after a weepy goodbye at the Denver airport. Sofia and her roommate seemed to be settling in. Then, I got an excited call.

"Mom, I need you to tell me what to do. I qualified for Doolittle. I can adopt him. Should I?" Those of us who have had an older teen live for this moment — that time when your child, who "knew it all" before going off to college, suddenly wants your opinion! But Sofia had called me while I was in a crowded Orlando restaurant, and I blew it.

"I can't tell you what to do. This is your new family and your new life. He'll be a big responsibility, but as pets go, cats are great companions. No one knows for sure how they'll act or if it will work out, but you won't know if you don't try. My advice is to take your roommate to meet Doolittle. If they like each other, do it."

I knew she needed this big, furry beast in her life, but I didn't want to tell her what to do. I didn't tell her that Doolittle reminded me of the cat that Sofia had loved when she was a little girl. Rascal was a huge, brown tabby I had adopted a few years after Beepers, and he became my favorite cat ever. He was loving, cuddly, and kind, and when Sofia came along, he slept in her crib and let her dress him up and carry him around like a doll. He died when she was only five years old, and I cried for days. Something about Doolittle's demeanor almost made me feel that Rascal was with us again, to be reunited with Sofia.

Sofia did adopt Doolittle, and he bounded out of his crate and into her heart the day she brought him home. He loves to cuddle with Sofia, and he follows her around the house, telling her all about his day. He defends her from any bugs that enter the apartment and greets her friends when they visit, just as Rascal had done many years before.

Going off to college away from home is hard. I'm so grateful to Denver Cat Company for bringing Doolittle into Sofia's life. And the feeling that Sofia has her own "Rascal" now, in Doolittle, makes my days of missing her just a little bit easier.

~Keturah Mazo

46

For the Love of Maggie

In ancient times, cats were worshipped as
gods; they have not forgotten this.
~Terry Pratchett

From the day we met, Ralph and I were like peas and carrots. We enjoyed the same things, talked until our jaws hurt, burst into laughter over the silliest nonsense, and each thought the other hung the moon. It was almost perfect, except for a slight difference of opinion.

I wanted a cat.

He didn't.

"What do you have against cats?" I demanded.

"Grandma's cat bit me when I was six. I don't like them."

"You're such a baby," I giggled. "Most kitties are wonderful."

Over the next few months, I used every sales technique I knew to get him to say yes.

He wouldn't budge.

Then one day, a stray calico appeared on our front porch and helped me close the deal. She was carrying a heavy load: a tummy packed so full of kittens that we could feel her belly writhe as they jostled for space.

"I think Dorothy would be a nice name," my new husband remarked, stroking her fur as the mom-to-be snuggled against him.

Amazing.

A few days later, Dorothy made us grandparents, and our home was never cat-less again.

Six years ago, we adopted a nineteen-pound gentle giant named Simon. White with black spots, he's gorgeous and a world-class cuddler.

If Simon had a résumé, his profession would be "surface tester." Moving from chair to bed, sofa to floor, Simon is all about comfort.

For the first few years, he was alone much of the day, but didn't seem to mind. We made it up to him by showering him with love when we returned from work.

Then, out of the blue, Simon began to mope. I knew he wasn't sick because he ate like a horse. He groomed himself fastidiously. And he certainly didn't lack for attention.

But something was off. He'd stare out the window for hours. Playtime didn't interest him.

"Get him a friend," suggested my friend Aimee. "He's probably lonely and bored. Imagine being the only one in the house who understands what meow means."

She had a point.

After a ninety-second family discussion, we went to the animal shelter to find a buddy for Simon. A volunteer led Ralph and our daughter Julie through the cage area, while I was directed to the Kitty Kat Room. Inside was wall-to-wall adorableness. I sat down, and I was claimed within seconds by a young tabby named Sid. He purred, bumped my chin, and settled into my arms. Of course, my heart melted.

I was about to announce that the search was over and I'd found Simon's soul mate when Ralph and Julie barreled through the door making the same claim.

Sid's competition was a ten-month-old female named Maggie. She had big green eyes, long white whiskers, and black fur with white spots — the opposite of our white-fur-with-black-spots Simon.

"Please, can we take her home?" Julie begged.

When she heard the word "home," Maggie poured on the charm… for them. But she wouldn't let me near her. After fifteen minutes of coaxing, I was over it.

"C'mon, guys, she doesn't like me. I found a sweet, little boy next door. Let's get him." Their distraught faces made it clear that we weren't adopting Sid.

"I hope you like me better when we get home," I muttered, loading her into the car.

When Simon met Maggie, his inhospitable growl conveyed the message that his home was his castle, and interlopers weren't welcome. Undeterred by his rudeness, Maggie strolled across the drawbridge and made herself comfortable.

For the first month, their spats were endless: tussling, swatting, and hissing. Once, when Maggie snatched one of Simon's catnip mice and dashed upstairs, he looked at me with bewildered eyes as if to say, "Why are you doing this to me?" One thing was certain. Our gentle giant was no longer lonely.

Maggie was a constant source of amusement, from her bowlegged sprints down the stairs to her sneak attacks on Simon while he was testing surfaces. She lay on her back like a dead bug as she watched TV, and licked the ice cubes bobbing in everyone's glasses but mine. Ralph and Julie lavished love on her and spoiled her rotten. I was permitted to feed her, but that was it.

Every attempt to show her affection was met with a firm rebuff. If I tried to pet her, she'd allow me to lightly touch the tip of a whisker or brush my finger over a tiny white paw before running away. I would cuddle with Simon and coax her to join us. She never did. She was so cute that I couldn't help but adore her, but a mom-and-daughter relationship appeared hopeless.

Then one day, I was cleaning out a drawer and came across Maggie's adoption paperwork. I opened the envelope and began to read. The intake volunteer had written "suspected abuse." Maggie's former owner was a woman. Her cage tag was also included. It stated that she was "due out" two days after we adopted her. *Due out.* My eyes filled with tears of pity.

When Julie found Maggie, she was frightened and unwanted. She wasn't in the Kitty Kat Room with Sid and the more adoptable cats. If we hadn't come along when we did, she'd have likely taken a sad, one-way trip across the Rainbow Bridge like so many before her. Perhaps in some small way, I reminded Maggie of her former owner and she couldn't trust me. It never occurred to me that events from her past might have been what kept us from becoming friends.

I knew what to do! Ralph brushed Maggie each night before bed, which was the highlight of her day. She'd wiggle around as he tickled her tummy and preen as he smoothed her fur. It was Maggie's idea of heaven. The next evening, I got the brush and sat down on the sofa. Maggie saw the brush, jumped onto the sofa, and meowed. I put the brush in front of her and she sniffed it and began rubbing her head against the bristles. Then she inched closer to me with an expectant look in her big green eyes. It was an invitation and a miracle. With each stroke, her impenetrable walls began to crumble.

Now Maggie follows me everywhere. She curls up next to me as I watch TV; she lies by my chair as I write. She drops a catnip mouse at my feet, expecting a game of toss and fetch. She wants the ice cubes in my drinks and burrows under our sheets at night.

I can't scoop her up and cuddle her as I do Simon. That's not who she is. There's still a line that I'm not permitted to cross, but at last my Maggie loves me. And the love of a cat is a beautiful thing.

~Michelle Close Mills

Purr-fectly Paired

We quickly discovered that two kittens
were much more fun than one.
~Allen Lacy

My middle son loves animals. For years, he wanted a pet — and not just any pet. He wanted a furry pet. But with infant twins in the house, taking on the responsibility of a pet wasn't high on my priority list.

However, when the twins turned three, we decided it was time. After much deliberation, we decided to adopt a kitten. We saw a flyer posted by a lady who rescues stray cats. She had found tiny kittens under a car, and she was now ready to give them away to their forever homes. *Perfect!* I took my four boys over to pick out a kitten after school. *One kitten. One sweet little fur ball.* Or so I thought.

We went to the cat lady's home and played with the kittens, trying to find the one that would be the best fit for our family. But as we talked with her, it became clear that she was not willing to give us just *one* kitten. We had to take *two. Two?* I had just gotten used to the idea of one pet! "Single-cat syndrome," she said. "Go home and look it up." Sigh.

So I looked it up. Apparently, single-cat syndrome was a real thing. Many kittens who grow up without a feline playmate can develop an aggressive personality. Nipping and clawing at children can become commonplace, not out of meanness necessarily, but out of an instinctive desire for cat-play. Kittens bite, wrestle, and pounce on each other.

It's adorable! But when a cat decides to bite, wrestle, and pounce on a child — not so adorable. All of a sudden, having two pets seemed less like a burden and more like a blessing.

"Great," said the cat lady when I told her our decision. "One for each of your twins, after all." We went to pick them up while the older boys were in school. Surprise! Two furry pets! We named them Vader and Obi because *Star Wars* is the thing in our house these days.

That night, after the kids were in bed and the trauma of a new place started to diminish, the kittens came out to do their thing. They pounced. They chased. They wrestled. They were so happy and cute! Then they curled up right next to each other and went to sleep in companionable comfort. No single-cat syndrome here.

I understood. I had seen it before, after all. My twin boys are the best of friends. They invent games that no one else understands. They pounce. They chase. They wrestle. And ever since my twins were babies, they have been my best sleepers. Like most twin mamas, I laid them side-by-side in the same crib when they were tiny. Somehow, they knew they had their best friend there, and they slept easily and peacefully in that comfort.

Yes, having two cats has been wonderful for the cats' sakes. But having two kittens has been particularly wonderful for our family, too. For one thing, the cat lady was right — one for each twin. Daytime playtime with the cats is even-steven, which is a nice benefit for twins.

There are much deeper benefits, as well. For instance, my twins and their brothers have learned how to care for the cats collectively and as individuals, in a way that would not be possible with just one in the house. There's no competition for who will take care of Vader or who will play with Obi, as I feared there might be. Instead, I've watched the boys learn empathy by gauging what the cats' unique moods may be. Sometimes they're playful, sometimes cuddly, and sometimes they just want to be left alone.

And because both cats may not be feeling the same way at the same time, the kids have learned to respect each one individually. This is a valuable life skill that will translate to dealing with humans for years to come. And it's especially helpful in a household that contains twins, who naturally tend to be seen as a "set" when they actually are not.

Having our cats has helped all my kids learn selflessness and responsibility, as well. The cats share bowls and litter boxes, much like my twins share clothes and cups — out of convenience. Therefore, my kids trade responsibility for the cats' food, water, and cleanliness, forcing them to take turns and think about equality and service.

Getting two kittens was definitely the right decision for our family. The cats are happy. The people are happy. And we're even more keenly aware of something we already knew — having two is never a burden; it's always a blessing.

~Melissa Richeson

48

Old Cat New Calling

*There are many intelligent creatures in the universe
and they are all owned by cats.*
~Author Unknown

Petey first came into the clinic where I work as a vet tech for a "sick kitty appointment." His orange-and-white coat was very thin and had black flakes like he was flea-bitten — but he had no fleas. He was emaciated and his eyes were slightly sunken. The tests showed he had developed diabetes and had other issues.

A new family member — a firstborn human baby sister — had recently been introduced to his household, and Petey had gone on a hunger strike. He was fading day by day. He had lost five pounds from his twelve-pound body. His owners were frantic. They had tried everything.

Days later, I looked at the schedule for the next day of appointments. I saw Petey's name in purple. Purple in our clinic means euthanasia. My heart sank. That night I was unable to sleep; I woke my husband begging to keep him. My husband pointed out the obvious: we had two big dogs and that wouldn't be a good environment for Petey to rest and recover.

I went to work the next day with a heavy heart. Around lunchtime, I finally broke down and told my co-workers what was on my mind. They all agreed with my plan. I called Petey's owner and asked her if she would surrender him to me.

Luckily, his owner answered the phone and was elated at the call. There might be hope for Petey! His mother of nine years had been weeping for days and seeking solutions for months. I could tell that she was grief-stricken and just didn't know what to do. I also knew that I could help, and that this kitty still had a future.

The first step in Petey's recovery was to keep him at the hospital for a few weeks. I had to get his insulin regulated if he had any hope of being adoptable. I was basically stalling while getting the word out to clients about him.

After a while, I got tired of seeing Petey caged up. One of my co-workers let him out one day, but we all knew that the boss would probably not be okay with another clinic cat. We already had one who lived there full-time. Nevertheless, we let Petey stroll around, and my twenty co-workers and I acted as if nothing was different. We made no effort to point him out to our employer, Dr. Greg. We pretended the cat was invisible. Dr. Greg said nothing, and we did not ask what he was thinking.

Petey was in heaven! He quickly showed us "The True Petey." We discovered he liked to crawl up and knead, suckle, and purr on the shoulders of staffers. He didn't discriminate. He would happily accept head rubs and treats from anyone. He did not even mind big, slobbery dogs, as long as they kept their distance.

Somehow, it became a done deal. Petey became our second official clinic cat. In his former life, he was a house cat who had never encountered other animals, especially dogs. Now they are a regular part of his day as he supervises the entrance of a large veterinary practice with five doctors and many furry visitors.

Patients and their humans enter into an expansive and open lobby with a wide, circular counter. Petey has a spot front and center, stretched out like a sunbather. Sometimes, he sits near the computer keyboard; other times, he hangs out near the waiting-room fireplace. You might find him dozing on the doctor's desk or enjoying a snooze in the arms of staffers on break. He works the room, so to speak. Petey, who has been renamed "Pete," particularly likes playing in his water bowl, scooping the liquid out with his paw and then licking it off.

Pete also delights in splashing the toilet bowl water. You might find little paw prints on a wet seat — be warned.

Even though my fellow employees and I were silent about Pete's presence, he did not go unnoticed. Within a month, twenty-five clients asked to adopt him. At that point, we were all in love with our new Allisonville Animal Hospital "Goodwill Ambassador." Finally, I told all the staff that he would not be put up for adoption. Technically, he's now my cat, though others claim him as "ours."

Our other clinic cat, Joe, is around seventeen years old. Joe is a black shorthair. He keeps a low profile and mostly resides in a back office, looking out the window. He is very happy to greet strangers and request a scratch under the chin or behind the ear, but people must come to him — the opposite of Pete's "in-your-face" approach as he patrols the hallways and common areas to make friends.

As for the boss, Dr. Greg, I had every hope he would fall for Pete like everyone else. It took about two-and-a-half weeks for him to finally acknowledge and agree that Pete is a part of the office management. The prodding of another vet, Dr. Ward, helped to move this along.

This white-and-orange wonder is petted by around thirty people a day. We have a "Donation for Pete" set up where clients read about his story and donate money for his special food and insulin. Pete's rich already. He looks it, too. His hair has grown back, and his eyes are bright and eager with anticipation.

As for the previous owner, she follows me on all social media platforms and "likes" every picture and video of him that I post. She did reach out to me via text when this first happened and told me how appreciative she was for what I did. Pete inspires me, too. He has touched hundreds of hearts and given hope to other impaired animals and people, as he redefines his life and rises to his potential.

~Meredith Engerski

49

A Band of Brothers

*It is impossible to keep a straight face in
the presence of one or more kittens.*
~Cynthia E. Varnado

We already had a stray cat. But Eggroll happened to bond deeply with me — and only *me*. Unfortunately, he merely tolerated my eleven-year-old daughter despite her best efforts. She fed, watered, and cooed at him, but it just didn't matter. He was a finicky, one-person feline.

One winter night over hot chocolate and a game of checkers, Emily handed me her Christmas list. She had just one wish — a kitten of her own, and preferably one that would not snub her. Then she announced that if she couldn't have a kitten, she would like a little brother.

Well, I'm a single mom, so the little brother idea was completely out of the question. But, a kitten… that I could do. We had room in our hearts and home for one more pet. So, I asked around the office about local animal rescues. My boss mentioned Special Pals, and I visited the shelter during my lunch hour. There were so many adorable kittens that I wasn't sure where to start.

"Those two are brothers," offered the shelter volunteer, pointing at two tiny fur balls. One was a tabby, and the other was gray and white. The tabby stuck his paw out of the cage and waved.

"Two? A pair of kittens? Good Lord, I need that like a hole in the head," I joked and moved on. But after looking at a half-dozen adoptable candidates, I found myself gravitating back to the brothers.

"Can I take just one, the one that waved at me?" I asked.

"They are such a comfort to each other," said the volunteer. "We'd really like to adopt them out together."

"Is there a two-for-one discount?"

"No discount," said the volunteer. "But they've had their shots. You'll just need to sign a form promising to have them neutered when they reach about five months."

"I see," I said, grimacing at the thought of two adoption fees and two neuters, which weren't cheap. But I could see how bonded the kittens were at twelve weeks, tumbling about at peak cuteness as if they had an acting coach. They melted my heart, and I could envision them playing with Emily. So I filled out the adoption paperwork on the spot. That required three personal references, my employment history, and my vet's contact information. If I passed inspection, the shelter would notify me within three days.

I felt a bit crushed leaving the brothers behind, but the delay gave me time to buy kitten chow, bowls, a cat carrier, an extra litter box, and some cat toys. I hid it all under a blanket in the back of my SUV. That way, if my application was rejected, I could return everything. I said absolutely nothing about the adoption to Emily, just in case it fell through.

My cellphone rang the very next day. I had passed muster, and the kittens were ready for pickup! Thankfully, my understanding boss gave me the afternoon off to prepare. I rushed home, set up all the kitten gear in Emily's room, and then brought the brothers home. The dynamic duo helped themselves to the litter box and began to explore their surroundings. Within minutes, they scaled Emily's bedspread and tumbled around on her stuffed animals — a perfectly seamless transition. I was so grateful the shelter volunteer recommended adopting them together.

Emily normally took the school bus home, but that day I arranged to pick her up.

"What's up, Mom?" Emily asked. "Why aren't you at work?"

"It's a surprise!" I answered.

"A surprise? What kind of surprise?" Emily asked as she buckled up.

"Oh, you'll see soon enough."

Finally, we pulled into the driveway. I told Emily that the surprise was in her room and to open her door slowly and gently. The look on her face was priceless when she spotted two kittens curled up together and snoozing on a blanket.

"Mom," she gasped. "Are they really mine?" She became so overwhelmed that her eyes welled up.

"Yes, sweetie, they are really yours!" I said, hugging her. "And they are brothers. What are you going to name them?"

Emily reached down to pet her new kittens and then proclaimed, "Checkers and Chocolate." It was my turn to sniffle when she reminded me that we had been drinking hot chocolate and playing checkers on the night she asked for a kitten.

The brothers stayed in Emily's room over winter break. Eggroll introduced himself by pushing his paws under the door. Of course, the brothers thought that was a hoot and did the same. After many days of playing footsie, we allowed all of our felines to meet and mingle.

We crossed our fingers that finicky Eggroll would bond with his new sidekicks and show them around the house. Sure enough, they became a trio. Best of all, Eggroll finally warmed up to Emily because the brothers hung out in her room a lot, and he followed suit.

Through the years, we've come to think of them as a merry band of brothers — Eggroll, Checkers and Chocolate. But, most of all, they are a part of our family. Adoption really does change lives, and we needed these cats just as much as they needed us. All three have infused comfort — and giggles — into our everyday existence, and we can only hope that others experience the same joy through adoption.

~Melanie Saxton

Lucky for Love

A cat assures its owner of good luck.
~Chinese Proverb

On a rainy December morning on Long Island, I drove thirty miles to Save-A-Pet animal shelter to look at kittens. Among the chaos of kids, barking dogs, and parents, I picked up a black kitten. She appeared to be six months old. She clung to me and purred as I petted her silky coat. How could anyone find a black cat unlucky? I had to take her home.

But I was just there to look. I didn't have a pet bed, food, or bowls for her. Furthermore, that night I was going out with Ed. We had been friends for quite a while, but this was our first "official" date.

I had to leave the kitten. "Goodbye, Muffin," I said and handed her to Kyle, the shelter volunteer.

As I drove home, sheets of rain beat against the car. And I cried tears for my kitten. *Why did I have to name her?* I thought. *Now, she is a part of me like a heart or a lung. I can't abandon her now. I should be excited about my date, so why am I sad?*

At home, I looked at the clock: 3:00 p.m. *If I hurry back to the shelter, there will still be time to adopt Muffin before it closes.*

I tore off my wet clothes, pulled on dry ones, and ran to the car. The rain had turned to hail. Golf-sized lumps of ice pummeled the vehicle. I struggled to see through the blurry windshield as I rushed back to the shelter to save my Muffin.

I must have looked like a madwoman when I got back, but Kyle brought Muffin to me. "She's been waitin' on you." I opened my wet coat and held her against my chest. She stretched her neck, stuck out her pink tongue, and licked me. Looking into her huge green eyes, my heart filled with warmth, love, and happiness.

"How did you know I'd come back?" I said to Kyle.

"Oh, you were hooked big-time. And the little girl, too." He scratched her head. "I'll get the adoption papers started."

"But I don't have any food, a bed, or a cat carrier." Through my shirt, I felt her heart beating. The winter chill was gone as she warmed me.

"No worries. We have some food and a box to take her home in," he said.

At the checkout counter, I signed Muffin's paperwork and paid a small fee.

The volunteer gave me a bag of dry food and put Muffin in a carton. He carried her out to the car for me and put the box on the passenger seat. Outside, the rain had stopped. A glimmer of sun fought through the clouds. Muffin let out some meows.

Kyle said to Muffin, "It's okay, girl. This nice lady's goin' to make you a good home."

Shivering in my soaked jacket, I thanked Kyle and opened the trunk. I put the food inside, closed it, and got into the car. Then I peeked inside the box. Muffin was gone!

I looked on the floor, under the seats, and in every corner I could find. No kitten. I ran into the shelter. I came back out with Kyle, and we went to my car. He pulled a lever on the bottom of the front passenger seat and pushed it forward. Muffin was huddled inside the small space.

"What are you doing in there?" I said. I patted her head. She peered up at me. Kyle picked up Muffin and put her in the carton.

"How did you know where she was?"

"'Happens all the time."

"Thanks again for rescuing us."

"Any time." He went back to the shelter.

I grabbed a blanket from the back seat, tucked it around Muffin, and made sure she had plenty of air. On the ride home, she cried. That was heart wrenching. Maybe I had made a mistake.

Inside my apartment, I gathered blankets and pillows. I made a place for her next to my bed and filled bowls with food and water. But she was not ready to take a nap. Muffin wanted to explore. Sniffing the air, she dashed under the bed, around the furniture, and into the kitchen. I got ready for my date even though I really wanted to stay home with my new kitten. It was too late to call Ed and cancel, but I thought that perhaps I should make a spaghetti dinner and invite him to eat in.

An hour later, I was dressed and ready. When Ed arrived I introduced him to Muffin.

She meowed, "Hello."

He kissed me on the cheek and I said, "Her name is Muffin. I adopted her about an hour ago. Would you mind if I cooked dinner? I can't leave her alone on her first night."

"Hey, Muffin. Sure, we can stay here."

We ate, laughed, talked, and played with her. I hoped there would be more dates with Ed.

Ed and I celebrated our thirtieth wedding anniversary this year. And Muffin, an indoor cat, lived for sixteen glorious years.

Often, we reminisce about the joy she brought us. Black cats are good luck after all — especially for love.

~Marilyn June Janson

51

Cade & Cally

The cat does not offer services. The cat offers itself.
~William S. Burroughs, The Cat Inside

escribing a half-grown female kitten with the unfortunate name of "Godfrey," the vet told me, "She'll do best in a quiet home." Godfrey was named after the road where she had been found. One of the clinic's employees caught the abandoned, starving kitten and brought her to the clinic for care. Godfrey's picture — posted to a pet-search website — had in turn brought me.

"She's very sweet and loving," the vet continued, "but scared by all the noise. It's not likely she'll ever be a social cat, but you'd be doing her a real favor by getting her out of here."

I was listening to the vet, but I didn't really hear her. A lifelong cat person, I was naïvely optimistic that I could bring this timid, little creature out of her shell. Plus, I had fallen half in love with her already. The scared kitten in the online photo, the pretty lady cat with the silly male name... all she needed was time, a new name — and me!

The vet's description turned out to be truer than my blind optimism. Callawassie (or "Cally" for short), as we named her, is a hide-under-the-bed-at-the-first-sign-of-trouble cat. She loves and trusts me, the person who "saved" her from the noisy vet clinic. She mostly accepts my husband and will allow him to pet her on occasion. She's also managed to bond somewhat with our older son, born five years after we adopted her.

That's it! No one outside our immediate family even believes she exists. She's not a lap kitty. She's not a follower. She seeks out attention on her own terms and otherwise hides out of sight.

I still believe we did the right thing in adopting her, but my hopes for transforming her have never been fulfilled. After ten years, I had stopped hoping for anything more — which is why her behavior following the birth of our second son has come as such a shock. Looking back, I should have realized that something magical was happening.

During my pregnancy, I would wake from a nap to find Cally curled up at the end of the bed, against the back of my legs or against my stomach.

"Whoa. Cally? Really?" I was surprised by the sudden change in behavior, but grateful. I thought that perhaps she knew I wasn't feeling well and wanted to help. Or, I admitted ruefully to myself, the more likely explanation was that my pregnant body was a tad warmer than normal and had turned me into an irresistible magnet for napping cats.

Within days of bringing baby Cade home from the hospital, however, I noticed that Cally was always present. Her home base moved from underneath our bed to Cade's bedroom. She was there when he had his diaper changed, when we did tummy time, when I nursed him or rocked him to sleep. She seemed utterly fascinated, even smitten, and no amount of noise from him — and he could raise the roof, believe me — would send her running.

At the end of the day, I'd shoo her out of the bedroom so I could shut the door while he slept. I didn't think that she would do anything, but I wasn't taking any chances. Cally responded by spending the night outside his bedroom door, just waiting for her boy to wake up.

I noticed her fascination, of course. My Facebook feed turned into a Cade & Cally show. "You won't believe this, but check out these two unlikely buddies!" or "Sorry for all the pictures, but this is bound to be short lived," I'd say. I figured that as soon as Cade was mobile, he'd cease to be fascinating and start to be threatening.

And so Cade learned to roll… sit up… crawl… and now walk. But he did it all under the watchful gaze of his feline friend. The bond they have — between the quietest, shyest member of our household and the loudest, most rambunctious — remains true. It is a beautiful thing to witness. Cally braves a world that frightens her in order to be by his side. In turn, she's teaching him how to interact with animals. If he gets too wild, she'll edge out of touching distance. If he's gentle, though, he's rewarded with the opportunity to give her pets and hugs.

Not long ago, he wasn't feeling well and had been snuggling with me on the couch. Upon waking, the first thing he saw was his "Cally kitty" on the floor at our feet. Immediately, he wriggled off my lap to sit beside her, draped one arm over her back, and gave a little sigh.

After caring for Cally for ten years, this turn of events still shocks me. We no longer have the "quiet home" the vet said she'd need, but it turns out we have something she wants even more: Cade.

~Megan Nelson

52

Miss Adventure

Cats like doors left open, in case
they change their minds.
~Rosemary Nisbet

e knew she wouldn't be a typical housecat when we first encountered Lylah. We had adopted her and a littermate at a street fair, quite by chance. A small bundle of jet-black fur, tinted with brown and smoke-gray undertones, the little kitten with large, amber eyes made it clear from the start that she would be marching to her own drummer.

Lylah was not a cuddly girl. Her medium-long fur was like glistening satin, and she quickly established her panther-like credentials by becoming the best mouser of our four cats. She was mischievous, always poking her nose into places that were supposedly off-limits. Our gang of four routinely spent their days exploring or lounging in the sun. But Lylah was a bit of a lone wolf, more interested in chasing lizards or field mice, climbing a tree, or rolling herself up in a carpet.

Our three other cats didn't always cozy up to Lylah, but that suited her just fine. While not interested in cuddling, she was very loyal to me. Every morning, she'd lick my face until she was satisfied that I was sufficiently groomed to face the world.

The years passed, and our furry family changed. Lylah lost her three feline companions and our dog wasn't really a suitable substitute. After a respectful period of time, we adopted Koka, a rambunctious kitten who turned out to be more of an annoyance than a partner. Lylah was not a happy camper.

Then, to make things worse, came our move from California to Michigan. The furniture went by van, Charles took the dog in his car, and I piled the two cats in mine. Off we drove, stopping along the way in motels that allowed pets. Everything went well until our fateful stay at Motel 6 in Laramie, Wyoming.

As we loaded the cars to leave Laramie, Charles opened the door to let our old dog out. I loaded Koka into his crate, and then turned to gather up Lylah, but she was nowhere to be found. She had slipped out beside the dog, quickly disappearing into a vast, open space behind the motel that was being excavated for a new development.

I was frantic. Charles put Koka and the dog in the cars, and then joined me in walking for hours searching for Lylah. Broken-hearted, we finally had to leave in order to meet the van with the furniture at our new house. We gave the office manager a description of Lylah and left my phone number.

Lylah had been wearing a bright, pink collar and tags, and was (blessedly) microchipped. I called the registry, Home Again, to report her missing and provide our new address in Michigan. Next, I contacted the Laramie Animal Control officer and designed a flyer, which was circulated electronically to all the vets and rescue groups in the area of the motel.

We prayed a lot. Lylah was a resourceful girl, an accomplished outdoor explorer and hunter. She had run away from home a few times over the years, and after posting flyers and searching our neighborhood, we recovered her every time. Yet this was different; we were driving in the opposite direction from where she had seen us last.

We continued checking in with Home Again and Laramie Animal Control several times a day from Michigan. The days stretched into weeks, and we could only hope Lylah would be found by some loving person who would turn her into the shelter, or adopt and love her for life.

Then, we got the call. Lylah had been found! According to the shelter director, Lylah had returned to the room we vacated after she tired of her great adventure. The door had been left wide open by the cleaning staff one day and she apparently slipped in thinking that we were there. When the door was closed, she was trapped without food or water, except for what she got from the toilet bowl.

Days later, the room was rented to another guest who asked for a pet-friendly room so he could enjoy the evening with his dog. As he related later, when he opened the door, a beautiful black cat with huge amber eyes was sitting on a chair staring at him. He shut the door and ran to the office.

"I didn't mean a room with a pet already *in* it… I brought my own!" he exclaimed. The manager quickly realized that it must be Lylah, and contacted Animal Control. They successfully captured her and turned her over to the shelter, where the director was almost as thrilled as we were.

Springing Lylah from a Wyoming shelter while we were ensconced in our new Michigan home turned out to be a bit of a challenge. She had to be checked out by a vet and then crated in an appropriate carrier. Then they had to find a volunteer to take her to the airport in Cheyenne… an hour's drive away. They found that amazing volunteer, who worked with dog rescues and was used to shuttling lost pets. He drove an hour from Cheyenne to pick her up, boarded her overnight at his home, and got her on a plane to Detroit. Home Again made all her travel arrangements and paid for her flight… all part of their service, as she had been found over 500 miles from our home. Amazing!

When we picked up Lylah at the Detroit Metro Airport, she was noticeably thinner. She was greeted by a very happy kitten and dog, not to mention the overwhelming affection Charles and I showered on "Miss Adventure," as we took to calling her. While she enjoyed the views of her new world from the many windows in our Michigan house, she never again appeared interested in venturing out into the world. That, and her new habit of drinking water from the toilet bowl, were the only reminders of her Wyoming travels.

First rescued at ten weeks of age, Lylah was rescued again at age fourteen. If cats truly have nine lives, I wonder how many she had before the two she shared with us. Lylah, our "Miss Adventure," will always be remembered as one of a kind!

~Sue Ross

53

Hospitality Cat

Meow is like aloha — it can mean anything.
~Hank Ketchum

was a half-hour late starting my morning baking routine at our family-owned bed-and-breakfast. I rushed to the back room and pulled out my mixing bowls and ingredients. Then I froze. *Oh, no! Mouse droppings!* I grabbed everything and dashed to the kitchen to shove the dishes in a disinfecting wash. Then I raced back and scrubbed the table and counters. Ugh! I could not ignore this situation. I double-checked the food containers to be positive nothing had gotten to them. Everything looked clean once again.

Crisis averted, I managed to get breakfast ready on time. After morning coffee with our guests, I set out to start the laundry. While I worked, I thought back on my unwelcome find from the morning. Our B&B is along a river in rural Washington. It is common to see a variety of animals, but none of them should be *in* my pantry!

Later that afternoon, I sipped a glass of iced tea while scrolling through social media. A pair of big, green eyes caught my attention. The eyes belonged to a cat. Not a kitten, but a young cat. His eyes spoke directly to me: "I will solve your dilemma." *No,* I thought to myself. *We can't do that. Our bed and breakfast has a no-pet policy. What would we do with a cat?*

As my day continued, I couldn't erase that little face from my mind. I gave in and called the number on the notice. After a brief phone conversation, I announced to my family we were going to meet a cat. We piled into the car and started our hour-long ride to the remote hunting lodge where the cat lived. I attempted to downplay the situation. "Don't be too hopeful," I said. Maybe this cat wouldn't work out. We required him to be an expert mouser, but he also needed to stay away from the guests and out of the guest rooms. As we drove, I relayed what details I knew about the cat.

He was six months old. He had no name. It appeared he was a skilled hunter, which is why the family that owned him needed to get rid of him. The cat needed rescuing. They lived in an area with an abundance of rattlesnakes. The cat had been seen hunting the snakes. He was young and naïve and didn't know that playing with rattlers could be the "curiosity that killed the cat."

We arrived at the turnoff for the dirt road that led to the lodge and bounced along over the rocks and ruts. Once we arrived, we piled out of the car and knocked on the door. A young lady answered. "We're here to look at the cat," I told her.

"Come in," she replied. "I will try to find him."

Soon, she returned with a huge, magnificent, tabby-striped, all-boy cat in her arms. We approached to pet him. Not impressed, his facial expression said, "Who are you people, and why are you touching me?" He was not mean, but it was obvious he wanted nothing to do with us. I had been sure our connection would be instant, so I was disappointed. After a quick family talk, we agreed to take him on a trial basis. We needed him to hunt mice. It would be better if he was somewhat aloof and didn't want to interact with the guests or us. Silent, but deadly — that would work!

Thus, the cat we named Oliver came to live with us.

He did hunt mice. In fact, I never saw one in the back kitchen after Oliver arrived. Hunting mice was Oliver's passion, but greeting and taking care of our guests became his life mission. Within one week of his arrival, he had the B&B schedule memorized. He showed up at check-in time to scope out the petting potential of the new arrivals. We provided specific guidelines to our guests regarding our no-pet policy and emphasized that these rules included Oliver. He had other plans. He felt positive it was his responsibility to examine each room as guests were bringing in their luggage. Maybe he wanted to make sure there was nothing that could potentially harm them hiding in their rooms. We worried our guests might find him annoying, but they did not, and he soon became very popular. Pictures and stories of him popped up on Facebook and in our guestbook. Our social-media friends and followers enjoyed the pictures I posted of Oliver. People dropped by during the day just to meet him.

Oliver took what he perceived to be his duty seriously, making sure that everybody came downstairs for breakfast at 8:00 sharp. If they were late, he positioned himself outside their door and waited. He followed guests up and down the stairs and took time to make himself available for petting therapy if needed. Petting always culminated in a reward of a deep, rumbling purr. For those who desired something rougher, he pounced, wrestled and played, but always kept his claws pulled back so he didn't hurt anyone.

As the days rolled on and summer turned into fall, our B&B reservations slowed. Soon, tourist season would end for the year. One morning, we had no overnight guests for the first time since Oliver had arrived. As I went through my morning chores, I could see Oliver running up and down the stairs. I wondered what he was doing. Then I stepped outside and looked up from the stairs toward the guest rooms. There was Oliver sitting on the deck above me with his head poking through the banister railings. He stared off into the distance, and then glanced at me and made a miserable little cry. Now I understood the problem. It was past 8:00 in the morning, and no people had come for breakfast. No guests were in the rooms. Oliver was searching for "his" people. He appeared confused and perplexed. Poor Oliver.

It has been almost a year since Oliver came to live at the B&B. He has learned to accept that sometimes there are no guests to pet him in the morning. He has achieved great success hunting mice. He has spent long "night shifts" patrolling the property and protecting his loved ones. But he has also captured the hearts of all who meet him.

Oliver is the embodiment of sociability. He puts the guests first and is ready to do his part to make their stay at our B&B special and memorable. Oliver is our very own hospitality cat.

~Connie Nice

Chapter
6

The Cat Really Did That?

My Heroic Cat

54

Mr. Princess

As anyone who has ever been around a cat for any
length of time knows cats have enormous patience
with the limitations of the human kind.
~Cleveland Amory

Growing up, one of the best things that ever happened to me was when my mother brought home Princess. She was gorgeous, a fluffy Creamsicle-looking cat with big, blue eyes and a sweet disposition. Only, when Princess went to her first vet appointment, we got a bit of a shock. Princess was a prince! But the name stuck. He was thenceforth known as Mr. Princess: household pet and my best friend. I could tell plenty of stories about him, but there's one that I return to, year after year. It happened when my sister Kiah was in diapers.

From the time she could walk, Kiah was nicknamed Houdini. The name was apt; she escaped every restraint we could devise, from car seats to high chairs. This included clothing. And despite child-locking every door on the house, she always seemed to get past those as well.

One blistering hot August afternoon, we decided to go for a swim. The pond was only a few minutes from our house, a short drive.

It did very little to cool us down, so once we were back at the house, we sat around in nothing but our swimsuits. Kiah was in her diaper. Even Mr. Princess lounged on the windowsill, looking uncomfortable. However, in our haste to get out of the heat and back into the house, my mother had left her wedding ring on the wooden swing set at the pond. Naturally, when she realized this, she flew from the house, promising to be back in a matter of minutes. We all nodded lazily. Even that little amount of movement felt like work.

I remember how pleasant it felt, lying on the couch with a warm breeze floating over me. I was drowsy after our dip, so much so that I was asleep almost as soon as I heard the back door slam to announce my mother's departure. And I would've stayed asleep there, under the fan, if Mr. Princess hadn't started howling.

I woke immediately. He had a deafening meow on a good day—even the vet called him a "talker"—but this was different. He was clearly agitated.

But we were hot and lazy, and my father yelled at Mr. Princess with as much energy as he could muster. The cat kept yowling, pacing the windowsill and getting louder by the second. The hairs on the back of my neck stood up. Something was very, very wrong.

Absently, I noticed that Kiah was no longer in the room.

Dad kept yelling, but Mr. Princess was screaming by now. I made my way to the window, hoping that I could calm him down by stroking his back or scratching his chin, but I was wrong. When I got to him, he was staring out the window, and for good reason.

My sister was toddling into the middle of the road, wearing nothing but her diaper and her curly, red hair.

The world stood still for a moment, with my cat slashing at the window screen, and my own shriek piercing the air.

There were cars out there, and they went too fast on this road. Mom and Dad always said as much. How could I get there fast enough?

I ran so fast out the front door and onto the asphalt that my feet burned. I felt like a streak of lightning. And when I got to Kiah, she was nearly to the center line. I scooped my gurgling sister into my arms and sprinted back into the house, my heart thumping.

Even once we were inside, I was shaking. I couldn't let go of her, even when she fussed and pushed against me with her little limbs. Mom was going to kill us when we told her.

She didn't, though. That night, she held Kiah in her lap a little longer than usual, and she fed Mr. Princess a whole can of tuna along with his normal food.

There is one big reason why my sister turned seventeen this summer, and that is Mr. Princess. He was a pretty cat with a silly name, but he saved her life. I have never stopped being grateful to him for that.

Mr. Princess died peacefully in my arms last year after fifteen years as my best friend. He was there for me through breakups and disasters, through high school, college, my first job, and even a car accident that we both came through unscathed. When I held him for the last moments of his life, I realized how lucky I was to have been his person.

There will never be another Mr. Princess.

~Stormy Corrin Russell

55

Up a Tree

*When a cat chooses to be friendly, it's
a big deal because a cat is picky.*
~Mike Deupree

O ur rescue cat, Mouse, had been Queen of the Hill for some
time when another feline entered her realm in the form of
a little, orange kitty. It was a ray of sunshine for our family,
but for Mouse, it was a home invasion.

We had found the stray one rainy afternoon by our back porch.
It had no tags and was in dire need of nourishment. Mouse did not
share our tender feelings for the interloper, even though we had rescued
her as well, adopting her from a shelter. She hissed and swatted at
the tiny thing.

The kids didn't want to take the kitty — named Peaches for its
bright, orange fur — to a shelter. Mouse would just have to adjust and
learn a little humility. She'd have to share some of the attention that
was heretofore exclusively hers.

The situation remained in standoff mode for several days. Peaches
quickly learned to be wary of the older, bigger cat. We all hoped that
Mouse would come around eventually.

Mouse had long since become strictly an indoor cat, showing
little interest in the outside world other than to watch the birds and
squirrels go through their antics around the bird feeder and a display
of peanuts. When she wasn't watching life pass by from the comfort
of a windowsill, she was usually stretched out across the middle of a

bed, drifting from one lazy dream to another.

I wondered if she had reached the point where she would observe a rodent or a beastly bug scuttling in front of her with no more enthusiasm than a yawn. But because of Peaches, we tried to make sure unattended doors were closed, worried that Mouse's intimidating tactics might cause Peaches to run outside. With kids coming in and out constantly, that would prove to be a daunting task.

Sure enough, on a November day when the weather was turning cold, Peaches was nowhere to be found. After an hour of searching, my wife heard a frightened "meow" from the back yard. Camouflaged among the oranges and browns of a tree's remaining leaves was the little pussycat, perched precariously on a high limb.

I was called upon to retrieve a ladder and attempt to coax Peaches down. Anyone who's ever had a cat up a tree knows that an accident is only one wrong move away. Peaches only climbed higher as I wondered how much a call to the fire department might be. Our son wanted to climb the tree, but I didn't want a broken arm or leg to complicate the situation.

Then, something amazing happened. Mouse, our lazy indoor cat, ventured from the house. She jumped on the tree trunk and started to climb, her seldom-used claws finding purchase in the hard bark. To my knowledge, Mouse had never climbed anything more daunting than stair steps. As the rest of us stood by, mouths agape, Mouse climbed to the limb Peaches was glued to.

"Don't you dare hurt that kitty, Mouse," my wife pleaded in a bit of a panic.

But that wasn't Mouse's intent. She was on a mission of mercy. She meowed at the younger cat and started back toward the tree trunk. It's hard to say what transpired between the two felines that day, but Peaches carefully followed Mouse down the tree. My wife and I each grabbed a cat and nuzzled it before returning to the security of the indoors.

Something definitely changed that day because Mouse approached Peaches later and licked her ears. The holidays were approaching, and we all had something unexpected to be thankful for — harmony within the household. An uneasy truce had been replaced with acceptance, by a feline who ended up showing compassion and courage when we least expected it.

~Troy Seate

Miraculous Mira

A cat is a tiger that is fed by hand.
~Vakaoka Genrin

My child's cry split the air like a sonic boom. We were having our usual Sunday morning biscuits in front of cartoons, just like we did every week. I had run to the kitchen to grab napkins while my husband handed out the food. In that quick moment, life went from happy and peaceful to terror-filled — at least until I returned to the living room.

My husband was in his customary place on the floor with tears of laughter streaming down his face, while my youngest son battled for his life... well, his biscuit. One of our new kittens, rescued from a storm drain during a flood, was inching her way across the living room with the biscuit wrapper in her mouth. The biscuit itself was about the same size as her, and she was moving slowly. But my son couldn't seem to get the paper away from her. His older brothers had joined their father in gales of laughter, and I couldn't help giggling myself.

The sight of this tiny kitten backing across the floor with a wrapper almost twice her size and a biscuit that weighed as much as she did filled our entire family with mirth. I just wish we'd had the presence of mind to snap a picture.

And this wasn't the only time Mira proved herself to be a food thief. One of her favorite items to abscond with was pizza. Even as a baby, she would try to drag pieces of pizza larger than herself out of the box. At some point, the boys figured out how to stop her, so she no longer got very far. Still, though, it was entertaining, if not exactly sanitary.

But that wasn't all there was to Mira. As she got older, she showed herself to be more and more like her grandmother, a calico that always seemed not quite completely cat-like. She didn't resemble her progenitor in appearance; Mira was a gray-and-black tabby with a white underbelly. But she had that same sense of family, of willingness to look out for people, that Kali had possessed.

Late at night, with the children in bed, my husband and I would sit in the living room and play video games or watch movies. We'd keep the lights off and burn lightly scented candles to provide a peaceful atmosphere. Always, Mira would join us. She'd rub her soft fur against our faces and then trot off down the hall to the boys' room. We watched on numerous occasions as Mira moved from one bed to the other, giving each child a gentle nudge with her head. She'd sniff them, and then she'd choose one to lie beside for a while. Throughout the night, she'd move from one child to another, resting a bit with each one.

Several years later, we moved to the neighboring town. The house was old and sat beside a cow pasture. In the spring, the scent of privet dominated the yard, and when it ceased to bloom in the hotter months, the odor of cows permeated everything. But it was a great place for the cats to roam, and Mira loved it. More than once, she chased the cows through the pasture, though we always wondered what she'd do with one when she caught it.

It was during this time that our family movie night was disturbed by a rattle and crash in the kitchen. Our Chinese food sat before us on the carpet, and we wondered why the aroma of General Tso's Chicken Shrimp Lo Mein hadn't attracted our resident food thief. Regardless of the meal, we could always count on Mira to be right there, doing what she could to commandeer some for herself. Our assumption was that she was outside doing cat stuff, so we let it go and set some aside for her.

Crash. Rattle. Thud.

We all looked at each other.

"What was that?" our oldest asked.

Their father sighed. "I'll go look."

He climbed to his feet and headed for the kitchen, but he didn't get any farther than the dining room. He stopped and jumped backward, and I was on my feet in a moment, food forgotten.

"Get the door open!"

It wasn't his words that spurred me to action, but the tinge of fear in his voice. I hopped across the living room, telling the boys to stay put, and wrenched open the front door. My husband passed me and opened the screen door that led outside from the porch.

"What...?"

I didn't get out the question.

Mira trotted out of the kitchen with a water moccasin in her mouth.

The snake was about four feet long and squirmed in her grasp. Black, shiny skin reflected the light, and the scent of reptile filled the living room. But no matter how much it wriggled, Mira held on tightly. She looked straight ahead to where we'd opened the way for her and carried the moccasin out of the house and into the yard.

She promptly dropped it in front of the steps and returned to the living room for some of our Chinese dinner. I guess she thought she'd earned it. We agreed.

Life with Mira was like that. She loved the boys fiercely, though it seemed, sometimes, like she was a bit confused that their kittenhood lasted so long. And don't think for a moment that she hesitated to treat them like her own. She'd swat them on the nose, the ankle, or whatever body part she could reach if she thought they needed to be disciplined. She continued to guard the house against snakes wriggling in through the kitchen sink drain, and she was always there with a soft purr or an encouraging head-butt whenever anyone in the house needed her.

~Lissa Dobbs

57

Gingham, the Hero Cat

Cats are cats... the world over! These intelligent,
peace-loving, four-footed friends — who without
prejudice, without hate, without greed — may
someday teach us something.
~James Mackintosh Qwilleran

'd never had a cat and never thought about having one, but how could I say "no" to the adorable child holding the box? It was a gift at the end of a wonderful school year. My eager third-graders huddled around, waiting to see if I'd accept it.

In the box were two six-week-old kittens curled up fast asleep. One was a calico and the other a gray tabby. I was assured they would grow up to be wonderful mousers. I sighed. *Me and my big mouth.* Just last week, I had told my third-graders about the mice in the straw bales skirting my trailer. In the box was their answer to my problem. I took the box and forced a smile. My students cheered. Soon, there were two litter boxes with two bags of litter, two water dishes, and two food dishes with two bags of kitten food adorning my desk.

Throughout the afternoon, the kittens dozed on and off. But when they were awake, they fussed and spit at each other in their box. They didn't seem to like each other despite being littermates. They'd fight until they wore themselves out. Then they would curl up as far away from each other as they could and fall asleep. At the end of the day, I carried the box home while my students trailed behind carrying the kittens' gear. The kittens slept soundly at opposite ends of the box.

When we reached the trailer, my dog, Sasha, joined the parade. Up the steps and into the trailer we went. The children quickly dropped the kittens' things and hurried away. I didn't have a clue what to do next.

The calico didn't get along with Sasha or me any better than she did with her brother. So a friend of mine adopted her. I named the friendly little guy who remained Gingham, and he was soon bedmates and best friends with Sasha. I always smile when remembering Gingham pouncing on Sasha's tail and waiting for a ride. The two of them spent a great deal of time together, and that became their favorite game. Sasha would lie down on the tile floor, and Gingham would pounce. As soon as he was stretched out on Sasha's tail, she would begin sweeping it back and forth. Even when Gingham was full-grown, Sasha still managed to give Gingham a ride on her tail.

Gingham, Sasha, and I shared many adventures over the years. One of the most amazing began quite innocently.

Late one night, I woke from a sound sleep and heard a light siss. I figured it was Gingham wanting out, so I told him "no" and rolled over. Sasha nudged my hand, and I reassured her with a pat on the head that all was well. I snuggled deeper beneath the covers and buried my head under a pillow. I dozed until I heard a thump. *What on earth?* Groggily, I uncovered my head and peered at the bedside clock. It was 2:00 a.m. Another thump. It was Gingham jumping at the bedroom door. He hated being locked out. When I didn't want to play with him or have him bite my toes, I'd just shut the door. But he'd never knocked so loudly or continuously before. Usually, he took "no" for an answer and went to the couch.

"Okay, okay," I muttered as I reached out and cracked the door. In he flew. "Settle down, or back out you go," I told him.

He raced around the tiny bedroom, jumping from the bed to the dresser and back. Sasha poked her head up from her spot on the floor at the foot of the bed. She grunted and settled down. Gingham took off out of the room. I had such a headache and felt so groggy that I was about to close the door when in streaked a gray tabby fur ball.

"Gingham, knock it off."

He raced around again, jumping on the bed and then the dresser. I groaned and put down my head. "Ow," I complained as Gingham began biting and tugging at my feet through the covers. I kicked, wondering at his weird behavior and why Sasha wasn't more upset. "Geez," I yelped, feeling my hair being pulled and pulled. I bolted upright. "Stop it, that hurts!" The room spun, and I stood dizzily at the side of the bed. Something was really wrong. I held onto the bedroom doorframe, and Gingham began biting my toes. "Gingham, have you gone completely nuts?" Then I heard the siss again, only louder. I staggered down the hall to the kitchen. The siss was coming from the stove!

Gingham kept biting my toes. "Okay, okay. I get it." I was starting to realize I might have a gas leak. I grabbed the phone and called Al, the volunteer fire chief.

He wasn't happy to be so abruptly wakened and snarled, "What is it?" Quickly and hysterically, I told him about the siss.

"Get out now!" Al yelled, fully alert.

I headed to the back door. "Sasha," I called when she didn't appear. Gingham was gone, too. I staggered to the bedroom and saw Gingham biting at Sasha and pouncing on her, trying to rouse her. I grabbed Sasha and half-dragged her to the back door. Gingham kept biting her tail. With the door open, I saw Al at my propane tank turning off the outlet valve.

"Hurry!" Al shouted.

I pushed Sasha down the stairs and onto the grass. Once we were safely out, Gingham quit his frantic actions and jumped in my arms. WHOOSH! The last of the propane caught on fire as it reached the automatic pilot lights on my stove. Al rushed in with a heavy-duty extinguisher.

Beyond Al, I could see the wall behind my stove blazing. Several blasts from the extinguisher did the trick. Thank God Al had turned off the propane on his way over. More than that, I thanked God for Gingham. With the bedroom door closed, I wouldn't have heard the gas leak. Sasha and I were so groggy from breathing in the gas that we would have been asleep when the stove blew, and the propane would have continued to feed the fire.

That little cat, an unwanted gift from my students, saved our lives. He was a true hero. The next day, he was happy with a few extra liver treats as a reward, but I would have given him the world.

~Sharon F. Norton

58

One of a Kind

Kittens are angels with whiskers.
~Alexis Flora Hope

My six-year-old daughter held out her hands to me with a hopeful look on her face. "Can we keep it, Mama?" she inquired sweetly. I looked in her hands to see a teeny, furry, black animal, barely breathing and not moving at all. It was a kitten, its eyes barely opened, and not even mewling. I was certain it would not survive the night, and furthermore, where had it come from?

Knowing there was a feral cat colony in our neighborhood, I had to ask my hopeful daughter, "Sweetie, where did you find this kitten? You didn't take it from its mama, did you?"

"No, Mama," she replied. "The neighbor's dog was loose, and I went out to help catch it. This little kitten was on the porch. I think maybe the dog had it. It's not dead, though. It moves sometimes."

Whether the mother cat had been moving her brood and lost one or the neighbor dog had gotten them, I never found out. But this baby kitten became the newest member of our family, even though I dreaded telling my children that it would likely die before dawn.

The kitten survived, and despite my misgivings, and with the assistance of the veterinarian and the pet-shop personnel, we learned to feed, burp, and wash him. We had to teach him to "go potty" and basically everything else required of a cat. Soon, the lump of fur began to have a "look" that reminded us all of a baby mouse. Therefore, his name became Mouse. Not a very regal name, admittedly, but it stuck.

Because Mouse was so dependent on the family for everything, we took him everywhere with us. He traveled in a large Rubbermaid tote lined with towels that he couldn't escape from. He had his own diaper bag that held baby bottles and formula. He even had a travel-size litter pan. We brought him to visit my parents in another state, tucked safely in his tote, and he became a fixture at every family event for quite some time.

Little Mouse grew into a lovely, sleek, black male with large, green eyes, and it seemed that he had decided to be the overseer and protector of those who had saved him. He would often sit up high on a ledge or windowsill and "survey his domain." He would choose the lap of one of us each night, and we remarked more than once that he was "making his rounds." When one of us was sick, Mouse would not leave that person's side until he or she felt well again. It was clear that we were *his* people.

One evening, while my husband was out for a long shift, I had put my son to bed and walked to the kitchen when I heard a blood-curdling scream. My son was screaming, "It's a man! He's trying to get in! Mama, Mama!" I dashed back to my son's room to find him in the middle of the bed, crying and screaming. He had heard scratching on his window screen. Knowing Mouse liked to survey his domain from windowsills, he threw back the curtain, thinking it was Mouse. Instead, my poor child came face to face with a man at his window.

Immediately, I called the police and my neighbors. My children and I went to a safe location in the house while my neighbors looked for the offender. Mouse came right away to comfort us, and growled at the door with every noise. Although neither the police nor my neighbors could find the man in question, there were large footprints beneath my son's window. Clearly, there had been someone there, but we never found out who or why. Oddly, Mouse never sat on that windowsill again.

After that incident, Mouse became more determined to spend time with my son. Understandably, my son often had nightmares, so we would often end up sleeping in his room with him. However, one evening when my husband was again out for a long shift and I had worked an extremely stressful second shift myself, I fell asleep on the couch. I awoke to Mouse pulling on the neck of my shirt and screaming like a crazy thing. Once I became more awake, I realized the house was full of smoke.

It was coming from my son's room. Mouse kept running there and back screaming. I darted into my son's room to find that he had turned on his bedside light, but kicked it over, starting a fire right there beside him on the mattress. Thankfully, I was able to put out the fire and drag the mattress outside. We were all fine thanks to this little kitten saving us as we had saved him. Had he not woken me, the smoke would have devoured us all.

Mouse had repaid the favor, certainly, and we were more than thankful. He was now more than family; he was our hero. We treated him like the king he felt he was, and he liked it. Even when we moved to another state, Mouse maintained his vigil over us, sitting at the top of the staircase where he could see us all.

Nearly fifteen years later, our sleek, little Mouse began losing weight, no matter what he ate. A trip to the veterinarian confirmed our fears. Mouse was a diabetic. Having medical training, my husband and I decided to try to care for the little guy as best we could. We injected his insulin and gave him IV fluids at home. As he grew weaker, we hand-fed him from a syringe. Although we were getting his blood sugar under control, we were losing the war.

One afternoon, he began to breathe poorly. We knew we had to make the choice all pet parents dread. Taking him to the vet for the last time, we gave him the gift of crossing the Rainbow Bridge and ending his suffering. Even today, pictures of him bring us to tears, but we bask in the joy and love he gave us as well.

We now have three new kittens, all rescues. They are all wonderful in their own way. However, I know there is usually only one "Mouse" in a lifetime, and I will always remember how much he blessed us. You just can't replicate that.

~Freda Bradley

59

Kitty and the Bear

Watch a cat as it enters a room for the first time. It searches and smells about, it is not quiet for a moment, it trusts nothing until it has examined and made acquaintance with everything.
~Jean-Jacques Rousseau

The bear cubs peeked through my office window every morning and tapped on the glass. The window was low to the ground, so they only had to stand on their hind legs to peer through, and peer they did. My office was at the back of the house, adjoining a small, screened porch that was in need of re-screening thanks to the antics of a large papa bear earlier in the summer. We coexist peacefully with bears in the Southern Appalachian Highlands — black bears, mostly — as well as coyotes, wolves, and an occasional mountain lion. Even in Asheville, the closest city to us, it is not unusual to hear about a high-school soccer match coming to a halt while a bear ambles across the field.

That summer, the three cubs passed our house on the first leg of a daily circuit through the woods with their mom. They always stopped and tapped on the windows and rolled about until Mama made her snuffy noise, calling them to be on their way again. They always made me smile, but they made Kitty — a handsome tuxedo cat who had adopted me when I first moved to the mountains some years before — absolutely frantic. She wanted to go out and play with them, and I wouldn't let her, knowing how seriously mauled she could get in the name of having fun. I also couldn't be too sure how Mama might react to another critter approaching her cubs. So Kitty ran back and forth between my desk and the back door to the porch, scratching at the door for me to let her out and letting out a sorrowful yowl when I wouldn't.

However, I am not one to obstruct the natural inclinations of critters, domestic or wild, so Kitty pretty much came and went as she pleased, at least when the bears weren't visibly about. She was an efficient hunter, could scurry up and down trees and clothesline poles with the best of them, and was as surefooted as a mountain goat on rooftops and fence rails. I am quite sure that, given the opportunity, she could leap tall buildings in a single bound, but I was in no way prepared for what she actually did one balmy summer afternoon.

I was at my usual station at the desk when I heard a commotion outside. I had let Kitty out a while before, and thought she had probably caught a squirrel, black snake, or some other prey that was putting up more of a fight than a mouse or mole normally would. So, I stepped out onto the porch and came to a dead halt. Kitty was facing down a large, male black bear on the ridgeline trail just a few yards away. I watched as Kitty took a few slow, low-to-the-ground stalking steps forward — and the bear took a step back. Then she took a few more stalking steps forward, and the bear took another step back, never taking his eyes off her. After about thirty seconds, the bear stood up on his hind legs, clawed the air for a few seconds, and turned tail and ran back into the woods. Kitty rushed behind him until he disappeared into the trees.

Of course, I was stunned by this performance, and spent several days twirling it around in my brain. It was obviously a freak occurrence, but what on earth had happened? Did the bear not know what she was? Did she have a funny smell for some reason? Did he think she was a skunk? Then, about a week later, I glanced out the window and saw a repeat of the same drama! I don't know if he was the same bear or a different one, but I do know that aside from our regular morning visitors, I didn't see another bear close to the house all summer!

As for Kitty, I still wouldn't let her go out and play with the cubs, but she took to greeting them paw-to-paw through the window every morning and forgave me for my overprotective eccentricities.

~Deb Louis

60

Ripple in the Snow

*Human beings are drawn to cats because they are all
we are not — self-contained, elegant in everything
they do, relaxed, assured, glad of company,
yet still possessing secret lives.*
~Pam Brown

Ripple, named for the ripple-like effect her tortoiseshell coat gave her, was a peculiar cat, to say the least. Maybe it was because of the way my mom found her: underneath a parked car, her beautiful tortoise coat covered in oil and grime, her ribs presenting themselves as large, spindly bumps on the sides of her body like her skin was pulled too tight. Whatever the reason, Ripple liked to follow my mom and dad everywhere they went, and once I was born she took a great liking to me, too.

Our house was just a mile from my preschool. My dad was legally blind and had been that way all my life. So instead of driving every day to my school, we would walk down a wooded path that was just over the road from our house. It was almost a straight shot except for one fork in the road a little way down the path. At the fork, we would take a left, which would take us the rest of the way to my school. If we didn't turn left, the path would lead us deeper into the thicket of the forest, far away from town.

Ripple would follow us down that path every day, her paws delicately stepping over every stick and stone, seemingly content just to be in our presence and to be included in the journey. Every weekday, my dad and I would get ready for our walk. Hand in hand, or sometimes with me on top of his shoulders, we would trek down that same unpaved path that weaved through the pine trees and the manzanita, our trusted feline companion following close behind. When we got to school, my dad would drop me off inside as Ripple waited patiently at the door. I don't remember what the other school kids thought of our cat, or if they even noticed her at all. What a sight it must have been to see our small troop walking down to the school building! After I was safely inside, my dad would then start his journey home, with Ripple following closely behind.

One day, it was snowing, and a thick cushion of white blanketed the northern California landscape, with more wet flakes falling at a steady rate. Still, we bundled up and headed out with Ripple following close behind. We walked for a while, our heads down to avoid the blowing snow. It was miserably cold and I was surprised that Ripple decided to accompany us.

My father and I did little talking, as our faces were pressed into our scarves. Because of this, when at one point a small sound broke through the snow and the wind, we looked at each other in puzzlement, wondering if the other one had said something and it was simply muffled through our winter attire. But no, as we listened more, we could make out a small mewing sound. It was barely audible, but still there, and it made us both turn around to see what was making that foreign noise in this white and forlorn landscape.

It was Ripple. No longer close behind us, she sat in the snow and the cold a good distance away from where we now stood. She was so far away, in fact, that I had to squint to see her little brown body in the fog of white. She was meowing so incessantly that my dad knew something must be wrong. But what was it? Was she cold? Had she had enough of the snow and sleet? We walked back to her, my dad confused and concerned. However, when we got to where she stubbornly sat, he realized something. She was standing in the fork in the road, the one where we were supposed to turn left. We had missed our turn, but Ripple had remembered. She tried to alert us the best way she knew how. And it worked.

We conceded that Ripple had a better sense of direction than we had, and we set off down the correct trail. This one would lead us to my preschool, not deeper into the woods. Ripple stopped her meowing as soon as she saw us going the correct way and followed us as usual all the way to my preschool. Then she went back through the storm with my dad to the warm house where, I'm sure she was praised and rewarded with a treat.

Ripple followed us many times after that until she passed away from old age. I have had many cats in my lifetime, but none as peculiar as Ripple. To me, she will always be the cat with the old soul, guiding us through the storm and protecting her family. For all those years, I had thought we were her saviors, but now I realize that she was the one watching over us.

~Kiva Arne

61

She Knew

It always gives me a shiver when I
see a cat seeing what I can't see.
~Eleanor Farjeon

Ten years ago, Kitty Kat — a gray cat with a white chest, white whiskers and white paws — arrived on our doorstep looking for food. For two days, she waited on our front porch for us to return from work, and then meowed to be fed. After a week of posting flyers on trees, no one claimed her and my husband agreed to let her stay and become part of the family.

Over the next seven years, I watched my husband and Kitty Kat bond. She waited for him to arrive home from work, and when he sat on the sofa to watch TV, she took her place beside him. Then, one evening, she crept onto his lap and went to sleep. I smiled to myself. For a man who was not raised with animals, he had developed a mutual friendship with Kitty Kat.

One morning, I awoke to find her sleeping on my husband's pillow. When he returned from his morning jog, he chided me for encouraging our cat to sleep with him. I laughed and assured him I had nothing to do with it. In fact, I had become secretly jealous of the attention she was lavishing on him and he on her. For the next week, she followed him up the stairs and into the master bedroom at night. Without an invitation, she leapt onto our bed and took her place on his pillow. She made sure to leave him enough space to place his head. Once he settled, she curled up and closed her eyes.

One morning, I awoke to loud meowing. Curious, I reached for my robe and descended the stairs. As I did so, I became aware that something was wrong. The house was silent except for Kitty Kat's meowing at the foot of the stairs to attract my attention. As I entered the dining room, she came running, almost tripping me, and stopped in the doorway leading into the kitchen. She turned and meowed loudly. I bent down and cradled her in my arms before entering the kitchen.

As I entered the room, I saw my husband lying on the floor in front of the kitchen sink. He was unresponsive and had no pulse. I dialed 9-1-1. But it was too late.

Three weeks later, I met a friend for lunch. When I told her about Kitty Kat's odd behavior and how she had stopped sleeping on his pillow after his death, she mentioned she had read how animals have an instinct about people and their health. I shrugged it off. How could animals know? Curious, I went online that evening and researched cats and their ability to sense serious illness in humans. I was surprised at the amount of information on the subject. An individual had recounted how the family cat had started sleeping on his wife's chest. Puzzled, she consulted her doctor and learned she needed surgery for a hiatus hernia. After the operation, the cat never slept on her chest again.

After my research about cats and their ability to sense illnesses in humans, I became a believer. I have no doubt that Kitty Kat had a premonition the week before my husband's passing. If only I had known then what I know now.

~Rosemarie Riley

Ellie, the Angel

Of all the things God created, from sunrises to
rainbows, to black holes and humor, cats
are the most fascinating to me.
~Jarod Kintz

My daughter was diagnosed with epilepsy her sophomore year in high school. She had a very difficult time dealing with the side effects of the medications and the fear of seizures. Because of this, she spent a lot of time alone in her room. One day, she came to me and asked if she could get a cat.

I was a little wary, since our last cat, although we loved her, had been a scratcher and very destructive, but I couldn't say "no" to my daughter given the tough time she was having. I began looking at the various shelter and rescue websites for an adult cat that had already been declawed and was litter trained. That's when I found Ellie at Father John's Animal House. The picture showed a sweet, white face with dark, expressive eyes. They described her as a lovable "mush" who loved to cuddle. Based on that description, my husband and I made the two-hour drive to see her.

As they pulled Ellie out of the cage, I gasped with surprise. She was *huge*! But as I held that giant, white pillow of cat, she purred with the volume of a small tractor, put one of her enormous, soft, clawless paws up against my face, and melted my heart.

The shelter volunteer then gave us her history. Ellie had been found in an abandoned home with several other cats. She had been adopted and then returned twice because of difficulties with the litter box. The thought of litter problems did make me think twice, but that motor-like purring and the quiet way she had settled her enormous bulk into my arms overrode my fears.

The smile that lit up my daughter's face as she gathered our new family member into her arms reassured me. From that day on, wherever she went, Ellie followed. My daughter's days of isolation were over. At night, I would check on her as she slept. Snuggled up next to her, Ellie would raise her head and look at me as if to say, "I've got this. I'm watching her."

As for the litter problems, she never had any problems at all with us. She has always been perfectly behaved. It's as if she knew the home she was supposed to go to and did what she had to in order to make sure that she got there.

One afternoon, when I peeked into my daughter's room, she was sitting on the floor writing in her journal with her back against her bed. Ellie was sprawled on the edge of the bed. Her head and one paw were resting lightly on one of my daughter's shoulders and her other paw was resting on the other shoulder. It was such a posture of protection, companionship, and love. I think this cat may well be an actual angel.

~Mary Fluhr Bajda

63

How Daisy Earned Her Middle Name

*Our perfect companions never
have fewer than four feet.*
~Colette

I n 2003, I casually mentioned to a friend that I wanted to rescue a black kitten from the pound. I'd heard that black cats and dogs were the last to be adopted because humans are silly and superstitious, and I tend to go for the underdog. Or, in this case, the "undercat." So I wanted a black cat.

The very next day, a tiny, sick, black kitten showed up on that same friend's patio. They couldn't keep her, and while they said she looked like she was about to die, I agreed to take the little creature. The vet thought she was six weeks old when I first brought her in because she was so small. But her teeth revealed she was actually six months old and very malnourished. She'd had a rough start to life. I set about fattening her up and making her feel safe and loved.

She had obviously been roaming the Indiana countryside for quite some time. Along with practically starving to death, she'd clearly had a run-in with a sappy tree and a serious tangle with an angry skunk. She had a cleft lip as well, and the vet thought perhaps she'd been rejected by her mother. I called her Daisy because she was the *opposite* of a flower. She was a mess — a skinny, sticky, very stinky mess! And I gave her the middle name of Serendipity because of the timing of her arrival. I had wished for her, and there she was. Daisy Serendipity.

Seven years later, Daisy and I had moved to D.C. It was just the two of us. She was my roommate, confidante, and my best friend. And we were very in tune with each other. I joked that we were co-dependent.

I started having trouble with kidney stones early in college, but they passed relatively easily then. In D.C., the issue got more serious, and I landed in surgery. My doctor removed almost eighty stones from my right kidney. The surgery left me feeling pretty awful.

Four days after surgery, I went back to work. As the day wore on, I became convinced I had swine flu, which was in the news that year. The pain started from the top of my head, and as the hours passed, that pain and stiffness crept down my neck and shoulders to my back and hips. I finally gave up and went home for the afternoon.

I just wanted to sleep. I didn't eat anything myself, but I fed Daisy before I climbed into bed with an ice pack at the back of my head. I fell into a deep sleep.

Hours later, Daisy woke me up by "push-pawing" on my cheek. I was accustomed to her pawing me, but this was different. It really hurt. When I groggily opened my eyes, I could see she was right in my face, nose-to-nose, her little mouth meowing like crazy. But I couldn't hear a thing. *Strange,* I thought. I grabbed the remote to turn on the television. Nothing. I turned the volume way up. Nothing. I got worried.

I sat up quickly and very nearly passed out. I knew something was incredibly wrong. I called 9-1-1 and realized as I waited on the phone that I could not hear it ringing or hear if anyone answered. I took my best guess and said, "I hope there is someone on the other end of the line. Something is really wrong with me. I thought I had the flu, but I feel like I'm going to die. I can't hear anything. I'm dizzy. I need help." I stayed on the line for a minute and then hung up.

I looked at Daisy, who was pacing and still meowing — not her normal behavior at all. I grabbed her long-term feeder (the kind that lets food out as they eat), filled it to the top, and turned on the water faucet to a thin stream. I wasn't sure how long I would be gone, but this felt like more than the flu, and I was worried about leaving her alone for days. Then I went to wait by the front door because I couldn't hear anyone knock.

Luckily, an operator had heard me on that 9-1-1 call, and an ambulance arrived quickly. The EMTs and I communicated the best we could. I could talk to them; they motioned to me. They took my temperature and blood pressure. Then they looked at each other and helped me onto the stretcher. Their look said it all. I got really scared.

In the emergency room, I remember a lot of people moving around me at an alarmingly fast rate. I remember a nurse with a cute, brunette bob, whose main job was to comfort me. She held my hand and tried to communicate what was happening. As they got my blood pressure to rise, I was able to hear again. And the nurse's face and voice were the only things that kept me from losing it. I heard some scary words. I saw some scary looks pass to and from medical team members. I remember a test in my wrist that was terribly painful. And then I woke up in the Intensive Care Unit two days later.

I had sepsis. It was, we believe, a result of the cleaning out of those stones in my kidney. My urologist visited me every day for my entire two weeks in the hospital. He felt pretty bad, but I didn't blame him. Things happen. The ER doctor visited me, too. And he said the team couldn't figure out how in the world I'd woken up at all to be able to call 9-1-1. My blood pressure when I arrived had been lower than 55/40. I should have died in my sleep.

"My cat," I said, smiling. "She woke me up."

"You probably stopped breathing a number of times and freaked her out," said the doctor. "Serendipitous. She's a hero."

Indeed, she is. And the fact that her full name is Daisy Serendipity was not lost on me.

~Kristin Ingersoll

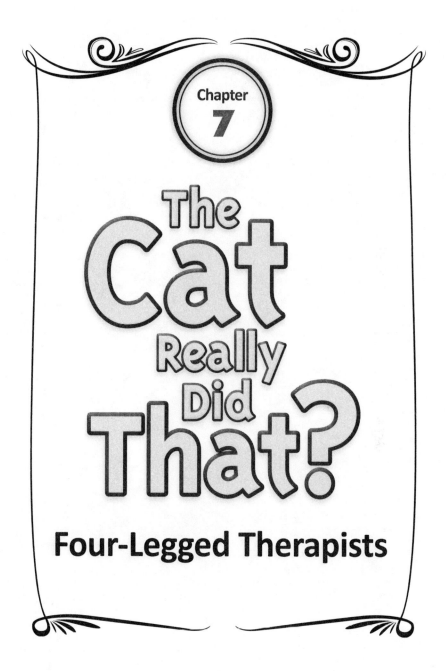

The Cat Really Did That?

Four-Legged Therapists

64

Hidden Voices

It is impossible for a lover of cats to banish these alert,
gentle, and discriminating little friends, who give us
just enough of their regard and complaisance
to make us hunger for more.
~Agnes Repplier

A s a volunteer for Colony Cats and Dogs, I've seen the best and the worst of people. Whether it's a hoarding situation or an abuse or neglect situation, the shelter always steps in to help. Colony Cats and Dogs is a cage-free, no-kill shelter. My task while I am there four days a week is to talk to the people who come in and educate them on the adoption process. I have seen many heartbreaking as well as heartwarming situations in my six years volunteering there. One adoption story in particular sticks out in my head; I will never forget it.

A young boy with golden curls had come into the shelter with his mom a couple days in a row. He was always so excited to be around the cats, but all he would do was shriek. There was such a bright glow on the boy's face that it was contagious. When I saw them at the shelter for the third day in a row, I had to talk to the mom. Walking up to her, I smiled and said, "Is there anything I can help you with?" Turning to me with a smile, she told me their story.

Her nine-year-old son was on the autism spectrum and had never spoken a single word in his life. While he couldn't talk, he did have a love of art, and he loved to draw cats. When his mom had heard about our shelter, she knew she had to bring her son in. I asked if they had any pets at home, and she said they did not. As a single mom of two, she was always working. The days that she was not working, she was running her son from one therapy session to another. Lately, though, her son had been very emotional, and the only thing that calmed him was spending time with our cats. After much consideration, she was strongly considering adopting a cat.

That day, her son fell in love with a little, black cat named Stevie. I was shocked that he was interested in her, given her appearance. Little Stevie had come to us after being severely abused. Some sick person cut off both her ears and let an eye infection get so bad that the eye needed to be removed.

The boy's mother kept trying to show him other cats, but he kept going back to Stevie. I asked her why she was steering her son away from this cat and she said she was worried about medical bills due to the abuse. I explained that all of our cats see a vet and are healthy upon going up for adoption. Stevie was truly healthy; she just looked different.

Two days later, the boy and his mother returned. She said, "My son has not stopped drawing pictures of Stevie. I talk about the zoo and seeing other animals, and he just points to his drawings. Every time I say Stevie's name, he smiles and claps his hands. What do I have to do to take this cat home?"

I sat down next to the boy and asked him, "Would you like to take Stevie home with you tonight?" He had such a glow in his eyes and was smiling from ear to ear. Giving me a huge hug he looked at his mom in disbelief, looking for confirmation of what I had asked him. His mother nodded her head and the boy shrieked.

After about five minutes, I had all the paperwork done and Stevie was in a carrier ready to go.

Later that night, we got a happy update on Facebook from the mom:

Tonight we adopted Stevie from your shelter, and tonight my nine-year-old autistic son said his first word EVER. Holding

Stevie he looked at me and said "cat." Did we rescue Stevie, or did Stevie rescue us?

I cried so hard, the words became blurred. Sometimes, we just need a pet as much as that pet needs us.

~Stephanie Jones-McKee

65

The Pair

There are few things in life more heartwarming
than to be welcomed by a cat.
~Tay Hohoff

Overhearing a soft-spoken mom, I turned to see a gorgeous, little girl of about six. She wore her long, auburn hair in a braid down her back, and the turquoise ribbon that secured it matched her jumper.

"My daughter's name is Emma. She rarely speaks and will often jump up quickly and hug herself if she feels afraid. She's autistic, you see. We need to find a cat that isn't put off by her mannerisms, but she truly wants a pet. We're not allowed to have dogs in our complex."

"Hi, I'm Kathleen, and I think I can help you," I stated as I reached out my hand.

"And I'm Michelle," she added as she shook mine.

"I've been a volunteer here for many years, and I know the cats quite well. I'm wondering if Emma would do well with an outgoing personality or one that is gentle but well socialized. Let's walk around, and I'll introduce you to our residents. May I hold your hand, Emma?" I asked as I knelt down to her level.

"She's really not comfortable with strangers," Michelle explained. Little Emma suddenly jumped behind her mother's back, and I felt her fear.

"I'm sorry that I startled you, Emma," I whispered. "Let's go meet Marty." Marty was an orange tabby, about four years old, and quite a character.

He loved attention, but he hadn't been adopted because he had only three legs. "Marty was dropped off in a cardboard box outside our back door," I told Michelle and Emma. "He was terribly ill with an infection from a wound on his leg. Unfortunately, that leg was amputated."

"Emma, look," Michelle said as she pointed to Marty. Marty was rubbing against the cage door, hoping to get a lovely scratching session. Emma stood still with her eyes on her pink shoes. "I don't know if this is going to work out," Michelle told me.

"We currently have thirty-two cats," I explained. "Perhaps one will get Emma's attention."

Emma's eyes remained on the ground as we moved from cage to cage and I pointed out various candidates.

"Goodness, I'd love to take them all," laughed Michelle. "Do you think it would matter if we picked a female over a male?"

"The males tend to be more social, but that is not a hard-and-fast rule. Here's Shadow. He was shy on arrival, but has turned into a fine boy."

Again, Emma showed no interest, but then her chin lifted as she stared across the room. "She appears to like one on the other side of the room. May we?" asked Michelle.

Emma was staring at Thomas, and my heart fell. "Thomas has been here for two years," I explained. "He has remained aloof even though we work with him each day. As you can see, he's flattened himself against the back wall, and he's quivering a bit. I don't think Thomas will work out for Emma."

Emma continued staring at Thomas. "Yes," she whispered.

"Emma, Thomas is a very frightened cat," I warned. "He doesn't play, and he doesn't like to be cuddled."

"Yes," stated Emma once again as she reached her small hand toward the solid gray cat in his cage.

I believe in miracles, and I witnessed one then. For the first time in his stay at the shelter, Thomas came forward to the front of his cage. "Pretty, pretty," cooed Emma as she gently slid her hand through the bars. "Yes," she said for the third time.

Several other volunteers and the shelter manager came forward.

"My, my... will you look at that?" the amazed manager noted.

As I turned back to Michelle, I saw that she had tears in her eyes. "Could we possibly adopt Thomas?"

Emma looked into my eyes as she took my hand.

Two months later, I received an envelope at the shelter. Inside were two photographs of Emma and Thomas. The first showed Emma asleep in her bed with Thomas curled up under her chin. The next showed Emma placing Thomas's food bowl on the kitchen floor as a confident, shiny, gray cat approached.

Dear Kathleen,

I can't thank you enough for the precious gift of Thomas. Emma and he are inseparable. Thomas is as sweet as can be and has come out of his shell.

When Emma is frightened, Thomas does not run away. He tends to stand quietly by her side.

Emma is talking a bit more, saying words that relate to her pet such as kitty, treat, play, and fun. She attends school each morning and her teachers say she is progressing nicely. Of course, Thomas perches on the back of the couch, awaiting her arrival home.

Please share the photos and note with your kind colleagues. We couldn't be happier!

With fond regards,
Michelle

~Kathleen Gemmell

66

Man's Best Friend

Cats are designated friends.
~Norman Corwin

Cats aren't exactly known for being "man's best friend." Our son and our cat, despite having both been adopted as babies, typified that relationship. It wasn't for lack of trying on Alec's part, but Princess never wanted much to do with him. It's hard to blame her. Princess was already six years old when Alec joined our family, and a haughty teenaged cat and a loud human baby were probably not destined to hit it off. But it didn't stop Alec from trying.

As a toddler, Alec trailed after Princess, trying to show his affection with hugs. Once, he followed her behind an armchair. We couldn't see what happened, but there was a yelp of feline indignation and a squeal of pain from Alec. He emerged with a scratch to remind him, we assume, that it isn't polite to touch a cat without her permission.

As they grew older, Alec kept trying to get close to Princess. Despite sometimes deigning to play with the laser lights or string he tempted her with, she resolutely refrained from climbing into his lap when the family watched television. As an only child, Alec often wished he had someone to share a room with. But no matter how much Alec wished Princess would sleep in his bed, she continued to curl up next to my pillow every night instead.

Nothing Alec could do seemed to change her first opinion of

him — until years later when he was on the cusp of becoming a teenager himself.

Alec had been diagnosed with epilepsy at age four. He had absence seizures — two- to three-second staring spells that most people never noticed. Medicine kept them well under control, but when he turned twelve, his seizure activity increased. This time, increasing the dosage of medicine didn't control the seizures, and he was admitted to the hospital for a week for testing.

My husband and I took turns staying at the hospital with him while the other went to work. I took the first shift, and when it was my turn to come home a few days later, Princess meowed happily when I walked in the door. I petted her and gave her some attention, but she kept up with her yowling. I checked her food — the other reason she sometimes vocalized — but it was full. So I headed toward the back of the house to the bedroom to unpack my overnight bag. Princess followed, caterwauling all the way.

When we reached the hallway between the bedrooms, she stopped in front of Alec's door. I could count on one hand the number of times Princess had been in his room in the four years we'd lived in the house, but she refused to move on. She turned in circles, eyes trained on me, meowing all the time. It may be fanciful, but I swear she was asking where Alec was.

When we all came home several days later, Princess wound herself around all of our ankles and mewed and purred until everyone in the family had petted and talked to her. That night, when we sat down to watch television, Princess jumped onto Alec's lap for the first time. He was cautiously optimistic. "Maybe she's starting to like me, Mom."

But after a dozen years of Princess mostly ignoring Alec, I wasn't getting my hopes up.

While he was in the hospital, Alec began having different types of seizures than the small ones he'd had most of his life. Two months after his hospital stay, he had a tonic-clonic seizure, formerly known as a grand mal seizure, as we were getting ready to leave for school. Then he had another a week later at wrestling practice. Seizures can be scary to witness and even scarier to experience.

Alec was understandably nervous about having another seizure. Like most worries, it seemed to grow bigger at night, and it often took Alec a half-hour or more of tossing and turning before he could fall asleep. The worst part is that sleep-deprivation can trigger seizures. Staying awake worrying about having a seizure was actually putting him at a higher risk of having one. We tried everything to help him relax, but nothing seemed to work.

One night, shortly after Alec went to bed, we heard him talking to someone. I tiptoed back to his room and peeked in. By the light from the hallway, I could see a little lump of black fur on the blankets beside Alec. Princess was keeping him company. He stroked and petted her, speaking softly as he settled down on his pillow.

Smiling, I tiptoed back to the living room to tell my husband. Five minutes later, Alec was asleep. Curled up by his pillow, Princess snoozed, too. For the first time in a long time, Alec had fallen asleep easily. Princess stayed in his bed the whole night that night and many nights afterward.

After twelve years of keeping him at paw's length, Princess finally decided to be friends with Alec when he needed her most. Just like a true best friend.

~April Serock

67

Did My Rescue Cat Extend My Life?

Cats are endless opportunities for revelation.
~Leslie Kapp

"Frank, I really do not want to take home a cat this young." I was seventy-four, and my middle-aged roommate had decided on a beautiful but pudgy one-and-a-half-year-old at the local shelter.

"Look at her," he said. "She's like a classy lady from the 1950s. She's got little, short white gloves on her front paws and little white knee-highs on her back ones. And she moves gracefully for a cat her size."

After she had tapped us both, in turn, on our hips, I noticed her lovely tortoise or calico (I couldn't decide which) head and back, some tabby striping on her sides, and her pretty face. But what caught my attention was the fluffiest white bib from her throat, down her belly, to her tail, and on her underside, with an occasional swirl of chocolate. Her belly looked like a hot-fudge sundae.

I noticed that she did not associate with the other cats in the room. She sort of hid behind the open door. After her first tap, she ignored us. Seeing her large size, we quickly realized that when we first entered, she tapped us because she thought we were attendants and might have some treats.

Yes, she was eye-catching, but was I ready for a new cat? And was I prepared for one so young?

Our household's most recent cat had died only a few months before. We had agreed to wait at least six months to get another. But Frank had medical issues and wanted the feline comfort and companionship. I was seventy-four, though, and having some physical difficulties. Stooping and bending for litter duty was reasonable, but hunting and playing with a frisky, young kitty was probably not in the cards for me.

I loved cats, but I really wanted one that was about five years old, and thus more settled and sedate. On top of that, the house was awash with clutter. A frisky, young cat would be hard to deal with, knocking things over and hiding heaven knows where.

In the end, I told Frank I'd go along with his decision. We took her home, and the scared little thing immediately squeezed under a twin bed in one of the bedrooms of the old, doublewide mobile home.

Three days later, after a constant offering of cat treats, she came out, quickly found and used the litter box, and then hid from us again. For the first week, that's all she did — come out, eat, use the box, and retreat.

Then she began exploring, very carefully, but she still refused to let Frank near her. It broke his heart. He had picked her out, but she was terrified of him. She would allow me to reach down near her to put down food. She would walk through the house. But if he came near her, she ran.

Meanwhile, we noticed that she was shedding like crazy. Her hair was everywhere. I decided to try brushing her, which she agreed to as long as there were treats. She and I began a nightly ritual of fifteen minutes of brushing and conversation. She felt velvety and silky after each session. I mentioned this to Frank. That's when she got her name: Silkie.

Just over a year after she came to our home, Frank passed away from a massive heart attack. Silkie had never gotten over her fear of him, and we guessed that a man had mistreated her in the past. Now, with Frank gone, I was officially the only human caregiver for this shy little cat, who was not even three years old.

Doing the math shocked me. She would likely make it to at least fifteen. That was at least twelve more years. I was now seventy-five. This cat was still so needy and afraid that I could not imagine exposing her to another lifestyle change. That meant I would need to live to eighty-seven or so if I wanted to be sure she'd be all right. My health was iffy. Walking and getting up off the floor after our brushing sessions were tricky. I had a quad cane I used everywhere. My bones and joints ached often. I wasn't yet on any meds, but I was having a harder time talking my doctor out of them.

When Frank passed on, I realized that I had to change my eating habits. Frank was a typical "guy," and the fridge was stocked with beef, pork, sausage, provolone, and Swiss cheese. I didn't have much money, so I couldn't just toss things out, but I slowly replaced the bad foods with good ones.

The change in my food, plus all the running around I had to do after Frank's passing, had a nice benefit. I lost twenty pounds that first year. The extra activity coupled with the weight loss made a big difference in my mobility. Now, I only use the quad cane for really long walks. I walk farther, although not as far as I'd like. My knee rarely hurts these days.

And Silkie finally climbed on my lap after a couple more years, and I heard her purr for the first time.

She is still not the most affectionate cat I've had, but she has made great progress. She stays away from me when I cry, but she seems to know when I'm stressed and need a break. I will often drop things or feel stress building, and suddenly she's at my ankle, looking up with a little meow. I've learned to take this as a cue to stop whatever I'm doing and rest and recharge for a few minutes or a half-hour.

This month will mark four years since Silkie's arrival. I've kept off those twenty pounds that I lost. I walk better. I'm almost eighty and I only take one medication—a very low-level blood-pressure medication. I haven't taken a pain pill in over a year.

Has Silkie extended my life? Who knows? I do know she has

enhanced it, and I cherish each minute with this still-aloof, pudgy shelter cat that was everything I thought I did not want. She turned out to be everything I needed.

~Evelyn Shamay Mayfield

68

Healing a Broken Heart

When I am feeling low, all I have to do is watch
my cats and my courage returns.
~Charles Bukowski

About twelve years ago, my daughter's father moved over a thousand miles away without saying goodbye to her. When we discovered he had left, Danielle was inconsolable, hurt, and angry. No amount of hugs or explanations could heal her broken heart, and I was at a loss in knowing how to help her. Since she had a nurturing personality and a deep love for animals, I decided to cheer her up with something to refocus her attention — a kitten.

At the rescue facility we spotted a fist-sized, fuzzy, black kitten meowing at the top of his lungs. His green eyes were bright, and his pert, little ears — much too big for his small head — stood at attention. He was amidst his brothers and sisters, all variations of gray and white. He was the only black kitten in the litter, and he was the tiniest.

When Dani held him in her arms, it was love at first sight. The kitten curled belly-up into her arms and purred so loudly that he sounded like a baby freight train. "Oh, Mommy, I love him. Can we keep him?"

"What are you going to name him?" I asked.

"Spencer," she said.

Spencer proved to be acutely aware that his presence was healing for Dani. He was high-maintenance in his need for cuddles and petting.

If he wasn't getting enough attention, he would meow. It wasn't just a little mewling — it was a loud, piercing, mournful meow.

Keeping Spencer out of trouble, or rescuing him from trouble, was a twenty-four-hour job! I still laugh when I recall the time he got his head stuck in a hamster ball. The hamster got away safely, but poor Spencer looked like an astronaut roaming the moon.

My daughter took her role as kitty mommy seriously. She made sure he was fed, watered, and had clean litter. As the years passed, Dani thrived. Her hurt and anger turned into a positive energy that motivated her to achieve high grades throughout high school, so much so that she eventually got a full scholarship to college.

The drawback to going to college was that Spencer could not go with her. Instead, he stayed behind with my new husband and me. When Dani left, Spencer's neediness diminished, and he became a lazy cat who only occasionally wanted affection. When Dani would return home for long weekends, Spencer's mournful meows and need for love would reappear as if he found his renewed purpose.

Dani eventually moved off campus and took Spencer with her. Spencer easily fell into her routine without requiring so much attention. He would curl at her feet when she was studying, and she slept with the sweet sound of his purrs in her ear, always her vigilant and faithful cat.

Then Dani met her future fiancé, and he was allergic to cats. He would sneeze, wheeze, and become deathly ill whenever he was around Spencer. Since my husband and I were moving into an RV with a Bull Mastiff, we couldn't take Spencer. Dani's fiancé offered to get weekly allergy shots, but that was not a viable solution for a lifetime commitment. Dani began the painful task of seeking a new home for her precious Spencer, but after months of looking she had not found the right place for him.

Dani worked with fish and wildlife, so she was surrounded by fellow animal lovers. When a co-worker announced that his wife of ten years left him and his three children, Dani's heart went out to his daughters and son. She remembered her emotions when her dad left and how it devastated her. She also recalled how much Spencer helped her heal from the loss of her dad.

Dani asked her co-worker, "How are the kids taking it?"

"Bad. Very bad. I don't know how to stop them from hurting," he confided.

"Have you thought about adopting a cat? One who has experience in helping kids get over the loss of a parent?"

When my daughter shared her story, the co-worker asked to bring the kids over to meet Spencer. The minute they walked into Dani's home, Spencer started his mournful, pitiful, loud meow. He jumped into the arms of the smallest child, a four-year-old, who tried to comfort Spencer by saying, "It's okay, kitty. It's okay." Spencer rolled belly-up and started purring like a baby freight train.

"Can we keep him, Daddy? Can we take him home?"

It was love at first sight. Spencer was doing what he did best — healing a broken heart.

~Dawn Smith Gondeck

In from the Cold

Cats choose us; we don't own them.
~Kristin Cast

He showed up one night as my husband RJ and I were having dinner on the deck. The aroma of steak must have attracted his attention, and he tentatively climbed up the stairs to watch us. When my husband threw the leftover T-bone from our dinner toward him, the black-and-white cat attacked it like a dog.

Over the next couple of weeks, we'd hear him crying before he slowly crept up the stairs, stopping to watch from the top step. His body language said, "Don't come near me." But when food was thrown his way, he continued to devour it with obvious hunger. Anyone who knew RJ's distaste for cats would have been shocked, but he seemed to admire the way this skinny creature attacked the scraps, stating, "That cat eats like a dog."

As summer turned into fall, the cat became friendlier, even coming over to rub against our legs. The high point happened when he started sitting in my lap for short periods. RJ said he could stay, but he would not have a cat in the house. We started calling him Tommy, and he took his meals by the sliding doors of the deck. As the nights grew colder, we sat outside less, and he would place his nose against the door and call for his meal.

Tommy became a staple in my life. If I didn't see him for several days, I became concerned. The days grew shorter and colder. Then winter arrived with snow and frigid temperatures.

After a particularly heavy snow, I left RJ working on files he'd brought home from his office and mushed my way into town for groceries. Thank goodness we had a 4-wheel drive since the store was miles away. When I returned, RJ was still working, but he'd pulled another chair over beside him. The wooden chair now held Tommy, curled up in a ball and purring when RJ reached over to pet him.

"What gives?" I asked.

"Well, it is so cold outside, and he looked pitiful sitting at the door watching me. I decided he could come in and get warm."

When bedtime rolled around, RJ checked the outside thermometer and decided the cat couldn't go back out into the below-zero cold. "He can stay in the house, but he will not be allowed on the bed."

"Where is he going to sleep?" I had had cats previously, and I knew that what RJ said and what the cat decided would likely be different.

"I'll fix him a bed." RJ got the clothesbasket from the laundry room and pulled towels from the linen closet. He placed the new bed beside ours and put the cat inside. He reached down and scratched Tommy's head until they both fell asleep.

Of course, I woke up in the middle of the night, and the cat was on the bed snuggled between us. Discovering the new sleeping arrangements when he awakened the next morning, RJ shrugged his shoulders and declared, "If he's going to be a house cat, we need to get him to the vet for shots."

Over the next several years, Tommy came and went as he chose, but he always showed up at dinnertime. RJ had a small dish of vanilla ice cream each night, and his new buddy always got a taste, too. On winter nights he would curl up on one of our laps while we watched television.

Then my husband had a stroke and passed away. The house bustled with out-of-town family and friends, but the cat was nowhere in sight. Once everyone had departed, Tommy showed up.

On the first night in a now-quiet house, Tommy wandered through the house calling for my husband at bedtime. I lay in bed listening to the pathetic cries. He gave up after about an hour, jumped on the bed and came over to me. My heart broke when he buried his head in my neck and made a strange sound for several minutes. Yes, cats can grieve and cry.

He shared my grief, and we became closer, snuggling each night to comfort each other. There was no question when I moved to another city that he would, too. The outside cat became a housecat. He still loved the ice cream RJ used to share with him, and he continued to sleep with me every night. But old habits die hard, and when others came into the house, he disappeared.

My kids encouraged me to start dating, so I eventually worked up the courage to take the first step. One of the gentlemen who a friend introduced me to asked me out. When he walked me to the door after an enjoyable time, I invited him in for coffee. While I made our coffee, he sat in the living room, and a visitor came down the stairs.

Tommy walked over and sniffed this stranger who dared invade his space, and I waited for him to bolt. Instead, the cat climbed into my date's lap and made himself comfortable, purring over the petting he received.

The end result of cat approval was that we married a couple of years later. Tommy slept with us until his passing, which we both grieved.

A lot of years have passed and a new cat has entered our lives. But memories of Tommy are still in my heart. I thank that cat every day for sharing the love of my first husband, and for his immediate approval of my new one.

~L.M. Fillingim

70

My Shadow

A cat pours his body on the floor like
water. It is restful just to see him.
~William Lyon Phelps

I guess I was lonely. I was going to school and working full-time to pay for it. I had my own studio apartment, which meant no roommate drama, but I started to yearn for companionship.

On my birthday, I decided to get a puppy since I missed my childhood dog so much. I certainly couldn't afford a purebred like the one I had when I was little, so I went to the local Humane Society. When I arrived that Saturday afternoon, it was a cacophony of sound with all shapes and manners of dogs demanding attention.

I spent thirty minutes walking among the dogs and finally talked myself out of one. I decided they were too big for a studio, and too young for me to take on housebreaking, considering my busy schedule.

Dejected, I was heading outside when I saw a small glass door I had not noticed before. There was a sign saying there more pets inside. I figured I could use a few more puppy kisses for the road and opened the door.

I ended up in the cattery. Walking up and down the rows, I saw dozens of sleeping and disinterested cats. They certainly weren't moved by my presence; most barely flicked their tails in acknowledgment. But there was one who was different. Each time I passed his cage, he slapped a black-and-white speckled paw at me.

I wasn't really there for a cat, but figured he should at least be rewarded with some affection for his persistence. I stopped on my next pass and rubbed behind his ears. His luminous, green eyes roved over my face. A volunteer saw an opportunity, opened the cage, and handed him to me. The black-and-white fur ball immediately broke into a purr louder than my blender. He proceeded to open his mouth and rub his teeth and gums all over my chin. It was a little wetter and smellier of a greeting than I expected, but it did the trick.

My new friend and I went home. He scoured my apartment with head bobs and slinky moves under the kitchen table. He peered into the toilet, watching the water swirl and dabbled his paws under the stream of water from the sink. He burrowed through the pillows on my bed and finally ended up napping on top of my desk while I worked on my computer, his head resting on the mouse. He followed me every time I moved, so I named him Shadow.

That first night after my lights went out, he promptly jumped on the bed, kneaded my shoulder a few times, and buried his nose in my hair as he curled up on me. He slept there every night for two years until I met my future husband and got married. My husband banished him from the bedroom. Seven years later, Shadow magically reappeared on my shoulder the first night after my divorce. He kneaded and snuggled in as I cried myself to sleep.

Shadow embedded himself in my life. When I was sick with a cold, he would give my shoulder a break. He would curl up between my legs, facing me, and open his eyes periodically to gaze on my face. When I took a government job and spent evenings with paperwork spread across the apartment floor, he would settle in on the least-needed piece of paper and watch with rapt attention. I would reward him periodically by running a pencil under his sheet of paper. The fluff on the back of his neck would puff up, and his eyes would dilate in excitement as he pounced repeatedly on the pencil.

He made friends for both of us when I was too shy to do so. I had gotten the notion in my head he might like to go outside. However, I didn't want him to run off or get hurt, so I opted to try a cat leash. He took to it like a duck to water, eventually sitting very still by the door each time so I could buckle it around his little body. He walked regally outside around the apartment complex, pausing to crouch excitedly in the green grassy areas when a bird's shadow would pass overhead. Neighbors were drawn to this curiosity — a cat on a leash — and I ended up meeting and befriending everyone in the complex because of Shadow.

When I adopted my daughter and placed her on the play mat among the toys, he would sit at the edge of the mat and watch her attentively. Occasionally, a ball would roll too close to him, and he would bat it back in play for her. At night, he would circle on the rug by her crib until she fell asleep.

Shadow took all the bumps of my life in stride. He rode quite calmly in the back window of my Chevrolet for the fourteen-hour move from Texas to Alabama. His head would bob at rest stops, taking in the sights. He rode just as quietly on the move back from Alabama to Texas ten years later when I left in defeat.

Like the stars, he was the one constant in my orbit for seventeen years. He was there through a marriage, a divorce, the adoption of my daughter, ten moves, my graduation from college, a layoff, three dogs, and the deaths of my grandfather and my sister. He saw many of the great moments, but he was the only one who saw all my worst moments — my tears, anger, embarrassment, loneliness, shame, sickness, and fear. He was there every day, rubbing his open mouth on my chin and purring like an engine.

I remember opening the blinds at the back door on his last day. A warm spot of sun appeared on the floor, and he pulled himself to it like so many times before. He curled up on his back briefly, those luminous green eyes taking me in for one last time. It's a little bittersweet that my favorite Shadow faded out in the sun, and there's been no one like him in my little orbit since — not canine, human, or feline.

~Angela M. Meek

71

We Saved Each Other

Since each of us is blessed with only
one life, why not live it with a cat?
~Robert Stearns

was at the stove covering up the food I had just cooked to keep it warm when Chuck walked through the door. He was holding a pet carrier with the newest member of our family inside — Candy, a little tabby cat we found at the local animal shelter just days earlier.

Candy had been discovered in an abandoned building in upper Manhattan and was only about four months old. We saved her from a life of scavenging for food and warding off the other cats that prowled the streets of Harlem.

Bringing Candy home was one of the few joyful moments Chuck and I experienced that year. His mother had suffered a slow, painful death from brain cancer, followed only seven months later by his father's fatal heart attack. Chuck was only thirty-six, so young to lose both his parents. On some days, the overwhelming, crushing feelings of grief and loss left him physically and emotionally incapacitated.

Our relationship suffered considerably during that year. Most people our age still had healthy, functioning parents, and they didn't understand what we were going through. I had no experience with this either, and no idea how to help Chuck through his grief.

Chuck was so emotionally isolated as he tried to process his grief. He kept pushing me away. Oftentimes, he would zone out in front of the TV and say nary a word for hours. It was like he was in a far-off place that I just couldn't reach, like we weren't even living in the same reality. Sitting next to someone who doesn't even know you're there is a disturbing experience.

He also started having bursts of rage. I never knew when it would happen, and living with such volatility was almost impossible. I would always forgive Chuck after his waves of anger had subsided, and I believed that his behavior was temporary — that it was the grief talking, not him. I urged him to go to therapy, but despite my pleading, Chuck wouldn't make an appointment. Many times, I felt like giving up, but a part of me knew deep down that I had to hold on for Chuck and see him through the lowest point of his life.

It was under these circumstances that we agreed to adopt a cat from a local animal shelter. Looking back, I'm not sure why we thought it would be a good idea to get a pet. Our relationship was hanging on by a thread, and neither of us was in a great mental space to take care of an animal.

Nevertheless, we visited a few local shelters before we stumbled upon that brown-and-orange tabby cat. We chuckled as she slowly stretched her body before she came out to greet us, as if socializing with humans was a task one had to prepare for. She nuzzled against Chuck's leg in the visiting room, walking back and forth between the two of us. We decided to take her home and change her name from Juniper to Candy, for her sweetness and the sheer delight she brought to us.

Candy was very anxious in her new home. She hid under tables and would get into our bed and bury herself under the covers for hours at a time. But slowly she began to get comfortable. Chuck easily became the "favored" owner. Even though I worked from home and was with her all day, she would run toward the door in the evening as soon as she heard his footsteps on the stairs. Instead of entering the apartment with his usual sad frown, Chuck's face would light up when he saw Candy, and he would scoop her into his arms for a nuzzle.

Sometimes, I got annoyed that I was the one who took care of Candy all day but Chuck was the one who got all the attention as soon as he walked through the door, as if I didn't exist! But it was hard to resist the happy sight of Chuck and Candy together. He loved taking care of her and took responsibility for clipping her nails, giving her baths, and changing her litter. His favorite thing to do after work was lie on the couch and let Candy crawl all over him until she settled on his belly while he scratched behind her ears.

As Chuck's bond with Candy strengthened, Chuck became stronger as well. The softness and patience he showed toward Candy spilled over to his attitude toward others, including me. His angry outbursts occurred less and less frequently, and it seemed as if the dark cloud that hung over him for so long was finally lifting. With Candy, Chuck was completely present, attentive, and light.

As cute as Candy was, she also came with some behavior problems. She would scratch us when she wanted food and pee in our bed when we were out. As frustrating as these problems were, Chuck was patient in training Candy. He spent hours online searching for remedies and tried a bunch of different tips to make Candy more calm and trusting. At the same time that Chuck's depression began to lift, Candy's behavior started to improve as well.

It's now been three years since Candy became a part of our family. Candy's life changed dramatically when she was brought into our home, and so did ours. Chuck was able to crawl his way out of his depression and anger into a state of acceptance for the devastating loss he experienced. Our relationship not only survived, but we became closer as a couple once we were both able to process the events and learn from them.

Indeed, when we married in 2015, Chuck began his vows with this: "Brittany, you have made me feel more loved than I ever thought possible and helped bring me through my darkest times. Our road has not been easy, but that is how I know it is one I want to continue traveling by your side."

Of course, Candy made it into our vows as well. We promised to be a good cat mom and dad to her, and as a joke, Chuck promised to always love me more than her!

I often wonder what would have become of our relationship, and of Chuck himself, had Candy not come into our lives when she did. We may have saved Candy from a grim future, but she saved us as well.

~Brittany L. Stalsburg

72

The Nurse Cat

When I look into the eyes of an animal I do not see an
animal. I see a living being. I see a friend. I feel a soul.
~A.D. Williams

t was Halloween night. Witches, ghosts, goblins, and Darth Vader were trekking from door to door asking for treats. The phone rang; it was my friend Lilly, whose five-year-old son has autism.

"Hey, would it be okay if I brought James to your house to trick or treat? This is his favorite holiday, and he's all dressed up in his costume, but he can't go just anywhere, only to homes where he knows people."

"Of course," I told my friend. I knew that her son didn't do well with strangers or crowds, and though I'd been to his home many times, he had never been to mine.

A few minutes later, the doorbell rang, and I opened it to find James standing there in his costume.

"Trick or treat," he whispered. I dumped a large handful of candy into his bag.

"Can we come inside?" Lilly asked. "We already visited all our neighbors. This is our last stop."

I opened the door wide and invited them inside. James took two steps and froze, staring at my orange tabby cat, Lox. I glanced at Lilly. "What's up?"

"Because of his dad's allergy to cats, he hasn't been around them much, or really at all."

We watched as James stepped into the room with all the caution of a secret agent scoping out a possibly dangerous environment. Lox stayed still and didn't take his eyes off James. James plopped down on the rug and lowered his head to the cat's level. Lilly and I moved over to the couch and began chatting about the mundane events of our week. Every few minutes, Lilly looked over her shoulder to watch her son, who sat mesmerized by Lox. If one of them cocked his head sideways, the other one mirrored the movement.

Tears began welling in Lilly's eyes. She reached up and wiped away a stray tear. "In his whole life," she said, "James has never looked anyone in the eye. Not me, not his dad. No one. It's part of his autism." She pointed to Lox and James. "Since he walked in here, he hasn't stopped looking Lox in the eye. And Lox hasn't stopped looking at him. I've never seen a cat do that."

I explained that Lox was a nurse cat, and had been since the day we brought him home as a kitten. He sensed when someone was ill or injured or needed a loving paw. I couldn't explain it, but Lox knew with uncanny insight when someone was hurting or ill. He wouldn't leave the person's side until he or she was fully recuperated. I'm not sure he knew what to do with James, so he did what he knew best. He mimicked James and stayed with him until Lilly took James home a half-hour after the stare-a-thon began.

Lox was one of the most extraordinary cats I'd ever known. He was social almost to a fault. Whereas other cats would vanish when company visited, he preferred to be in the middle of the conversation. At every meal, he politely sat on a dining chair, watching us eat, never begging or intruding. He simply wanted to be with us.

We also witnessed Lox fall in love. We took in a stray mother cat and her kittens that someone had dumped in our neighborhood. The mother was thin and exhausted, and the kittens were hungry. Lox and Shayna (the name we gave her) bonded immediately. To give her time to rest, Lox would babysit the little ones several times a day while Shayna retreated to another part of the house. It was astonishing to watch the vast empathy Lox displayed for everyone, including animals he didn't know. Eventually, we found homes for the kittens, and Shayna stayed with us. She and Lox became inseparable. I don't think they spent five minutes apart until she passed away a few years later. I'd never seen an animal grieve before, but grieve he did, sleeping only in the places where she slept, eating little, if at all. He mourned like a human.

But it wasn't just animals he cared for and nursed. When my husband was recovering from shoulder surgery, Lox lay next to the injured shoulder, placing a paw lightly on the bandages, providing warmth.

A few years later, I suffered a near-fatal pulmonary embolism that required I spend several days in the hospital. I returned home to a fretting cat. As soon as I lay down on the bed, he was right next to me. He snuggled between my arm and upper body, with his head resting gently on my chest. Somehow, he knew that his body evoked a healing effect, something unexplainable, a sort of spiritual nourishment. Every hour or so, he would lift his head and look into my eyes, softly stroking my cheek with his soft paw. I could only interpret it as his way of checking on me. I would nod and tell him I was going to be okay. He would hunker back down and begin purring, lulling me back to sleep.

For weeks, he nursed me, and I slowly recovered. But as I recovered, Lox began his decline into terminal kidney failure. Lox had been in kidney insufficiency for a year, and he'd been doing well, or so we thought. Then, all of a sudden, his health turned, and he was dying before our eyes.

I wasn't allowed to cry as Lox entered his final days. The doctors had warned me against any activity, emotional or physical, that could cause the embolism to dislodge and travel back up into my heart or plunge into my lung, which could result in instant death. My dear, sweet cat was dying, and all I could do was grieve silently.

Finally, after watching Lox suffer over a weekend, we called the vet's office on a Monday morning and said it was time to bring him in. They prepped him and placed him on my lap. We kissed him and told him goodbye. In moments, he was gone. All the tears I had not shed gushed out. I didn't care what that embolism did. I'd lost my sweet kitty, my nurse kitty, an extraordinary little being that had made the world a better place through his simple acts of nurturing. He saved me, and he saved countless others, and I was heartbroken that I couldn't save him.

~Jeffree Wyn Itrich

A Furry Angel

*God made the cat in order that man might
have the pleasure of caressing the tiger.*
~Joseph Méry

M y husband and I had been married for about two years
when Nekko came into our lives. The first time I saw
him, I was visiting friends when I spotted a small, black-
and-gray cat stuck in a tree. I climbed the tree partway
and managed to coax the cat down. It jumped to the ground and ran
off when a stranger approached to ask why I was in a tree.

The next time I went to visit my friends, I found the same little
cat being tormented by three men who were trying to tie firecrackers
to its tail. I yelled for them to stop, but I'm a very small woman and
not very intimidating, so they just laughed and ignored me. I ran to
my friend's house and got her husband Charles, who is a very, very
large man. Charles chased off the men, but we were unable to catch
the cat. It had run off.

I told my husband about the small cat and its plight, and how it
was obviously a stray and in need of a home. My husband and I already
had one cat, and he said if I saw the little cat again, it was fine with
him if I brought it home. When I went to visit my friends again, I was
prepared. I brought a cat carrier and a can of tuna, and it was good I
did, because I saw the little thing again. It walked right over to the tuna
and didn't protest at all when I picked it up and put it in the carrier.

When we got home, I gave it a bath. The cat was covered in grease and mud, and I didn't want to risk bringing fleas into my house. I quickly discovered that the cat was a female, and rather than being black and gray, she was a lovely black and white. She purred loudly as I washed the filth from her fur, never protesting or trying to get out of the bath. It was as if she knew I was trying to help her, and she wanted to be clean.

While I was washing her, my husband asked what we should call her, and he began proposing names. He was studying Japanese at the time and suggested we call her Nekko, which is Japanese for cat ("neko"). I asked the cat if that was all right with her, and she seemed to purr louder, so Nekko it was.

A few days later, I took her to the vet for a check-up and to be fixed and get her shots. The vet guessed she was about two years old, and she was pretty healthy despite living on the streets.

Nekko soon became a very loving and affectionate cat. She'd greet me at the door whenever I came home from work and always loved to jump up on my lap while I watched television.

Several months later, we were visiting my father-in-law at his assisted-living center, and I saw a sign saying the center was starting a pet-visiting program. I spoke to the nurse in charge of my father-in-law and asked if I could bring Nekko for a visit. The nurse said Nekko could come if she was clean and well behaved. I began training Nekko to sit and walk while wearing a body harness and leash. As always, she was very calm and willing to please. In a matter of days, she was leash-trained.

I began bringing Nekko with us whenever we went to visit my father-in-law, and she soon became very popular with the residents at the home. She would walk down the corridor and let strangers pick her up and pat her. She would also sit on their laps if they wished.

During one visit, my father-in-law's nurse brought in a nurse from another floor and introduced her to me. She was a hospice nurse and had a patient, an elderly lady, who they didn't think would make it through the night. The hospice nurse explained that her patient was alone and had no family. She had been asking to see and pet a cat just one more time. The hospice nurse explained that her patient had owned many cats and had to give them all up when she entered the center. The lady had told the nurse that if she could pet a cat just one more time, she could die happy. The nurse asked if I would mind bringing Nekko to the lady's room and let Nekko stay with the woman. I agreed. I picked up Nekko and followed the hospice nurse to the room of a very old and frail woman named Martha.

Martha looked up as we entered, and upon seeing Nekko, she broke into a smile. I walked up to Martha's bed and introduced Nekko, then put Nekko on the bed and tied the end of the leash to the bedrail. I told Nekko to stay and be a good cat. Nekko immediately walked onto Martha's chest and knelt down facing her. Martha began patting Nekko and talking to her, and Nekko began to purr very loudly. I stayed for several minutes to be sure Nekko was behaving and then left to go back to my husband and father-in-law, with a promise from the hospice nurse that she'd return Nekko to me.

Two hours later, the nurse still hadn't returned with Nekko, and I was wondering how I could politely retrieve her. Suddenly, the hospice nurse appeared holding Nekko and crying, accompanied by my father-in-law's nurse and another nurse. The hospice nurse said that Martha had passed a few minutes earlier, but she'd died smiling. The hospice nurse went on to say that she'd left Nekko with Martha while she'd gone to check on other patients, stopping in every few minutes to check on them both. The nurse said that every time she stopped in, Nekko was loudly purring and looking into Martha's face.

The nurse had then been tied up with another patient longer than she'd intended, and a good thirty minutes had passed before she could return to Martha. When she'd gone back to check on Martha the last time, she'd found Nekko sitting upright at the foot of the bed and mewing softly. The nurse went to check on Martha and discovered that she'd passed. The hospice nurse said that Nekko was surely a little angel for she'd sat perfectly still and purred nonstop for Martha, making Martha's last hours on earth very happy.

The nurses all thanked me for bringing Nekko and said that she was welcome back any time. Nekko continued to accompany us to the center, and brought smiles and laughter to the residents every time.

~Leslee Kahler

Chapter
8

The Cat Really Did That?

Eight Lives and Counting

74

Everyone's Cat

As every cat owner knows, nobody owns a cat.
~Ellen Perry Berkeley

Someone was singing right outside my door, but when I looked, no one was there. A moment later, Mike opened his door down the hall. A sleek, striped cat darted between Mike's shins.

"Did he wake you? Sorry," Mike called down the hall. "Nobody can talk like a tabby Maine Coon!"

It was my first morning after moving into the apartment, and I was glad to make friends with someone.

While checking my mail, I ran into Mike again. He was tall and slender, with an elegant manner learned from his years as a Hollywood chauffeur.

"Glad you got a chance to meet Gizmo," Mike explained. "He's so old — he's been here longer than I have. If you hear him, feel free to knock on my door. But whatever you do, don't pick him up. He can be grouchy."

As the weeks passed, Mike proved himself to be an excellent apartment manager. He collected cans from all the tenants and used the recycling money to purchase new Christmas decorations for the courtyard.

Gizmo serenaded us morning and night. One day, I sat at the top of the stairs, and to my surprise, Gizmo slunk right up onto my lap. He coyly stretched out his white chin for me to scratch, neatly hiding away any grouchiness he might harbor. He let me scratch behind his ears, and then, in a flash, he had enough and was gone.

I learned to look forward to Gizmo's evening visits on the stairs. Sometimes, I "accidentally" spilled some coffee creamer into a pie tin next to my door, and often found myself leaning on the balcony railing as I watched him poke around in the miniature jungle of our courtyard.

And I was not the only one. There were haphazard jar lids placed near every other apartment. On a Saturday afternoon, I watched Gizmo take the stairs down to the first floor, sneak into the laundry room, and then visit three apartments in a row.

The lady who lived directly across from me could only greet me in Ukrainian, but Gizmo seemed to understand her perfectly. The two gentlemen who wore Hawaiian shirts as their constant uniform were often seen scooping him up and passing him to one another. Gizmo's grouchy reputation was apparently just a ruse. Even the college professor on the other side of Mike's place was friends with Gizmo, often leaving out scraps of eggplant and prosciutto.

That season, Mike purchased a giant, inflatable snowman, and we both laughed over its odd movements as it deflated each evening. Gizmo would walk toward it tentatively and then dash away. A few minutes later, he'd repeat the whole process.

Soon, glitter snowflakes gave way to whirligig hearts spinning across the lawn — a constant source of fascination for Gizmo. Eventually, flags and sparklers lined the walkway. When the Los Angeles weather melted into scorching heat, that's when Mike knocked on my door to deliver the bad news.

"There was an accident," he told me, solemnly. "One of the neighbors watched it happen at the intersection… It was horrible. I could barely recognize him."

He shook his head before adding, "I've chosen to bury him in the courtyard, just under the jade tree."

I didn't know what to say. "I'm so sorry, Mike. He was everyone's cat, really."

I thanked Mike for telling me. Until I was by myself, I didn't realize how I felt about Gizmo. I curled up on the couch and remembered how Gizmo surprised me by showing me his tender side. I thought about his plaintive song, and how he often seemed to be telling me something. What was he always trying to say?

That evening, I raided the cupboard for something special. Way in the back was a box of gourmet chocolate brownie mix. Tears spilled while I mixed the dark batter. If Gizmo had been my cat, then maybe I would have built a Gizmo-specific armor around my heart. But Gizmo was as much a part of life here on Moorpark Street as the constant *whoosh* of Los Angeles traffic or the smell of jasmine in the spring. He was not an incidental cat, as I had thought. Gizmo was essential to everything here.

While the tray was still baking, I went online and made a donation to the Burbank Animal Shelter in Gizmo's name. I printed a little certificate and added it to the plate of brownies. Maybe someone else's incidental cat would benefit.

Then I walked down the hall to deliver condolences to Mike. As the door slowly swung open, I was surprised to see so many faces crowded into his small living room. There were matching Hawaiian shirts on the couch, and the college professor was leaning her elbows on the kitchen counter. Even the Ukrainian lady was there, dabbing her eyes. I passed around the plate and marveled at all these people — Gizmo's people.

We spent the evening telling stories about Gizmo, the many times we mistook his voice for a baby's cry, or a bird, or a stranger waiting outside the door. I always thought of Gizmo as a stray, but now I saw how wrong I had been. We were his family, all of us, together.

Summer changed to fall, and Mike returned to his usual rounds, staking tiny, glowing pumpkins along the walkway. He shimmied up the lamppost and attached a witch who seemed to have collided with the pole while riding her broomstick.

One evening, in the early darkness, Mike saw me walking upstairs and beckoned me to come closer.

"You'll never believe who's here," he said, raising his eyebrows ominously.

I shrugged, and then he told me what happened: "I was up early one morning because I have so much trouble sleeping these days. I heard a sound, but I thought, *No, that can't be what I think it is.*

He had my full attention.

"I pulled back the curtains, and there he was!"

"Gizmo? How?"

Mike shook his head with wonder.

"Then, who's in *there*?" I thumbed toward the courtyard.

"Dunno. Rest in peace, whoever you are," he called out to the grass.

Sure enough, the next day I watched Gizmo curling around Mike's legs as he set out a fresh tray of food.

"See this notch in his ear? See that white patch on his chin? Yup. None other."

I leaned my head back and laughed.

That night, as I busied myself making dinner, I was thinking over Gizmo's life and death, and life again.

When I heard him outside the next morning, it was uncanny how his voice sounded like language, and his message seemed perfectly clear: *Do not despair! You are not alone,* he seemed to say, *and neither am I.*

~Robin Jankiewicz

75

The Cat-fish

There are no ordinary cats.
~Colette

I sauntered toward the old barn and idly glanced around, expecting to see our barn cat. Ginger normally met me midway from the gate and meowed to remind me that it was suppertime. Her rambunctious kitten was generally close behind. Oddly, there was no sign of either.

As I opened the barn door, an unexplainable sense of dread flowed through me. I tried to rationalize that Ginger had probably taken her new kitten out on his first hunting expedition. A faint mew from their favorite sleeping spot dispelled that hope.

Ginger and her kitten were snuggled together in a tight little ball that only cats can accomplish. She raised her head, and dejectedly laid it back down. I picked up her limp and lifeless kitten. He struggled to lift his head, which was swollen to nearly twice its normal size.

I grabbed the kitten and sped down the highway toward the vet clinic, which was eighteen miles away. Dr. Wyand was locking the door to his clinic when I arrived, but he turned back without question and unlocked the door as my car approached.

After careful examination, he parted the kitten's soft orange-and-white fur to reveal what looked like puncture marks on the head and neck. He then repeated the demonstration on the other side. While it was of no significance to me, Dr. Wyand nodded knowingly. The kitten had been attacked by a hawk, and the puncture marks were from its talons.

After a long pause, he said, "I can treat the infection, but I have no way of predicting what permanent damage he might suffer." He opened the eyelids to reveal nystagmus, an involuntary oscillation of the eyeball that indicates neurological damage. Dr. Wyand broke the silence and said, "He obviously put up the fight of his life to get away from the hawk. He deserves a chance to put up a second fight."

Two days later, the swelling had reduced considerably, but the once playful, energetic kitten remained weak and wobbly. We had done what we could and now he needed to heal. Only time would tell how much neurological function he would recover.

I knew Chico would miss his mother, but recovery in the barn was not an option. He could not walk more than a couple of steps. His front legs would go in one direction, and his hind legs in another.

Chico would lose his balance in the litter box, so bathing him in the bathroom sink became our daily routine. One day, when I placed him in the sink of warm water, he began moving his legs. It was a swimming motion that showed actual coordination, and our first sign of what might be true progress.

Over the next several weeks, his coordination improved, and the need for his bath routine ceased. He could now walk relatively well, but he had not fully regained his ability to travel in a straight line. His hind legs often trailed off at a 45-degree angle to his front legs. Seeing a cat toy and being able to go directly to it was a feat that eluded him. But he was equally happy to stumble over one of his favorite toys when he least expected it.

The next goal he set for himself was the sofa! The synchronization required for jumping had not returned. Christmas Day, however, offered Chico another opportunity. A gift box sitting adjacent to the sofa was low enough for Chico to jump on, and from there he made it to the sofa. It was another milestone in his recovery.

One night, after a particularly stressful day at work, I decided to take a nice leisurely bath. After I filled the tub, I decided to get a glass of wine, and when I returned to the bathroom, I was shocked. Chico was swimming in the bathtub. Did he know that water was good therapy? Did he miss his playtime in the sink? Or, more likely, did he try to jump onto the side of the tub, and a lack of coordination landed him in the water?

Regardless of the reason, swimming in the bathtub became a routine. While I preferred he didn't swim *before* I had a bath, we had an agreement that he could have his therapy session afterward.

Because Chico was deaf as a result of the neurological damage, we taught him to walk on a leash at a young age. He wasn't allowed to wander on his own, so we went for walks in the grassy vacant lot next to our house, and I took him to the farm to visit his mother. He learned to enjoy riding in a vehicle.

By summer, other than the deafness that he had learned to accept, he was pretty much a normal cat and very much a part of the family. When it was decided that we should go on an RV adventure to see the Pacific Ocean, Chico was included without question.

He found his favorite spot on the dashboard of the RV and entertained many a service-station attendant by trying to catch the squeegee through the front window. In the evenings, we stayed in RV parks and would take Chico, wearing his harness and leash, for a walk.

After a long day inside the RV, I took Chico for a walk along the shore when we reached our final destination. He was normally a very obedient cat on the leash, but this time he kept tugging and trying to get closer to the water. It became clear that he was determined to experience the biggest bathtub he had ever seen!

And why not? I walked out into ankle-deep water and let Chico enjoy his now familiar dog paddle. He seemed unconcerned with the occasional small wave. After several minutes, I decided it was time to end the adventure. I cradled the soggy cat in my arms as we headed back to the RV. I was unaware of the semi-circle of people who had lined up along the beach and were watching us. As I approached them, I felt that I owed them some sort of explanation, so I blurted out, "But he WANTED to go for a swim!"

So if you ever hear of what sounds like a far-fetched story about a woman from Canada who took her cat to swim in the Pacific Ocean… well, that cat tale is actually true!

~Brenda Leppington

76

The Loner

Fiercely feral or determinedly domesticated, the cat
does the deciding and the humans do the abiding.
~Author Unknown

Our family moved to Sarasota, Florida when I was ten and my sister Nikki was nine. Our new home had a beautiful lake behind the back yard, with woods on both sides. Nikki and I loved feeding the wildlife that visited the lake: Mallard ducks, whistling ducks and the resident Pekin duck, which had been left behind by the previous owner.

One particular morning, Nikki and I noticed a small, brown tiger cat watching us from a distance. As soon as we approached it, the cat darted back into the woods. This went on for about a week. Our mom suggested we put dry cat food on our back patio and see what happened.

That worked. We put out food, went to school, and came home to find the food was gone. We were so happy that our new friend, whom we named Brownie, had decided to join our "Breakfast Club." Every morning before school, Nikki and I would go out to feed the ducks, and Brownie would always watch from a distance, waiting for breakfast to be left on the patio.

Our mom used our new interest in the feral cat as a teaching tool and made us each write a report on feral cats.

One morning, when I was about to open the back door, Nikki called out, "There's Brownie!" Sure enough, Brownie was sitting on the patio, and behind the cat, scampering around in the tall grass, were four adorable, black-and-white kittens. Nikki and I could not believe our eyes! Brownie was a mommy.

Six months passed, and the kittens got bigger and stronger. Not one of them looked like its mother. Each kitten had some pattern of black and white in its coloring. One kitten, in particular, stood out from the rest. It was the largest of the kittens, and it had long hair and black lips. Yes, it truly looked like someone had applied black lipstick.

Nikki and I also noticed that this kitten was extremely elusive. While the other kittens allowed us to pet them, this one always waited until we were inside to come over and eat. He never played with the other kittens. It seemed to me that he liked being feral and was not going to be turned into a pampered, domesticated cat.

From the research we did for our mother, we knew we had to humanely trap, spay, neuter and vaccinate each of the cats, including Brownie. Mom introduced us to a local feral-cat rescuer, and soon our volunteer days began. Nikki and I were able to successfully trap and return to our back yard all but the cat with the black lips.

To our family's amazement, all the cats stayed by our home for many years to come. Each had its own personality, and Nikki and I gave each one its own name. We named the elusive one Duma, meaning "pride" in Polish. Unlike the others, Duma would disappear for weeks and return unexpectedly, with what seemed like a prideful attitude. Nikki and I always worried about Duma when he was gone, all alone in the woods with a major road nearby.

Then came that day we all dreaded. Nikki and I were putting out everyone's breakfast when we looked up and saw Duma was limping across the back yard. He was dragging one of his front paws. He still would not come close to us, so we quickly put out his food, went inside, and hoped he would come and eat.

As we watched out the window, Duma came closer, and then we saw the extent of his injury. His whole left shoulder area was bloody and not moving at all; his paw was badly mangled. The other cats appeared fearful as he approached them.

Nikki and I started to cry, as we knew in our hearts that he was too feral to allow us to help him. Duma became even more elusive, striking out at any of his cat family that would try and comfort him. Several weeks passed, and one morning we watched Duma walk slowly into the woods after he ate. Nikki and I were sure this would be the last we saw of him. By now, his long hair was matted and dirty. It was just too painful for him to twist around and clean himself as cats do. His paw looked infected, too.

Five years passed with no sign of Duma. Nikki and I were active with our local feral-cat rescue program. Once a month, on a Sunday morning, we would head to a local vets' office at 6:30. Six veterinarians and twenty other volunteers would donate their time to spay/neuter approximately 100 feral cats that had been trapped throughout the county. All the cats, after passing their post-surgical screening, would be returned to the area where they were trapped.

One particular Sunday, Nikki and I were helping to clean up after a very successful surgical day when one of the vets came out of the recovery room and announced that they had a cat that could not be released back into the community. This cat had to have a front leg removed due to an old injury. Its paw had been worn away up to the ankle joint. The vet went on to say that this cat was very "wild" and would not permit anyone near his cage. The cat would be euthanized if no one felt they could foster him safely.

I couldn't believe what I was hearing. Could this be Duma? I ran and got Nikki. We made our way to the recovery room and convinced the vet to let us see the cat. He warned us that this cat was extremely aggressive and not to put our hands near the cage. As we got closer, we could see this large, black-and-white, longhaired cat pinned to the back of the cage with fear.

I softly called out "Duma" and the cat raised its head. Nikki and I began to cry as soon as we saw those beautiful black lips. He began to purr, louder than anything I had ever heard. The vet was amazed. We told him the whole story, and even though he was impressed with Duma's response, he warned us not to get our hopes up. He said this cat has been through some pretty horrible times, and would probably never be able to be domesticated. We called our mom and took Duma home that day.

It has been four years now, and from the minute Duma's eyes met Nikki's and mine in that recovery room, he has never been elusive or showed one sign of being aggressive.

Our back patio is now screened in and Duma lies there all day, watching the ducks and his littermates, who are still around. They will lie right next to him with only a screen separating them.

And now, our formerly feral feline seems to be just as happy to lead the life of a domestic housecat. When Duma sees Nikki or me getting ready for bed, he jumps right up on one of our beds and settles in for the night. One thing's for sure: Duma's in charge of his own life!

~Tori Cleaves

Dog People

A dog, I have always said, is prose; a cat is a poem.
~Jean Burden

"A kitten just fell out of the hayloft." It was a simple statement, but one that didn't sink in as I brushed my horse in our small barn.

"What?" I asked my husband, Mike. I was busy getting ready to train with the horse and slightly annoyed by the interruption.

"There's a kitten on the ground."

Sure enough, right beside my horse's front right hoof, lay a mewing day-old kitten. It was mid-October, and the temperature was in the fifties. Mike gently picked up the little thing and said, "It feels cold."

Earlier, we had heard what we thought were birds chirping. Instead, it was the small kitten, squeaking. It fell fifteen feet from the hayloft and landed right in front of my husband. Had it fallen a few minutes earlier or later, neither of us would have been there.

The day before, Mike and I had decided that we would be done with cats once our eighteen-year-old cat passed away. Our children were grown, and I was tired of litter-box duty. Besides, we now lived on Mike's family farm that was close to Route 9, a death trap for any feline that frequented the outdoors. And we considered ourselves to be dog people anyway.

After we found the tiny black kitten, whose eyes were still closed, we searched the hayloft upstairs. There were no more kittens, and the mother cat, who we suspected was the black cat we had seen around the barn, was gone, too.

We took the kitten into the house and set up an electric heating pad under a green afghan my aunt had made me years ago, I snuggled the kitten while we called area shelters and researched how to care for her. I learned that if we could find another nursing mother cat, she might accept the kitten as one of her own. Many telephone calls later, we learned no one had a nursing mother cat. I researched online and found a homemade kitten formula recipe that I made and fed to the kitten with an eyedropper. The kitten was hungry and ate quickly. Then the little ball of fur yawned, stretched, and fell asleep on the warm afghan in my lap.

The next day, I visited our neighbors in search of the mother cat. One of them knew the mother because she lived behind their house. The kitten's best chance for survival was to reunite with her mother so I brought the kitten over there. The neighbor promised to make sure the mother cat accepted the kitten. I didn't know if the kitten would survive, but my husband and I had done what we could.

That winter we had record-breaking snowfall in Maine. It seemed snow fell every other day, sometimes more than twelve inches at a time. During one blizzard, I returned home early from my job as a child and family therapist. Mike was already home plowing and shoveling snow.

I came in the front door to find my husband standing there smiling. He asked if I remembered when we agreed not to have any more cats because we were really dog people. There on the kitchen floor was a tiny, black kitten playing with our large Lab mix, Luke. Mike explained that when he started shoveling the snow away from the barn doors, he saw a kitten running inside. He found her sitting on the steps to the hayloft. She did not run when he picked her up and placed her in his coat. He couldn't believe she just sat there in his coat, happy to be warm, purring while he finished plowing snow.

The kitten appeared to be eight to nine weeks old. Could this be the same kitten we had helped earlier in the fall? The kitten playfully batted Luke's ears, although the Lab looked a bit nervous and uneasy. Upon closer investigation, the kitten's eyes appeared to be glued shut. They were severely infected. The drainage crusted over the fur surrounding her eyes, and she could not open them.

I washed the kitten's eyes gently with warm water until she could open her eyes. A quick trip to the veterinarian provided antibiotic ointment for her eyes, de-wormer and her first shots. We named her Phoebe.

Phoebe quickly became part of our lives. She adored the old afghan—the green one we had used when we first rescued her—which happened to be on our king-sized bed on colder nights. As soon as I got done brushing my teeth and walked to my bed, a black flash would bolt onto that blanket for some playtime.

Soon enough, the tiny, black kitten became a beautiful, sleek cat that I dearly cared for. We always made sure that our windows had screens in them in the summer so she could not get outside due to the closeness of the major roadway. But we had a family member staying with us who took out a window screen to place a fan in the window. One day, I noticed Phoebe was not around and found the window upstairs left open. I searched for her for weeks, to no avail. I feared she had been injured or killed on the road.

About a month after Phoebe disappeared, I was in the barn feeding the horses when I heard a loud crying sound. It sounded familiar. I called out, "Here, kitty!" The cry grew louder. I looked up toward the eaves of the barn—the same place where a newborn kitten had fallen two years earlier. There, peering down at me, was a sleek, black cat, meowing loudly.

I ran up the hayloft stairs and called out, "Phoebe!" She came running, and I picked up my thinner but unharmed friend. I carried her out of the barn and inside the house so I could get a better look at her. It took me a moment to realize I was repeating "Thank God! Thank God!" as tears sprang to my eyes at the return of this dear pet.

A little underweight, but unharmed, Phoebe jumped onto the

old green afghan on the couch. All was well with the world again. I loved this cat, no doubt about it. I guess we really weren't just dog people after all.

~Janet Anderson-Murch

78

One Lucky Cat

A cat is a puzzle for which there is no solution.
~Hazel Nicholson

Gus joined our family when our son was five, and they were instantly inseparable. Gus roamed the neighborhood as he pleased, but nights were spent on Jordan's pillow.

Then, the summer before Jordan's junior year, we moved from New York to Colorado, living in a rented house for about six weeks before buying our home in the mountains above Boulder. We moved in on the Jewish New Year, which was in mid-September that year, and experienced a major snowstorm that first night. When Jordan opened the door to get more firewood, Gus ran out to explore. Nothing unusual there.

But he didn't come back.

All that night, we called. Normally, we'd call his name and clap our hands, and soon we'd hear the bell on his collar coming closer.

After everyone else was asleep, I set my alarm and got up every two hours to open the back door and call. Nothing. Once, I even pulled on my boots and went out, thinking I'd heard Gus crying. I followed the sound to a small, snow-laden bush where I imagined he was huddled, cold and scared. I found a fox. We looked at each other in the moonlight before it ran off. I returned to my warm bed for another two hours.

The next day, we searched everywhere, meeting several new neighbors along the way. They expressed concern for Gus and told us, "Up here, cats and small dogs tend to have short *but happy* lives."

In the dawning hours of our second Gus-less day, Wayne saw a mountain lion on our front porch. When I awoke, he said it had probably "come back for seconds." I was horrified and convinced he was wrong.

We went out several times that day, trudging through the deep snow and yelling until we were hoarse. We continued searching as what became one of the coldest and snowiest winters in years descended on "our mountain."

By December, we were pretty discouraged.

The house was coming together. Jordan was settling in at Boulder High. Wayne's home office was taking shape, and I loved my new job. We no longer went out calling for Gus, and Wayne was sure he wasn't coming home.

Then, on the last night of Hanukkah, just as Wayne and Jordan were about to head up the mountain and out of cell-phone range, Wayne's phone rang. It was a woman saying she'd just found a cold, hungry, injured cat seeking shelter in her barn. Wayne turned the car around.

She was holding him when they arrived. He'd been there when she came in to feed the llamas. Jordan cradled him while she explained that she knew Gus was loved because, when she put out food, "He spent at least half a minute looking between her and the bowl, clearly conflicted about which he needed most: food or a hug." He chose the food, but let her pick him up immediately afterward.

Gus was severely underweight, had a large puncture wound on the right side of his neck, and a broken "elbow" joint on his left front leg. It had been shattered, and he'd been holding it up for so long that new bone had formed, ensuring it would never unbend. The vet wanted to amputate. We wanted to wait until his wounds were healed and he gained some weight, so we headed home with our personal Hanukkah miracle.

Based on where he was found, we concluded that Gus had been heading toward the house we'd rented when we first arrived, which, having been the end of his cross-country journey in the moving truck with Wayne, he must have decided was his home. That cat had traveled about eighteen miles and crossed a major highway to get there. He'd worn his collar the whole time, its bell alerting predators to his existence while warning off any smaller creatures he might have eaten himself.

Eventually, Gus recovered and was his old self again — bounding up trees and chasing impertinent deer and foxes off his property. In honor of his surviving the loss of one of his proverbial nine lives, we changed his name from plain old Gus to Gus-the-Miracle-Cat.

We never did amputate his injured leg. He used it for balance and, when sitting on one of our laps, patted our faces gently, but only with that paw.

The mystery of the puncture wound was solved, too, about eight weeks after we got Gus home. We found a lump under his fur, so we took him to the vet, who was shocked to discover it was a .22-caliber slug!

She theorized that someone had been using a sign for target practice, and the bullet had ricocheted, causing the puncture wound. The impact had knocked Gus over, and the fall had broken his leg. That explained both his injuries, but nothing explained how he survived two months alone in the snowy backcountry, except that Gus is one lucky cat.

Gus enjoyed ten more years of adventures before dying quietly at age twenty-two. His ashes are spread over his mountain.

~Lisa Napell Dicksteen

79

Old Tom

*A cat has nine lives. For three he plays, for three he
strays, and for the last three he stays.*
~English Proverb

t was a sun-washed Tuesday in late September when I met old
Tom. I had responded to a call from an elderly neighbor, Mrs.
Winter, who was badly crippled with arthritis. Her voice was
halting and apologetic. "It's about this cat…" she said, and led
me outside to meet the biggest, oldest, ugliest, sickest alley cat I had
ever seen.

He lay on a splintered board on the paint-blistered porch behind
Mrs. Winter's house, one paw stretched out in pain. His ears were
scabbed black from ear mites. Two deep, blood-encrusted cuts ran
down his tabby-striped back. His face was oddly distorted, the mouth
pulled askew, apparently the result of some fight.

"Old Tom's been coming around for sixteen years," said Mrs.
Winter. "Never lets me pet him or nothing. But I leave a little food
out. And some water. Kind of cheers me up to see old Tom. Now he's
so sick…" Her birdlike voice trembled. "I'm afraid he might die."

I wasn't sure what to say. I didn't know Mrs. Winter well. I'm
single, and my freelance work kept me too busy to socialize much in
our neighborhood. Finally, stumbling a bit, I said, "Sixteen years is
pretty old for a cat. Are you sure it's always been Tom?"

"Oh, yes. My friend Mrs. Giraldi — before she had her stroke last
year — she used to visit. She always said Tom's gone through all nine

lives and then some."

As if he felt our attention, the cat lifted his head and stared directly at me. His yellow eyes were hard and shiny.

I gave in. At the very least, I could ensure that Tom was humanely put to sleep. "I'll take him to a vet I know," I said. Gingerly, I picked up the cat. Too sick to fight, he stiffened when I jarred his injured paw, but otherwise was quiet as I deposited him in my car.

"He might not make it," I warned.

Mrs. Winter nodded with tears at the corners of her eyes. "Old age and hard times never licked Tom before. No sir. Hear me, old Tom? You can't just give up."

At the vet's office, Dr. Abbot said, "Is this a candidate for kitty heaven?"

The old cat stared at me, and then blinked. I surprised myself by saying, "Not yet. Let's see if we can save him."

"Are you sure? This old cat isn't your responsibility. And vet bills…"

"I know. But still, do what you can."

I returned to the animal clinic a week later. Tom was sitting up, his paw bandaged. Under medication, the cuts on his back had started to heal. Only his ears were still in bad shape, black and nearly deformed from years of infestation from ear mites.

"I can treat his ears at home," I said.

"Okay," said Dr. Abbot. "But this is a feral cat. I don't think you'll make a pet of him."

"I know."

I borrowed a large dog crate and set it up in my basement. For a month, Tom lived there, learning to use a sandbox. Morning and evening, I treated his ears for the mites. It wasn't easy. Every time I opened the door to the crate, Tom backed into a corner until I moved a safe distance away. Then, stealthily, he would poke his head out, until slowly one paw would emerge, then another. At last, with a certain weathered dignity, he would stand beside the kennel. Like an old soldier at parade rest, I thought.

Tom's body began to fill out, although his ears continued to itch. Still, I decided, he was in good enough shape for a visit with Mrs. Winter.

When she came into my house, her eyes grew young in their gladness. "Will you look at old Tom? It's a miracle!"

The bent old lady and the veteran alley cat eyed each other. "I guess it just makes sense to stay alive when someone cares, don't you think?" she said.

I moved Tom upstairs. He no longer retreated when I approached, but he still didn't let me pet him.

The week before Thanksgiving, an envelope arrived, full of wrinkled bills and a short note. "I been saving my money," read the crabbed handwriting. "I want to give you something for keeping old Tom."

I counted the bills. Nearly fifty dollars! From a woman who lived on a very tight income. "Well, old warrior," I said to Tom, "what should I do about this?"

Tom still didn't come close, but when I talked to him, his yellow eyes would lock on mine, and he'd tilt his head as if listening.

"I'll hurt her feelings if I return the money," I said. Instead, I wrote a letter.

Dear Mrs. Winter:

Thank you for bringing me help when I needed it. Your money is going to a shelter for stray cats.
Your friend,
Tom Cat

P.S. Barbara invites you to Thanksgiving dinner.

On Thanksgiving, Mrs. Winter wore a pink, silk dress that smelled faintly of camphor. Shyly, she offered a bowl of homemade cranberry relish. Tom didn't come close enough to be petted, but he stayed in the same room when we sat down for dinner.

"He's doing pretty well," I said.

"Old Tom. He's no quitter, that's for sure."

When I replied, "I'd say the same for you, Mrs. Winter," she almost blushed.

After I took her home, I cleaned up the dinner dishes, and then settled on the living room sofa. Tom sat three feet away as usual. "You're a good ol' cat," I said.

Suddenly, I felt a peculiar weight in my lap and heard a strange, rumbling noise. It was Tom! And he was purring! For a moment, I was too stunned to move. Gingerly, I placed my hand on his back. He didn't flinch. He just looked at me with his tough, yellow eyes.

~Barbara Bartocci

80

When Friends Meet

Cats come and go without ever leaving.
~Martha Curtis

Blended families. The transition is not easy. Concessions have to be made — so much to be gained and… sometimes lost.

One side of this new marriage had a cat; the other had a little boy with asthma and an allergy to cats. They tried to find a home for the cat, but no one would take him, and regretfully, I couldn't. So, the cat went to the shelter, and the boy's breathing improved as a result.

Almost a year later, my granddaughter — who had shared her room for a short time with the cat — went with a friend to visit his grandparents. They had a black-and-white cat, like the cat her family had before they had to give him up.

The cat rubbed against my granddaughter's legs, jumped into her lap, licked her chin, and gave her an affectionate head butt. It was like a friendly "how are you" or "nice to see you."

The grandmother was surprised. "I've never seen him do that before," she said.

My granddaughter scratched the cat behind his ears and ran her hand down the length of his body and along his tail to the crooked tip she knew she would find there.

"Where did you get him?" she asked her friend's grandmother.

"From the shelter at the Humane Society," the woman replied.

"We've had him about a year now."

My granddaughter smiled. Meeting an old friend will have that effect. "His name is Charley," she said.

~Deborah Lean

81

United by a Myrakle

There is, incidentally, no way of talking about cats that
enables one to come off as a sane person.
~Dan Greenberg

My husband and I were looking for a new brand of kitty litter to try. We drove twenty-five miles to Eugene and chose one of twelve pet stores there.

The kitty-litter aisle in the store was forty feet long, making our choice complicated. We did not want pine litter, as it is hard on my and the cats' breathing. We had tried the newspaper brands, and crushed walnuts were not to our liking. We were not sold on the clumping brands because they attached to our Persians' long fur, and could end up in their digestive tracts when they groomed.

We were reading bag after bag of clay and crystal litters, trying to figure out what to do. Whenever someone pushed their grocery cart up to the litter section, I approached them like the "kitty-razzi" and interviewed them about their choice. "Have you used this brand long? Does it hide the odor? How often do you change it? Do you have long- or shorthaired cats?" Everyone smiled and gracefully answered our survey.

Then a beautiful, blue-eyed woman with shoulder-length white hair, reminiscent of a white Persian cat, tossed a bag of litter into her cart. I noted her kind face and proceeded to ask her my list of questions.

She told me, "My name is Linda, and we have two shorthaired cats."

I quipped, "Oh, you look like someone who would have Persians."

She stopped, caught her breath, and said quietly, "We did have two. We loved them. But Myrakle died a year ago."

I was stunned! I felt I already knew the answers to my next questions before asking them, but I tearfully choked out, "Was she a rescue cat? Was she orange and black? Was her full name Ms. Myrakle?"

"Yes," said Linda.

What were the odds?

"We fostered and named Ms. Myrakle for the Humane Society," I said. "It took three days to gently clip off all her tangled fur. When the last fur ball was clipped off, she could finally extend her back leg. It had been held back by the tangled fur. She lifted her head from my lap and looked into my eyes as if to say, 'Thank you!' Then she slowly stretched her leg fully out for the first time in a long time."

Linda was nodding her head in recognition. I continued to reminisce about Ms. Myrakle, and told her, "She never fought with our cats, and she accepted my daughter's two dogs. But we had to give her back to the shelter when I had surgery. We were so sad. We always wondered what happened to her, even after all these years."

In fact, just that morning, I had been reminiscing about Myrakle while looking at the newspaper article I had written trying to find her a loving home.

Now crying, Linda recounted her life with Ms. Myrakle: "Four years ago, I told my husband Gene that I wanted a cat for my birthday. We saw Ms. Myrakle on the shelter's website. Persians have lovely personalities — and we liked how her name was spelled — so we went right over and adopted her. She was elderly and had only a few teeth, so we knew she would be a challenge. Gene would get down on the floor and hand-feed her soft foods. We both loved her. She was the sweetest cat."

I nodded in sympathy. Linda said, "While driving here, I was thinking about Myrakle because she died a year ago this week. I miss her and our other cat. They both died the same week during the Christmas season, but a year apart."

Then what she said next stunned me again: "Our other cat's name was Angel."

I had to grab her litter-filled shopping cart for balance! As the author of the online "Angels and Miracles" newsletter for twenty years, teaching others to "Expect Miracles" (also the name of my first book), this divine encounter by the kitty litter was an unexpected, overwhelming joy.

For a day that started off normally, it had a remarkable, miraculous ending!

Linda and I felt that Ms. Myrakle's love brought us together to assuage our grief and thank us for the gift of loving her. I was thrilled that Myrakle had found a loving home.

As soon as Linda arrived home, she told her husband, "I had the most amazing thing happen at the pet store." He said, "Oh, no!" and began looking around for a newly adopted pet! She laughed and told him that it was "someone" she met.

Linda and I are now good friends, united by a cat in heaven.

~Mary Ellen Angelscribe

Passion and Compassion

A kitten is the delight of a household. All day long a
comedy is played out by an incomparable actor.
~Jules Champfleury

Shortly after dawn on an otherwise ordinary morning in late June of 2016, heavy raindrops began to fall across much of West Virginia. Within moments, torrential rain began in what was later called a catastrophic "thousand-year" flood, sweeping away cars, houses, and bridges in a mighty deluge of raging water and mud. In the path of the destruction were hundreds of thousands of animals, among them three newborn kittens.

Nearly a thousand miles away, Janet Swanson's phone rang. A lifelong ardent animal lover and philanthropist, Swanson has been volunteering with the American Humane Rescue team since the devastating EF-5 tornado almost wiped Moore, Oklahoma off the map back in 2013. After she was told of the newest humanitarian disaster, Swanson began laying out plans to mobilize with the famed rescue program, which began its work more than 100 years ago rescuing wounded war horses in World War I Europe. It has been a part of the rescue effort in virtually every major disaster since, including the Great Ohio River Flood of 1937, Pearl Harbor, 9/11, and Hurricanes Katrina and Sandy.

Deploying to a disaster zone is hardly glamorous. The work is vitally essential and in the end gratifying, but it is also exhausting, dirty, and hazardous. Volunteers live in one of five giant American Humane Rescue vehicles, sleeping in bunks after arduous eighteen-hour days coaxing frightened, starving, and often ill animals out of trees and wreckage, surrounded by stagnant water, sharp rubble, and downed power lines.

Janet was trained and prepared to deal with all these conditions, but was still shocked when she saw the magnitude of the destruction created by raging waters that in some places crested at twenty-six feet over flood levels.

"It was terrible," she said. "There was mud everywhere. The people who came to us for help had heartbreaking stories about losing their homes. They brought in their pets who needed attention after having been in floodwaters. In some cases, they had lost one of their pets to the flood and brought in a surviving cat or dog. All the people who came were so glad we were there. They were truly grateful to be able to get the necessary care for their companion animals."

Swanson was one of a corps of ten highly trained volunteers and animal doctors who deployed to rescue and make sure veterinary care, food, and plenty of love made their way to the lost and abandoned animals whose owners' homes were destroyed. Using one of the fifty-foot American Humane Rescue trucks as a base of operations, the team set out to find animals missing in the flood zone and set up a mobile veterinary clinic to provide first aid, wellness checks, vaccines, and food for sick and hungry pets, treating more than 100 animals in one day alone. The rest of the team scoured the area for lost and injured animals.

That's when a volunteer found a trio of tiny kittens huddled together on the lid of a trashcan in the middle of a creek bed. Tragically, their mother was gone. When the small litter of animal orphans arrived at the safety of the mobile clinic, the kittens were trembling, covered in fleas and ticks, and swollen from painful parasitic infections. They were hungry and dangerously dehydrated.

After giving them emergency veterinary aid, the team provided the feeble kittens with around-the-clock care, even sleeping with them and waking up every three hours to bottle-feed them, slowly nursing them back to health. Because of this tireless dedication, all three kittens made full recoveries. The tiny creatures stole the hearts of all the American Humane responders, and they were passed around with big smiles during the daily briefings and debriefings.

But a serious problem arose. The kittens were still extremely young and the surrounding area had been destroyed, which meant there was no local foster care network left to take care of them. The rescuers discussed the situation. One of the trio, a tortoise-shell cat with warm, grateful eyes, had touched Swanson's heart. Naming her "Hava" (a variant of the Hebrew word for "Love"), she agreed to take her home and adopt her.

"I had never adopted a baby that young," said Swanson. "Almost every companion animal I have ever had was an older rescue coming either directly off the streets or from a shelter. These kittens would only be two weeks old on the day we left and need frequent bottle feedings as their mother had been lost in the flood. When I heard that there was nobody to take care of them, I agreed to take one and got a crash course in bottle-feeding, with a full sheet of instructions on just what to do and how to do it."

American Humane Rescue veterinarian Dr. Lesa Staubus ended up taking the two other brothers with her, so all three found good homes in which they could finally relax after their ordeal.

Since the rescue, Hava has been doing great. She is now part of a loving family that includes four cats, two dogs, three parrots, and a bunny — the perfect environment for a lively and curious cat.

When they were rescued, Hava was the first to do everything and was always the most adventurous of the three kittens. She would explore everything first, before her brothers, to the point where the rescue team would laugh and dubbed her the "nosey" one, always wanting to check everything out.

Janet said she continued to be that way once at her house. She says, "She is now a happy, healthy girl who will soon be a year old. She still comes to me every day, just to be held and cuddled the way she did when she was a little one. Stories like hers are why we do what we do at American Humane, and for her part, Hava has lived up to her name, returning love to me every day."

~Dr. Robin Ganzert

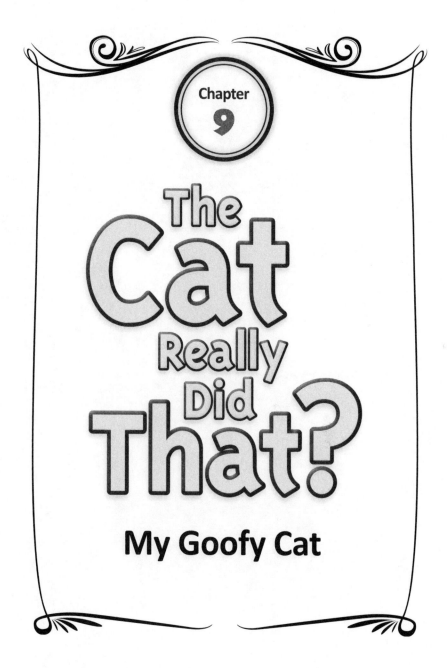

Chapter

9

The Cat Really Did That?

My Goofy Cat

Fashion Diva

Cats do not have to be shown how to have a good time,
for they are unfailingly ingenious in that respect.
~James Mason

When Vinny, a chocolate European Burmese, moved in with me, I had no idea that he loved wearing clothes. It all started when Vinny was training to become a registered therapy cat with Love on a Leash. I thought the nursing-home residents we visited might enjoy seeing him wearing some cute things. So, a bandanna here and a bowtie there led to Halloween and Christmas outfits—and Vinny was all for it. He even wore his Halloween pumpkin costume, including the stem hat, for our entire one-hour visit! I think he enjoyed the extra attention and reactions from the residents.

I know not everyone approves of clothing on pets. Let me say immediately that I do not in any way force this on him. Also, he only wears apparel under close supervision.

Vinny enjoys dressing up at home, too. He purrs when modeling, and he seems to know when to pose for the camera. He's even been known to photo bomb when I try to take pictures of my other cats! Vinny loves being the center of attention.

One Halloween, I entered Vinny in our local Petco's costume contest. I found an Egyptian crown and necklace for cats, and a friend made him a kilt and neckpiece. Vinny liked his Egyptian Pharaoh costume. The only problem was that he kept tripping over the kilt! At Petco, he was directly up against the dogs in the costume contest... and he won first place. I was so proud! The next year he placed third, as a peacock. The year after that he was back in first place again, as Zorro.

Vinny now seems to have developed his own opinions on what is "cool." Petco recently had a big clearance sale on apparel. Vinny was thrilled when I brought home seven new outfits and he happily modeled them. However, the *Star Wars* Yoda hoodie was not really his style (or maybe green is not his color!). He definitely liked Darth Vader, studded skulls, and faux leather better. Despite the purring, my little boy apparently likes looking "bad." I don't tell him, but I find most of his things in the dog section. Vinny is a big boy, 11–12 pounds, and usually wears a dog's size medium.

Recently, Vinny decided to help me with my fashion sense, too. I had a beanie-style winter hat. Vinny apparently decided that the pom-poms looked dorky, so he chewed one off. Immediately, I cut off the other pom-pom. It's definitely been fun and interesting living with a male feline fashionista!

~Leanne Froebel

84

Here's Looking at You, Kid!

An ordinary kitten will ask more questions than any five-year-old.
~Carl Van Vechten

was about to install a full-length mirror on the back of my bathroom door, but needed a different screwdriver. I leaned the mirror against the wall and went to retrieve the proper tool.

When I returned, my bull's-eye-patterned, orange rescue cat was seated in front of the mirror, staring intently at his reflection. I smiled and waited to see what he thought of that "other cat" in there.

Gently, Simon reached out with one paw and patted the glass. Then he pressed his nose against the nose of his reflection and gave it a quick lick. Next, he walked around behind the mirror and came out the other side, looking rather befuddled.

"What's the matter, my sweet little genius?" I asked him. "Can't you find that other orange cat?"

He meowed. Ever since I brought him home from the shelter, he meowed at me whenever I ask a question. He's pretty quiet most of the time, but when my voice goes up at the end of the sentence, he nearly always has an answer.

He turned to look at me, tilted his head, and turned back to the mirror. "Meow?" He nosed the reflection again and reached out, tentatively at first.

Suddenly, he reared up on his hind legs and started batting at his reflection, effectively shadowboxing with an image he could not beat. His rights and lefts came swiftly: Bam! Pow! Kerplunk!

I leaned against the bathroom counter and laughed like crazy.

Simon looked over his shoulder at me. I couldn't decide if he was asking for help or imploring me to stop laughing at him.

I swooped him up and carried him to the kitchen. "I'm sure that other cat has learned his lesson," I told him. "And you've earned a treat."

Setting him on the floor, I opened the cupboard and got out his box of special snacks. While he enjoyed his reward, I went back into the bathroom, closed the door, and installed the mirror — positioning it just a little higher than I'd planned.

I didn't want the little guy traumatized every time he followed me in there!

~Jan Bono

85

Cat Got His Tongue

The smart cat doesn't let on that he is.
~H.G. Frommer

Several years ago, I got a call from a fellow cat lover about some kittens in dire need of a home. Originally, there had been a litter of seven, but now only two females — a solid black mini-panther with golden eyes and a fluffy, longhaired, speckled girl — hadn't been placed. My friend was desperate to find someone to take these last two, so my husband Dan and I agreed to adopt the pair. Nervous but excited, we headed out with our cat carrier to pick up the newest members of our family.

Upon arriving at the shelter, we learned that one of the other kittens — an orange-and-white-striped male — was suddenly homeless again. "His adoption fell through," we were told. "The woman who was going to take him had to change her plans, so he has nowhere to go."

The little guy looked at us with big, sad eyes that were as blue as the April sky. His sisters seemed heartbroken, too, sharpening their cries as we gently took them away from their brother and loaded them into the carrier. Through it all, he sat quietly, looking back and forth between his departing siblings without making a sound. The thought of this tiny, scared kitten languishing alone in the shelter was too much to bear, so Dan and I agreed to take him as well. We named the girls Harriett and Jane, and the last-minute addition to our crew was dubbed Raptor.

From that very first day, Harriett was incredibly vocal. She would meow loudly to complain about an empty food bowl, growl at the neighbors' dogs, and coo like a pigeon when we stroked her fluffy mane. Jane was less noisy but still voiced her feelings, meowing softly when she was hungry or scared or just needed a little attention. Raptor, however, was almost entirely silent. Every now and then, he emitted a nearly inaudible purr, but other than that, nothing. At first, we thought he was just shy or scared, but after a few weeks, we began to worry there was something wrong with the sad-eyed, little fellow.

We took him to the vet, but a thorough exam revealed no physical issues, and the doctor told us not to worry. "Some cats are talkers, some aren't," she said after pronouncing him healthy. "Or maybe he's just letting his sisters speak for him."

We were reassured by the vet's report even though we didn't get any real answers. In every other way, Raptor seemed fine. He loved napping in the sunlight and chasing Jane and Harriett through the house, and he never passed up a meal. Still, we remained concerned that maybe he was suffering in some way we could not detect.

Then, one afternoon a full two years after the cats came into our home, we finally heard from Raptor. My husband and I had taken the three of them with us on a drive. Jane and Harriett were nuzzled together on the passenger-side back seat while Raptor curled up behind Dan, who was driving. About a half hour into the trip, a truck cut in front of us, and Dan slammed on the brakes, hard enough to send a startled Raptor onto the floor. We pulled to the side of the road and shut off the engine to make sure everyone was okay.

Harriett and Jane were sitting bolt upright and blinking at us, not sure what had just happened. Raptor, however, was quite animated. He jumped onto Dan's lap and unleashed a truly unprecedented cacophony of meows — not long, howling mews, but rather a continuous out-burst of loud yapping sounds. Neither of us speak Cat, but we clearly understood his message: "What was THAT all about!?! Seriously, you should be more careful on the road! Your driving is terrible! Do you realize you just flung me off my comfy chair and onto the FLOOR? What do you have to say for yourself, human?"

The cat we thought incapable of speech was reading Dan the riot act! I couldn't help but laugh, which made Raptor turn toward me and give one last, gruff "hurumph!" before returning to his seat and resuming his curled-up position.

Dan smiled and gave Raptor a quick apology before starting the engine and continuing our drive. Then he looked over to me and said, "Well, I guess if this is the first thing he's had to complain about, then we're doing a pretty good job as cat parents!"

~Miriam Van Scott

Chicken Soup
for the Soul

Velcro

One must love a cat on its own terms.
~Paul Gray

y husband John and I headed for the local shelter to find the perfect fuzz ball to entertain us in the evenings after work. I had my mind set on a female, maybe a tiger cat or a black one with white mittens.

As I cooed over the assortment of kitties, I noticed John in conversation with the attendant in front of a cage containing a full-grown, sand-colored tabby with a brilliant pink nose. "He just came in," the scrub-wearing lady said. "We have his shot records; he's fourteen months old and neutered. The family said he's too big and jumps on them, whatever that means. People surrender pets for some of the strangest reasons."

"Is he friendly?" John put two fingers through the cage bars despite the signs warning: Do Not Put Fingers in Cages. The tabby revved up his purr and rubbed his face on John's knuckles.

Uh-oh, I thought. *This isn't going in a kitten direction.*

"Let's take him to the visiting room," the attendant said, catching the scent of a possible adoption. She hauled the long, leggy cat out of his cage and tried to corral most of him in her arms.

"Um," I ventured. "Will he get much bigger?"

"No. He may put on a pound or so, but he's grown."

"He's great!" John said, as the cat, now on the floor in the little room, threaded himself around John's legs in figure eights, pausing for an occasional emphatic head bump. "I think he likes me."

That did it. Fees paid and papers signed, I drove while John held the cat, whose legs dangled off his lap.

Once home, the name game began. Stretch? Magic, for Magic Johnson? Longfellow? Nothing seemed right until the cat named himself. While vining around John's legs, he kept positioning himself behind my husband's back. If John turned to face him, the cat circled around again, looking up at his back.

Then, with a swift, vertical cat leap, John had a fifteen-pound, sand-colored burdock clinging between his shoulder blades.

Velcro was named on the spot, and the habit, which we found was a persistent behavioral habit, was termed, "Doin' a Velcro."

Fortunately, I knew a young cat's relationship to humans is often that of a kitten to mom-cat, so when Velcro began his circling routine, a quick tap on his nose with my finger and a hiss would stop him. He was also an ankle-biter, but the same corrections promptly nipped that habit in the bud, too.

However, Velcro did have a sense of when he might get away with some fun, and we had to be on the alert. One day, a less-than-favorite female relative stopped by unexpectedly and inconveniently. As we stood in the living room, Velcro began his circling routine. For a moment in time, John and I exchanged furtive and rather devilish glances, but reason won out. A split second before the leap, as I saw Velcro crouch, I short-circuited the cat's plan with a nose tap and a quiet hiss. I gathered him in my arms stifling a laugh, as I said, "And this is Velcro!"

"No need to introduce me to the cat," said Aunt Agnes, lowering herself even more in our esteem.

Perhaps Velcro had his own opinions about some people, but in another setting he thrived, making friends and behaving like a gentleman.

We began taking him to our car dealership for the working day. He enjoyed the car rides, watching out the windows and jumping over the seat to the back windshield when a big truck passed. He was a man's cat, indeed, with a passion for semis.

At the office, he contented himself with getting comfortable on the bookkeepers' desks. They didn't mind the laid-back cat sprawled on their journals or vehicle-registration work. They just pulled what they needed out from under him and propped the work against him. He had his own cardboard cave for nap times, never tried to leave the office, and had a fan club of customers. "Doin' a Velcro" was not a problem at work.

At home, he was a house cat unless John invited him for a walk around our pond. While the man fished, the cat sat. When the man moved thirty feet, the cat followed. Just the words, "Velcro, want to go walk around the pond?" and the cat was up for an hour of companionable fishing time.

If only his original family had known how to discipline him, he wouldn't have landed in the shelter where adult cats are passed over for amusing, little fur balls. But then we wouldn't have had the fascinating and enjoyable years we had with him — once he stopped "doin' a Velcro."

~Ann Vitale

87

On a Mission

In a cat's eye, all things belong to cats.
~English Proverb

M y kitten climbed my leg like a lemur. "Miss Skitters! Get down!" I grimaced as I felt the razor-like claws.

I set the bag of French fries on the table and pulled her off me. Miss Skitters' eyes locked onto the bag like a heat-seeking missile to its target. She scrambled. I snatched the bag. Miss Skitters leaped. I couldn't believe I was battling an adorable, gray-and-white kitten.

"No!" I said firmly, pointing.

Miss Skitters relented. Sort of. Yowling, she stalked me to the couch and intermittently attempted to nab French fries. I put her in the bedroom and shut the door.

That was only the beginning. My husband and I quickly discovered that this cat loved to eat. Anything. Potatoes, onions, lettuce. Miss Skitters never met a food she didn't like. Every edible item required Fort Knox-style containment. She struck unattended consumables like a ravenous bear at a picnic ground.

One day, I forgot and left a package of hot-dog buns on the counter. I returned to the kitchen to find her in a frenzied feeding. Guttural sounds rattled in her throat. Bits of buns spewed from her mouth. As I grabbed her, she snagged a surviving bun and wrapped it between her front legs.

Although we kept food under lock and key, Miss Skitters mysteriously started packing on pounds. Finally, we discovered that while we were bringing home the bacon, she was eating it. Literally. While we were out, Miss Skitters was creating a buffet beneath our bed. Its existence remained unknown until I heard rustling one afternoon. I peeked under the bed and discovered Miss Skitters with her head shoved into a plastic bag. She was gnawing at an accumulated smorgasbord of rotten hot dogs, rib bones, and other delectable items. She had managed to get into the garbage can in the cupboard beneath the sink. That got locked up, too.

A couple of years later, we adopted a calico cat. My husband placed the cat bowls on opposite sides of the room — a good strategy until Miss Skitters slinked over to scarf down Little Buddy's food, and then returned to polish off her own afterward. We had to start standing sentry over meals.

During a visit from my sister, Miss Skitters pulled off one of her stealthiest missions. While we were at work, my sister decided to vacuum. The closet that housed the vacuum cleaner also stored the cat food. Since Miss Skitters popped things open and closed with her paws, we always placed a chair in front of the door. My sister accidentally left that door ajar. Halfway through vacuuming, she remembered and hurried to the compromised location. The door had mysteriously closed. My sister opened it to find Miss Skitters inside the cat-food bag inhaling kibble.

During the entire twelve years of her life, Miss Skitters' desire for food never ceased, nor did her cunning ability to obtain it. She pilfered a donut here and a pizza slice there, shamelessly accomplishing her mission to the very end.

~Lisa Mackinder

88

Pumpkin's Magic Sweater

Some people have cats and go on to lead normal lives.
~Author Unknown

"Y ou have the most adorable cat!" "How in the world do you get her to sit for these incredible photos?" "My cat would never let me dress her up like this!" My friends on social media are continually in awe of pictures I post of our furry little feline. I usually respond to the comments with a thank-you and a winking emoji.

We adopted Pumpkin as a tiny kitten from our local feed store where people are encouraged to bring kittens or cats in need of homes. I'd been dreaming of an orange tabby for years; when I spotted Pumpkin, it was love at first sight.

I have read that there are far more male orange tabby cats than there are females — about eighty males to every twenty females — so Pumpkin was special from the very beginning.

Because of her orange coloring, and the fact that it was nearing Halloween, we decided that Pumpkin would be the perfect name for her.

Soon after bringing our beautiful, big-eared, little kitten home, we made an appointment with the local veterinary clinic to have her spayed. When we picked up Pumpkin after the surgery, the vet handed me a plastic cone collar to protect her stitches.

As I slipped the unappealing apparatus over her tiny head and tied the gauze laces, she looked up at me with those big, pleading green eyes, and I caved. Off it came, and I was forced to find an alternative solution to protect her incision.

That first day, the kitten was too groggy to be bothered with checking out her sutures. However, I knew she couldn't be trusted during the night.

To keep the cat cozy, I put her in the new pink, knitted turtleneck sweater I'd picked out especially for her at the pet store. Coincidentally, it was long enough to completely cover her fragile surgical site. "Hmm," I mused, "this might just be the answer."

I took her to bed that night, where she lay next to me without moving an inch — very similar to a swaddled newborn baby. It worked perfectly!

There was no need to put the sweater on her during the day since I could keep an eye on her, but she wore it every night and never once stirred in bed.

A couple of weeks after Pumpkin's incision was completely healed, we woke up to about six inches of fluffy snow. I grabbed the sweater, slipped it over her head, and out the sliding glass door we headed, eager to capture some photos of the kitten's first snowfall.

I set her down on the snow-covered patio where she sank quickly and was nearly buried in the deep powder — not exactly the picture I had in mind. So we ventured about the acreage checking out other sites for our first wintertime photo shoot. I posed her on an old, snow-covered log, and later atop a huge, snowy rock with a backdrop of snow-covered shrubbery. She was so well behaved, remaining magically motionless — like a statuette. I couldn't have asked for a better little model.

When we returned to the house, I set the kitten on the kitchen floor where she sat motionless.

"Oh, Pumpkin, I think you may have gotten too cold," I cried as I ran for her blanket on the couch. When I set it next to her, she made no attempt to lie down; instead, she just sat there staring at me.

I thought it best to ignore her for a few minutes while I grabbed a cup of hot coffee and some freshly baked chocolate-chip cookies.

The coffee warmed me up in a hurry, which prompted me to wonder if maybe Pumpkin was too warm as well.

I scurried across the kitchen to find her still sitting motionless. After carefully pulling the sweater over her tiny, furry head, I watched in amazement as she quickly darted off to her food and water dishes.

We took more pictures outside in the snow the following day, and she was just as cooperative as the day before. She certainly appeared to be a lovely, sweater-girl model in the making.

Throughout the holiday season, I captured adorable shots of our little sweater-clad feline sporting everything from reindeer antlers to Santa hats. Whether beneath the brightly decorated tree, on Santa's lap, or posing with the grandchildren, Pumpkin never tried to escape the camera's flash.

Then, one day, it dawned on me — Pumpkin *always* remained exactly where I left her until I removed her sweater. She not only refused to walk while wearing the sweater; she wouldn't budge an inch. Instead of lying down when she got tired, she simply fell over. No amount of bribing could coax her into taking even a single step.

I decided to conduct a little experiment to determine whether she was trying extra hard to please me while dressed in her photo-shoot attire, or if the sweater was actually responsible for her exceptionally compliant attitude. After posing the sweater-less kitten on the wooden landing of her scratching post, I grabbed my camera and squatted down just in time to capture the unexpected photo — an airborne feline!

Following several failed attempts to get a good picture, it became painfully apparent — all the magic was in the sweater! She was completely mesmerized while wearing it, forcing her to stay wherever and however I chose to place her. So much for my beautifully behaved kitten!

On the bright side, the sweater has worked to my advantage for nearly a decade, and she has never once resisted when I put it on her. However, until this day, I have not divulged my secret as to how I'm able to photograph Pumpkin in a variety of awesome poses; rather, I've allowed everyone to believe it is simply her sweet, gentle nature.

I feel a bit guilty for keeping the secret all these years, and can only hope our little, furry girl's photos will continue to be appreciated on social media now that I have let the cat out of the bag.

~Connie Kaseweter Pullen

89

The Great Chicken War

People that don't like cats haven't met the right one yet.
~Deborah A. Edwards

When I first saw Cloud, I wasn't sure what to think. With his overly large eyes, his extra long tail, and the bits of fluff popping out from his ears, he was a strange sight. In fact, I even scrolled past his picture on Facebook. My childhood cat had just passed, and I was broken-hearted, but this strange, little creature didn't seem like the right one to fix it.

A week later, his picture popped up again. He was days away from being taken to a pound, where he might have faced a grim future. With teary eyes, I showed his picture to my grandma, with whom I was living at the time, and asked if we could bring him home to live with us. The house seemed lonely without a cat, even with our three dogs.

Reluctantly, she agreed as long as he would count as my Christmas gift and I kept his litter cleaned. That seemed like a good deal to me. Plus, I'd be lying if I said I hadn't also wanted to get him to impress my new boyfriend, who loved cats too.

Within a few days, the kitten came home to live with us. I was incredibly happy until I realized how absolutely crazy kittens are. His favorite thing was to silently wait by my face as I slept and then sink his sharp, little claws into my face as I woke up. I quickly learned the best course of action was to pull a pillow over my face and sit up before opening my eyes. It was a lesson learned the hard way, of course. Luckily, it was something he grew out of.

Unfortunately, my grandma's dogs were not as lucky as I was. The Cocker Spaniel, in particular, was a favorite plaything of Cloud's. He would lie in wait for Puddles to walk by before silently leaping from the shadows to grab onto the dog's neck and nip his ear. At first, Puddles thought this was great fun. Finally, someone actually wanted to play with him! The other two dogs were party poopers that never wanted to do anything but eat and nap.

Puddles enjoyed the attention until Cloud got older. His claws got sharper, his teeth got bigger, and he became far more accurate with his attacks. Eventually, Puddles learned his best course of action was to ignore Cloud altogether.

This strategy worked for a short time, but Cloud was determined to find another way to get the dog's attention. That's when he realized that all of Puddles' love and devotion were going to his yellow rubber chicken. He was always playing with it.

One day, while Grandma and Puddles were playing fetch, she threw long, and the chicken accidentally landed in the bathtub. Cloud saw this as an opportunity to strike. He ran faster than Puddles and hopped into the tub before the dog even knew what was going on. Puddles began to sniff frantically for his toy. He knew it went that way. When he finally caught onto the scent, he realized where it had landed. As soon as he leaned his face over the side of the tub, WHAP! Cloud, who was sitting on the chicken, smacked him right in the face.

That began the Great Chicken War. Every opportunity after that, if Cloud noticed Puddles had left the chicken unattended, he would strike. Sometimes, the dog would run around the house for a good ten minutes looking for his chicken.

But Cloud's favorite time to attack was when Puddles was outside. You see, the dog wasn't allowed to take his toys outside because he would never bring them back in. He would just drop them in front of the door in order to be able to grab them easier on his way in. We had a fenced-in back yard and a door that led right to it from our house, so the dogs were allowed to run around for a while, and then they'd scratch at the door when they wanted in.

So, whenever Puddles was outside and staring in through the

glass, Cloud would come over and sit right next to the chicken, just letting Puddles know that he could touch it whenever he wanted to. He would stretch over it, slap at it, and even lie on top of it. Thinking back on it now, maybe it was also Cloud's way of being spiteful because the dogs were allowed outside, and he wasn't.

After peaceful negotiations — also known as the purchase of an additional chicken — the Great Chicken War came to an end. That wasn't to say Puddles didn't steal whichever chicken Cloud dared to sit by to add to his growing toy horde, but things were far less tense between the two. It was no longer the end of the world for Cloud to touch the chicken.

Eventually, Ian and I moved away from Grandma's house, and Cloud became an only child. He seemed nervous at first, but quickly became his crazy self again, only now we are the targets. He always knows how to make me feel better with his crazy antics. I may not have known it when I first saw him, but he was exactly what I needed. And he even outgrew his funny looks and became quite the handsome cat! I wouldn't change him for the world.

~C. E. DeRosier

90

The Voice of Authority

Cats are independent, by which I mean smart.
~Dave Berry

We like to think — despite much evidence to the contrary — that we are in charge of our cats. It's not true, of course. We just flatter ourselves with the illusion that we're in charge. And if we believe in that illusion a little too much, we can find ourselves in a lot of trouble.

Fortunately, we don't really need to be in charge of our cats because our cats are quite capable of directing the course of events themselves. I learned that lesson on an occasion when our elder cat demonstrated — in no uncertain terms — that she was the one in charge of a situation.

This happened a long time ago, during one summer when I was home from college. My mom had decided that all the window screens in our apartment needed to be cleaned. That meant the screens would have to be removed, and all of our home's windows would need to be wide open during at least part of the day.

That presented a problem because it meant our cats, W.T. and Gus, would have to be kept away from those open windows, lest they got too excited and tried their luck at some two-story skydiving. Since both my mom and my sister were going to be at work all day, that meant it fell to me — and me alone — to corral the cats into the safety of the bathroom, the only room in the apartment that would escape the open-window treatment.

When the window washer arrived, I sprang into action and began the roundup.

I grabbed W.T. first. She was a veteran member of the household, and the days when she would resist such treatment were long in the past. She calmly acquiesced to her fate, allowing me to carry her to the bathroom and close her into temporary detention without a struggle.

Gus, on the other hand, was having none of it.

Our Gus had only been with us about a year at that point, and he was still young, nervous, and mildly distrustful. Indeed, the confinement plan had been conceived for his sake in the first place, since no one took it for granted that the excitable Gus would have the sense to avoid jumping out of an open window.

Unfortunately, Gus had been paying attention when I picked up W.T. and placed her in the bathroom; he knew something was up, and he was determined to avoid a similar fate. As soon as I made a move to grab him, he took off.

As you surely know, chasing down a young, nervous cat all by oneself is nearly impossible. And our apartment's layout made things worse, allowing Gus to make an easy escape every time I tried to corner him. Soon, Gus and I were going around in circles, with me chasing him from the dining room, into the hallway, through the kitchen, and back into the dining room.

All the while, Gus was yowling louder and louder, and running faster and faster through the circuit of rooms. My own panic rose in tandem with his. I could easily envision this frightened cat bolting straight for the nearest escape should the window washer choose to open the wrong window at the wrong moment.

I had no hope of catching Gus, and I knew it. Out of breath and lagging behind, barely able to call Gus's name to beg him to stop, I was just about to give up, break off the chase, and tell the window washer to cancel the job. But then, as we passed the bathroom door, the voice of authority intervened.

From within the bathroom came a call that brought Gus to an immediate halt. He turned and faced the bathroom door, answering the call with an uncertain cry of his own.

From behind the door, W.T. responded with another call — a

distinctive, drawn-out meow that was clearly both reassuring and commanding at the same time. While the two cats shared another vocal exchange, I caught up to my runaway cat. I opened the bathroom door just wide enough to see W.T. standing near the doorway. She meowed again, and Gus — suddenly calm and relaxed — obeyed her unmistakable command and entered the bathroom. I shut the door and breathed an immense sigh of relief. The cats were safe, the work could go forward, and I had a chance to sit down and catch my breath.

A skeptic might say that W.T. did not call Gus into the bathroom. One might contend that Gus just heard the voice of another cat, and in his panic sought the company of another of his own kind. Simple instinctual behavior, and nothing more.

I tend to be a skeptic myself, but I can't agree with that opinion. I witnessed this event, and I know what I saw and heard. W.T. did not just randomly meow from the bathroom; everything in her behavior indicated that she recognized what was going on and took charge of the situation. I could hear it in her voice. And, thankfully, Gus could hear it, too. Otherwise, I might still be chasing him through those rooms.

No, we are not in charge of our cats; they are in charge of themselves. And, when necessary, they can run the show on their own. I know that now, and I am grateful that, when I was faced with an unsolvable problem, the voice of authority was there to save the day.

~Stephen Taylor

91

The Designing Cat

Who hath a better friend than a cat?
~William Hardwin

Kit Cat was a lovely calico cat of medium build and size who I'd found as a two-day-old kitten in a packing box full of kitchen towels on our back patio. She had a disposition as lovely as her face, and she was so sweet that anyone who met her instantly adored her. She became my mother's constant companion and best friend, and at times, my mother referred to the cat as her third child.

In addition to being very sweet and loving, Kit Cat was crazy about string. If string came into the house, she'd mew plaintively and beg for it until it was given to her. Light brown twine was her favorite kind, and she would run through the house with it in her mouth, letting out trilling meows for a good fifteen minutes straight.

After happily running about with her string, she'd settle down in the middle of our long front entry hall and just stare at it. During this string-staring stage, no one was allowed to touch or move her string — not my mother or the other cats in the house. If anyone came near the string, they'd get a paw swipe and a dirty look.

After a long period of analysis, Kit Cat would begin to arrange the string on the floor, sometimes using her right paw, sometimes her mouth. She would slowly arrange her string into intricate circle designs, often taking over an hour to do so. When she was finally satisfied with her design, she'd sit back and meow loudly until everyone in the house came to examine and praise her creation.

The finished string creation couldn't be moved or touched, or Kit Cat would become visibly upset and go sulk under my mother's bed for several hours. As a result, the family learned to tiptoe around her string-art creations until Kit Cat became tired of them and dragged the string off to her special hiding spot behind the sofa. After a few months of string art, my mother began taking photos of Kit Cat's masterpieces, and would display them on the refrigerator next to my brother's or my art. If a friend or neighbor stopped by and spotted one of the photos, my mother would simply say it was a photo of her third child's artwork.

~Leslee Kahler

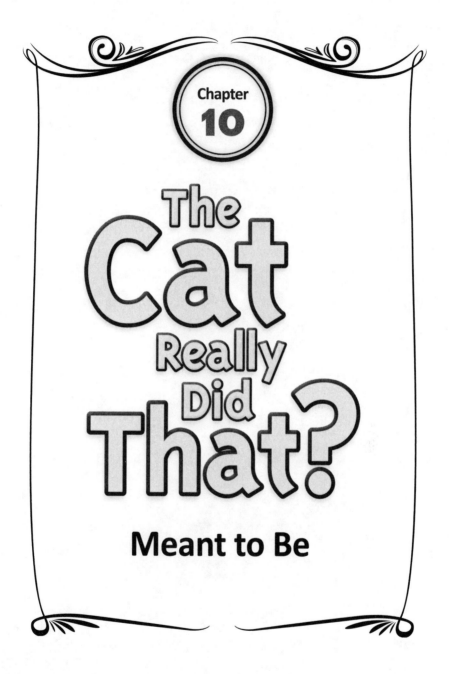

Chapter
10

The Cat Really Did That?

Meant to Be

A Series of Miracles

How we behave toward cats here below
determines our status in heaven.
~Robert A. Heinlein

y mom was diagnosed with metastatic cancer this summer. She was happy and full of life the day my daughter graduated from college. She walked two miles, navigated the tortuous hills at Lehigh University, and took pride in her granddaughter graduating as the first Engineering-Psychology major at Lehigh.

The next day, my mother had a CAT scan. The results showed that she had a large tumor in her lung. The following morning, she bled into her kidney, and we were in the emergency room. She had metastases in her kidneys, liver, and hip. One day later, the PET scan confirmed the devastating final blow: she had metastatic lesions in her brain.

Almost immediately, she said, "Aim, I need to put the cats to sleep. I don't want you to have to deal with this. You can't take them, and you won't be able to find a home for them because they need to be together." My mom loved animals, but she loved these two cats desperately. They were her "girls."

I begged her not to put them to sleep. I wanted her to have as much time and happiness with them as possible, and somehow I convinced her to wait. And, honestly, changing my mom's mind was no easy task.

My mom passed away only five-and-a-half weeks later. We watched her lose her ability to drive, her strength, energy, and independence. Every day, she lost another small piece of herself. What she didn't lose was her dignity, her pride, and her ability to speak her mind. She spoke openly about how there is "no blueprint for how to die."

She spent time with us, loved us, and cried and laughed often. She taught us many things, but perhaps the greatest lesson she taught us in those few weeks was that even in the most horrific of circumstances, one can find a reason to get up and get out of bed in the morning. Everyone deserves to be treated with dignity, in life and in death. She modeled true bravery and courage. She was the family matriarch, the family comedian, and everyone's greatest supporter and champion. We miss her profoundly each and every day.

As predicted, we tried endlessly to find a home for her adored cats. We asked everyone we knew, advertised, e-mailed, and called at least fifty nonprofits all over the country, often with no response. What I didn't know was that seventy percent of cats and sixty percent of dogs are euthanized when their owners pass away.

At the time, our beloved fifteen-year-old cat, Chocolate, was being treated at the Veterinary Specialty and Emergency Center. I asked one of the vet techs if she knew of anyone who might take my mom's cats. She suggested contacting Tabby's Place in Ringoes, New Jersey, although she thought they only rescued cats from shelters. I wrote an earnest, heartfelt e-mail to Angela Townsend, the Development Director, telling the story of my mom and her "girls." Angela doubted they would be able to take my mom's cats, but offered to speak with her board of directors. The thought of not being able to find a home for my mom's cats was unfathomable, and we were close to losing all hope. A true miracle happened a few days later when Angela called and informed us that Tabby's Place would be willing to take "the girls."

My husband and I brought them to Tabby's Place. What an amazing facility! Tabby's Place is a cage-free sanctuary that provides impeccable care to cats coming from otherwise hopeless situations. Most of the cats are adoptable, but they may stay there and be cared for their entire lives if not adopted. In a true collaborative effort, volunteers make a huge contribution, and each cat is a cherished member of the Tabby's Place family.

A few weeks later, I was in my living room when Angela called. She asked if I was sitting down. My heart sank: *Was something wrong with one of my mom's cats?* She told me the following story.

A woman had walked into Tabby's Place inquiring whether they had a pair of cats whose owner had recently been unable to care for them. It was not a common question, for sure. The staff informed the woman that they had three sets of cats meeting that description, each coming from very different circumstances. The woman then asked, "Are any of these cats both female? All my life, I have wanted to have two female cats and name them Thelma and Louise!"

As hard as it is to believe, my mom's cats were named Thelma and Louise!

The woman did not know this! How could she have? The odds of this are seemingly astronomical. It was improbable that Tabby's Place would take them at all, doubtful that seven-and-a-half-year-old cats would get adopted, unbelievable that they would be adopted together, and astronomical that the amazing couple who adopted them would be looking for two female cats to name Thelma and Louise!

I hung up the phone with tears streaming down my face and looked up. As I did, I felt my mom say, "You did a great job. I'm so proud of you, honey. I wanted Thelma and Louise to be together in a loving home." Yup, this was definitely my mom's work from up above.

In the blockbuster movie *Thelma and Louise*, the title characters are both strong women, just like my mom. At one point, Thelma says to Louise: "You're not gonna give up on me, are ya?"

This story is about not giving up. I will forever be thankful that somehow I convinced my mom to keep Thelma and Louise with her for those short weeks. A few days before she passed away, I helped lower her to the floor so she could lie with them and say goodbye.

I am forever grateful to the many people who never gave up on us: To Brooke from VSEC for telling us about Tabby's Place. To Angela, for being an actual angel and offering Thelma and Louise a new home.

And to the anonymous couple who opened their hearts and home to give Thelma and Louise their second act.

~Amie Gordon-Langbein

93

Harley and the Angel

You are my cat and I am your human.
~Hilaire Belloc

O n a rainy spring day about ten years ago, there was a knock at my front door. A very small boy stood there holding an extremely small ball of fur under his chin with both hands.

"We can't keep him. My mother said to bring him here because you love cats," the boy said. "If you don't take him, she's gonna give him to the dog catcher."

I looked at the boy's sorrowful eyes and saw his little heart was breaking. I had just rescued two litters of kittens, and my house was currently overflowing. I needed another one like I needed a migraine — but what difference was there between fourteen cats and thirteen? I took the tiny tom from the boy and promised I would find him a good home.

The little tom was barely weaned, but he was a fighter. From his extensive fur and coloring, he looked like a baby Maine Coon cat, which meant he would eventually be a huge tom — if he made it. The problem was that he was younger than the rest of the kittens in the house. He was so small that I could hold him in one hand.

The little guy got along with every animal in the house — kittens, dogs, and grown cats. As the weeks went by, I slowly found homes for all the other "rescues," but at the end of the month, there was no taker for Little Tom. He still had not grown much in size, only in girth and fur. I was just beginning to think he would become a permanent resident of our house when I got a call from a friend.

She asked if I had any kittens left because a friend of hers had just lost his twenty-year-old tomcat and was devastated. He wanted a new cat, but he was — well, how did she put it? "Special. He's sort of rough around the edges." She said that I had to meet him to understand. But if I had a kitten, she could guarantee this man would be the best pet poppa ever. She added, "Don't judge by appearances."

Now, I was curious. I told her to tell her friend about Little Tom. If the kitten was what he was looking for and he could guarantee a good home, I really did not care what he looked like. Since she also rescued animals, I knew she would not recommend him if he was not a viable pet person.

He was set to come see Little Tom the next evening after he got off from work. I was curious. What could be so different about this man?

The questions all ended with a roar in my driveway the next evening. When I came to the door to see what the noise was, a huge bear of a man in biker leathers was walking up the path to my porch. I stood in awe as he approached. He had to be a minimum of 6 feet, 4 inches tall and 240 pounds. His long hair was pulled back in a ponytail, and his beard covered his chest. His arms were a living display of tattoos. He held out his hand, and I shook it tentatively.

"Hi. I'm Jake," he said. "Sara told me you've got a kitten."

I invited him into the house and told him to wait in the living room. I went to get Little Tom, debating whether to go through with this or not.

Everything changed in one second when the tiny tomcat met the giant biker. The man melted like an ice cream cone in July when he took off his sunglasses and laid his blue eyes on the tiny tom. He reached for him, and the little cat virtually flew out of my hands and immediately snuggled in Jake's beard, purring like a motorboat and kneading his paws into the man's chest.

If there was ever love at first sight, this was it. It was probably the strangest pair I'd ever seen, but love knows no reason. We sat down and had some coffee, and Jake told me about his cat who had recently passed away. He went out to his bike and brought in a small cat carrier for Little Tom, and we exchanged e-mail addresses with promises to keep in touch.

Jake named the kit Harley, and sent me photos over the years as he grew into the giant Maine Coon tomcat that I predicted he would be. I could see the cat was healthy and happy.

Then two years ago, I got a call from Jake. He told me that he had a job that took him away from home for long periods of time, and Harley was getting lonesome. Did I have another kitten that could keep the old guy company? Preferably a female?

As luck would have it, one of the feral cats next door had kittens that season, and they were ready for adoption. Two little girls were extremely friendly: a gray who I called Honey Bear and a beautiful, white-and-black Angora girl who I called Angel.

When Jake roared up, it only took one look for him to know that Angel was the one. He scooped her up and told me Harley would love her. He wouldn't be lonesome in the daytime anymore. After promises to send updates, he was gone again, roaring away with his new addition firmly secured in a cat carrier.

He's e-mailed photos of Harley and Angel twice since then. All is well with the two cats and their biker dad.

~Joyce Laird

94

Sushi to Go

Cats tell me without effort all that there is to know.
~Charles Bukowski

"I think our next cat should be a longhaired, black-and-white tuxedo kitty," my wife Judy said out of the blue one day, long before our Maggie left us. Elderly and much loved, our sweet, silver tabby was going to be hard to replace.

"What? Why?" I stroked Maggie's silky head where she lay in her basket, a place she rarely left anymore. I couldn't imagine holding out for a specific type of cat when the time came. I knew whoever it was would need to be longhaired, like Maggie. Shorthaired cats tend to make Judy wheeze. But I wasn't even sure I'd ever met a longhaired tuxedo cat.

She shrugged and said, "I don't know. I just like them."

"Well, we don't need to think about that now," I said, listening to Maggie's faint purr.

Of the two of us, I was the one who required a cat in my life. Judy had come to love Maggie and tolerated the previous cat — an ornery fellow I'd brought to the relationship — but she was happy to live without a cat, too. So it was funny to hear her muse prematurely about our next cat.

I put the conversation out of my mind, thinking, *We'll just find a good one at the shelter when we're ready. One Judy's not allergic to.* That's how we'd gotten Maggie years ago, when she was just a year old. And for now, she still needed all our love and care.

After she died, I was too busy grieving to think about another cat.

"I don't know if we're ready," I told a friend who stopped by about a month after Maggie's death. We hadn't even talked about visiting shelters yet. But she wanted to tell us about a homeless cat she had befriended.

"He's been hanging around our porch all winter," she said. "I can't take him in. We already have too many critters to take care of." With a dog, cat, guinea pig, and flock of chickens—not to mention two young children—she was tapped out. "He's such a nice cat, and we've tried and tried to figure out where he belongs. But no one in the neighborhood has claimed him."

She told me that her kids and husband adored the cat because he was sweet and funny. Both cuddly and playful, she said. "Not a mean bone in his body." The kids had christened him Sushi because he sort of resembled a sushi roll.

"Won't they miss him? Sounds like he's your outdoor cat."

"I think he'd love to live in a house," she said. "He's always sitting on the windowsill and looking in with these big, green eyes. He has the most enormous eyes I've ever seen on a cat." She assured me that her family would be on board because a loving home would be the best thing for Sushi.

"Well, he'd have to pass Judy's allergy test," I said. I remembered our search for Maggie. The long-suffering Judy held cat after cat in the shelter while I fell in love left and right. It took weeks to find one that didn't make her instantly sneeze. "He's longhaired, you say?"

The next Saturday, Judy and I drove over to meet the cat. "Just call 'Sushi-kitty,' and he'll come," our friend had assured us. I started down the path to the back yard, calling "Sushi-kitty, Sushi-kitty."

"Now don't get your hopes up," said Judy for the umpteenth time, settling in on a wicker porch chair.

"Here he comes!" A feline shape had materialized. I saw intelligent green eyes, a crisp white blaze between them. I gasped. Sauntering up the path was a black-and-white tuxedo cat with luxuriant long fur.

I looked up at Judy, who stared down from the porch. "Sushi?"

she said, dumbfounded. "That's Sushi?"

I burst into astonished laughter. "Honey, I think that's the cat you ordered."

The dapper fellow walked up the porch steps, climbed onto Judy's lap, and draped his white paws over her leg as if he'd been there all his life.

"I don't think you're going to be allergic to this one," I said, plopping down across from her and grinning.

She wasn't, of course. Not to this cat, whom she'd seemingly invoked out of thin air.

I call Judy his favorite human now. Whenever she comes home, no matter where he is in the house, he comes running and makes his way onto her lap. He loves me too, of course. But he and Judy have an unshakeable bond because, after all, she called for him. Or maybe he called for her. Who knows?

~Shawndra Miller

95

Kindred Spirits

If purring could be encapsulated, it would be the most
powerful anti-depressant on the market.
~Terri Guillemets

I hadn't worked at the animal shelter long when an old cat, probably around thirteen, arrived. She had been declawed on all four paws, had an odd color in one eye, and a litter-box problem, which was why she was being surrendered to the shelter. This cat was absolutely beautiful, though. We named her Sally.

Sally was a sweet cat from the beginning. I took great pains to make sure she was well cared for. She always had a blanket to lie on and got a special kind of food. She would play sometimes, and that cheered me a little. She got a few looks, of course, but her inability to properly use a litter box always warded people away. Not to mention, she was old. How many more years did that cat really have left? Some days, I worried she'd never see daylight again.

Then one day, a glimmer of hope appeared in the form of an older lady. Her hair was white and her hands were wrinkled, but her eyes shone with such liveliness. She asked immediately about the old cat, never once looking at the others in the room. I'm not sure how she had heard about her, whether she had seen the cat in the paper or a friend had informed her of the feline's precarious situation.

This lady began coming in every day around 3:00 in the afternoon. While at the shelter, she would sit in front of Sally's cage and talk to her. I would occasionally leave the room, finding it rude to eavesdrop, but some days I stayed and listened. She'd tell Sally about her day, and talk about how if she came home with her, she'd have a good life.

Unfortunately, she didn't want to adopt a cat that was old and might not be around long. She worried about the cat's odd eye and other possible ailments, including Kidney failure. It was an understandable concern. My boss decided to get blood work on the cat, which the lady insisted she would pay for. At first, the blood work looked good, but a week later we had no choice but to tell her we had gotten a bad sample. We would have to draw blood again, and it would be at least another week before we had any answers.

I overheard the lady speaking to Sally that afternoon, and I had to leave the room as tears pricked my eyes at the soft, secretive words of one elderly citizen to another. "I know how it feels. I've had to get blood work done a few times myself." Sally blinked lovingly at the lady as she curled in her lap. The lady stroked her almost absentmindedly. "Don't worry. I'm old, too. I know how it feels."

After weeks of tender moments, agonizing waiting and many, many tests, the lady did end up adopting Sally. I secretly worried Sally wouldn't last another year.

A year later, I was proven wrong when the lady returned to the shelter and gave me several photos of Sally, whose name was now Cassie. She still wouldn't use the litter box all the time, but the lady didn't mind. She said a few messes were worth Cassie's company.

She told me she wanted me to know how Cassie was doing since she remembered that the old cat had been one of my favorites. She was right. I had been so concerned that no one would see past that sweet cat's age and her minor issues. All it took was one wise elderly lady to see the potential in another very sweet senior citizen. And just a bit of faith that everything would work out like it was meant to.

~Ashley Ledlow

96

Blue Eyes and Elbows

She clawed her way into my heart and wouldn't let go.
~Terri Guillemets

ate one Sunday evening, I was suddenly captivated by a pair of baby blue eyes! The Siamese cat, Cleo, had such a sweet, expressive face I figured the Petfinder website posting had to be an old one. Surely someone had already adopted her!

But what if she was still available? I had to know for certain.

According to the posting, Cleo was being featured at a Tampa Petco. All through the night, restless and unable to sleep, I counted the eleven long hours until they opened so I could ask about her. Over and over, I returned to look at Cleo's photo on the website — there was just something about those beautiful blue eyes.

When I made the call, a Petco employee gave me the great news that Cleo was still there, but then I was immediately cautioned.

"Cleo may have been spoken for, so I'll need to double-check with Mary, the lady from the rescue agency, who handles adoptions."

I provided my contact information as the waiting game began anew, and tried remaining hopeful while reminding myself that if Cleo had already found her new home, then maybe it was for the best. But I just couldn't get those blue eyes out of my mind.

Fortunately, Mary was prompt in returning my call. "Hi, were you calling about Cleo?"

"Yes! Is she still available for adoption? I hope so!"

When Mary didn't immediately respond, my heart sank. Was I too late? A few excruciating seconds passed as I waited, trying to be patient.

"Oops, sorry, I got distracted there for a minute," Mary laughed. "A kitten I'm fostering was shredding some newspaper. Anyway, yes, Cleo's still available. She's very petite and looks like a Siamese, but has the extra toes of a Hemingway cat."

"A Siamese Hemingway sounds adorable! Ernest Hemingway's home in Key West is the only place where I've seen a polydactyl cat."

"Oh, Cleo's quite special! I saved her and her three kittens in the nick of time just one day before they were to be put to sleep, and the little survivor was quick to show her gratitude," said Mary. "When I brought her into foster care, she not only nursed her own babies, but also four other kittens. At only eleven months old, her life has already been a busy one!"

But Mary also had something else to tell me.

"Listen, I must be honest with you. Cleo was born with misaligned front legs, so she's unable to walk on her toes like other cats."

I was stunned. My husband, Bill, and I had recently lost a beloved cat to an illness. Did we dare take in another with potential medical challenges, only to face heartbreak once more? My questions tumbled out as I tried to understand.

"Can she get around by herself? Will she need to be carried to the litter box and her food bowls?"

"Oh, Cleo's not disabled. She's just different and very adaptable," Mary quickly assured me. "She's learned to walk on her elbows instead of her toes!"

"That's hard for me to imagine," I said quietly.

Mary sighed. "So many people have seen Cleo's photo and were interested at first, until they came to see her in person, watched her walk, and decided not to adopt her. Trust me. She is healthy and very adoptable. All she needs is for someone to believe in her."

I sat quietly, trying to picture the sweet-faced cat with the beautiful baby blue eyes walking on her elbows.

"We understand if you need time to think about it," Mary said kindly. "But in the meantime, if somebody decides to adopt her, I'll have to let her go with them. There are so many homeless animals

we're trying to place."

I promised to call Mary back. After discussing everything with Bill, we were both touched by the story of a tiny cat with the big heart and lots of courage. We decided to give little Cleo the chance she deserved. Within an hour, my mom and I started on the seventy-five-minute trip to Tampa.

In my excitement, I forgot to call Mary to let her know we were on our way.

Mom and I drove down I-4 to Tampa, excitedly talking about Cleo. We wanted to give her a new name that better described her special legs and feet, so we tried out names like "Digit" and "Toes." I'd read that some polydactyl cats have what is known as "mitten paws," with an extra toe attached in a thumb-like appearance, so the name "Thumbelina" also came to mind.

Suddenly, a warning light flared. We were low on gas. After locating a gas station, I looked at my map, only to realize I had made a wrong turn! We needed to double-back. To make matters worse, it had begun to rain.

Rush-hour traffic ground to a halt as the skies opened up with a heavy rainstorm. The afternoon turned into early evening. Cellphone service failed to connect. I was in tears, upset with myself for not contacting Mary before we left home, frustrated for not paying attention to the map. *What if someone adopted Cleo before we got there?*

Finally, the exit sign came into view. We drove into the Petco parking lot and breathed a sigh of relief. As we entered the store, a lady walked past, wheeling a cart.

"I just adopted the Siamese cat," she said proudly, and pointed at the cat carrier nestled inside her cart.

My heart sank. We were too late. Tears rolled down my cheeks. As Mom tried consoling me, a store employee approached and asked if we needed help.

"We drove a long way to see Cleo, but a lady just told us she adopted the Siamese cat," I said, tearfully.

The employee smiled. "Don't worry! She adopted the last of Cleo's kittens, but Cleo is still here!"

We couldn't believe our ears! We followed the employee to a room with cages, all empty except for one.

Mary arrived with a smile and gently placed Cleo on the floor. When those beautiful baby blue eyes met mine, tears fell anew. As the little cat shuffled pigeon-toed on her elbows to joyfully greet us with sweet friendliness, Mom described the scene perfectly by saying that Cleo reminded her of a little girl trying to walk in her mother's shoes.

Cleo didn't protest when I scooped her up and lovingly stroked her special legs. From that moment on, she was ours.

Her large paws resemble catchers' mitts, so we decided to rename her Mitzi, and she never fails to amaze us with her adaptability. There's so much she can do! She can sit by tucking her longest front leg inside her hip to keep from toppling over. She can pluck toys from her toy box and bat them around by swinging her elbows like hockey sticks. She can sit up like a meerkat and daintily nibble treats from an outstretched hand. Most importantly, she can bravely overcome her challenges in her own special way, and she never fails to bring us joy.

~Lisa Faire Graham

97

Tea Cozy

If there were to be a universal sound depicting
peace, I would surely vote for the purr.
~Barbara L. Diamond

looked down at the furious, grey-and-white tabby and sighed. Feral cats never make rescue easy. Whether because of human cruelty or just an instinct to survive, most seem convinced that people are terrible predators who are looking to eat them.

So it was with Chicory. Taken off the street as an adolescent and brought to my home late one night, Chicory was terrified. She crouched under the sink in my bathroom and hissed. She mostly hissed at me, but she also tried threatening the toilet, shampoo bottles, and laundry basket for good measure.

"I hate this part," I said over my shoulder to the rescuer.

The lady nodded and sighed. "Do your best with her. We think she's hopeless."

Packing up the carrier, the rescuer turned to the door and said, "We can always send her to a big, heated barn with other cats, if need be. Some just can't be habituated to humans."

I shook my head and looked back at Chicory. "No, I think we'll be okay." The little tabby smacked at the toilet brush and then hissed as it fell over. "Well, we'll give it a go, anyway."

As soon as the front door closed, I turned to the cat and said, "We are going to get something straight, okay? I'm a vegetarian and in no way interested in putting you in my salad."

There was more hissing and a baleful glare. The look said, "I lick myself all the time, and I KNOW I am delicious. You can't fool me, horrible creature."

Shrugging, I left her alone with a cardboard box, a litter pan, and a small bowl of food. From experience, I knew it was best to give her some space.

The following months proved difficult. Chicory, or Chic as I came to call her, searched out every hiding place available, and then glared up at me from the shadows, with cold fury in her eyes. At the same time, she would anxiously watch my hands for any sign of tin cans. She rather liked those. She knew that I was the "Keeper of the Cans," and she would have to endure my presence to get any of the delicious fish she so prized.

In this, I was merciless. I refused to put down food unless she came close to me. Secretly, I was looking for the opportunity to pet her while feeding her treats, hoping to cement in her mind the maternal role I had taken on. Grooming was something a mother did, and a cat that will accept touch from a human is halfway to accepting that person as a friend.

But Chic was having none of it. As soon as the food was placed in her bowl, she would dart forward, grab it in her mouth, and disappear under the bed, leaving little blobs of salmon behind like a breadcrumb trail.

If I got down on my hands and knees and asked her how her dinner was, she would hiss, mouth full of fish, and retreat farther into the darkness.

"You are not Gretel, you know," I would say. "And I am not the witch, fattening you up for the oven."

There would be no reply, save the sound of smacking lips.

I had to acknowledge that she was a tough case, but I wasn't ready to give up. With as many toys and treats as I could afford, I tried to bribe her to come near me, if only for a few seconds.

"Who's my little sweetie?" I would ask, waving a toy at her. "Who's my little sweetie-girl?" But Chic only eyed my attempts with disdain and turned away.

It was the harsh Canadian winter that came to my rescue. Chic had taken up residence under the bed for warmth and would rarely leave, except for three times a day when the wonderful tin cans were in evidence. Then, braving the chilly air and the scary human, she would creep up to sit just beyond arm's reach, her eyes firmly glued on my face. If I tried to touch her, she would bend away from my hand, her spine a sine wave.

Sighing in resignation one frosty morning, I left her to her breakfast and made myself a pot of tea. Then, realizing I hadn't cleaned the cat box, I put the teapot on my desk and left the room.

When I returned a few minutes later, I found Chic perched on the desk beside my teacup.

"Hey," I said. "Whatcha doing?"

Chic looked at me, but didn't move.

I blinked. Usually, when caught stomping on the computer keyboard or nosing around my notebooks, she would fling herself off the desk and flee to the bedroom, but that day she held her ground.

I took a few steps forward, suddenly worried that something was wrong.

"Chic? Are you okay? Are you hurt?"

Still, Chicory did not move, but only glared at me, her face full of wild ferocity.

Slowly, I approached the desk and stared at her, uncertain what to make of her behaviour.

And then I saw what was happening and had to bite my lips to not burst out laughing.

Chicory had appropriated the hot teapot. She had wrapped her tail around the base and was sitting so that her little feet were pressed against porcelain. Her fluffy chest rested atop the lid, while her tiny belly squashed against the side.

Despite the little space heater that ran night and day, it seemed that the apartment was just too cold for her.

As I smiled, it struck me that my moment had finally come. Hoping I was right, I reached out and brushed my fingers across her ears. Torn between delightful warmth and insistent fear, Chicory sat perfectly still, uncertain as to what to do.

"Sweetie-girl," I said, scratching her chin. "Sweetie-love."

Confusion plain on her face, she studied me, and then, to my utter delight, Chicory closed her eyes and allowed me to pet her. It only lasted a moment, though. In a flash, she was gone.

It was enough.

Each day of the seven-month winter, Chic and I would meet over the teapot. Defiance in every line of her body, she clung to the pot, waiting for the dreadful touch she so feared, but unwilling to leave her wonderful warm spot. At first, she trembled under my hand. But as the days turned into weeks, she began to lean toward me and even purred once.

By spring, after the teapot had lost its allure, Chic and I had developed a morning ritual.

"Who's my sweetie?" I would ask, stroking her chin with one hand while holding a teacup in the other.

"I am," she seemed to say, her eyes half closed. "Yes, I'm pretty sure that's me."

Then one eye would open, and she would fix me with it.

"Remember when you used to want to eat me?"

~Alex Lester

98

Soul Mates

Every life should have nine cats.
~Author Unknown

The cat raised her head and stared at me through bleary eyes, releasing a soft, squeaky mew. She'd wedged her twenty striped pounds into a tiny kitty bed she shared with a small, orange kitten. She was bald from her withers to her tail where her fur had been shaved, and runny gook ran from her eyes and nose. I stroked her head gently as she squeaked again, the smallness of her voice a contrast to the enormity of her body.

The cat dropped her head back into the kitty bed, a soft raspy purr vibrating her white chest. I wasn't in the market for another cat — I already had one, Percy, and a German Shepherd named Tess — but this cat tugged at my heartstrings like I hadn't felt since my Blue-Point Himalayan, Mindi, passed away.

I knew better than to visit the shelter just to socialize with the cats. I can walk into one of those places, visit the dog kennels, and leave empty-handed. The cat room is a completely different story. Homeless, unloved cats bother me in a way no other animal does. I love all animals, and all unloved, abused animals hurt my heart, but there is something about a roomful of unwanted cats.

Maybe it's because in Wyoming it's easier to find homes for dogs. Few people want cats, and no one thinks cats are important enough to pay for the surgery of fixing them to prevent more litters. Cats are considered pests and vermin. They are used for pest control in barns, but otherwise they are overlooked. When I visit the cat room of the shelter, I know the kittens will find homes, and the friendlier adult cats probably will, too. They run to greet visitors who might be potential homes.

But a half-bald, twenty-pound cat with an upper respiratory infection has little hope.

I alerted a shelter employee to the cat's illness.

"I think one of the cats is sick. She has a runny nose and gooky eyes."

The shelter employee checked the cat and sighed, shaking her head sadly. "We'll have to quarantine her."

"Can you tell me about her?" I asked.

"Her name is Puckett. We named her after Wolfgang Puck, the chef, because she's so fat. We found her under a bush, her fur completely matted. That's why she's been shaved. We thought she belonged to someone because she's so big, but no one ever came to claim her."

I didn't think long about it. "I don't know if I can adopt another cat, but can I foster her?" I asked. "She's just so pitiful. I feel sorry for her."

The shelter employee's eyes lit up. "No one's showed her any interest. Would you like to apply to be a foster home?"

I agreed immediately. I filled out the application, interviewed with the volunteer who works with foster homes, and took Puckett home a week later. I had to keep her quarantined because she was sick, and I didn't want her to infect Percy. I kept her in my guest room with a litter box, food, and a water bowl, and I visited her every day. She ate and drank a little, but slept most of her days. Both Percy and Tess knew there was someone new in the guest room, and they both camped outside the room, sniffing and pawing under the door. Sometimes, I could hear Puckett mewing her high-pitched, squeaky meow behind the door, and Percy would respond, yowling in his deep voice. Tess snuffled underneath the door and kept vigil at night, waiting for the time she could meet the new guest.

After four days of isolation, Puckett finally had enough. When I opened the door one morning to feed her and give her fresh water, she pushed the door out of her way and marched out. Her eyes and nose were clear, and her coat was starting to grow back. She looked much healthier than she had when I first saw her at the animal shelter. She stopped to sniff noses with Percy, and satisfied that he was no threat, she stalked over to Tess and sniffed her as well. I held my breath, afraid she might have a problem with dogs. After several moments of sniffing from nose to tail, Puckett marched over to me and flopped on her side, purring and rubbing her head back and forth on the carpet, begging to be stroked.

Puckett, Percy, and Tess became fast friends. Any apprehension I had about adding a second cat to my household disappeared when I saw how easily Puckett fit in. She played with Percy, slept snuggled up to Tess, and shared my bed at night. Puckett and Tess developed a routine, a dance they performed every night, circling the kitchen side by side with Puckett directing the steps. When Tess reached one side of the kitchen, Puckett walked under her nose and turned her around to circle in the other direction. Then Tess would lie down on the floor, and Puckett would dance back and forth in front of her, running her tail under her nose.

Four weeks later, I had to leave town for a week. As Puckett wasn't officially mine, I had to return her to the animal shelter. When I returned a week later, they told me Puckett had fallen ill again and was in quarantine. By then, I decided that the shelter atmosphere was toxic to Puckett. There were too many cats crowded together in a small room, competing for territory, dominance, and attention from the few people they see every day. Some cats stress harder than others, and I could see that Puckett struggled at the shelter. The foster volunteer asked if I wanted to take Puckett home again when she was cured, and I agreed.

When the foster volunteer called me two weeks later to tell me Puckett was recovering, I went to pick her up.

The volunteer didn't even pretend to believe that I only planned to foster Puckett. "You're just going to adopt her, aren't you?"

"Yep," I said.

"It's Buy One Get One Free Month. Do you want this one, too?" She pointed to the cat I held in my arms. I'd picked her up and cuddled her while I waited for Puckett to get vaccinated.

"Sure," I said.

Those shelter employees sure know a sucker when they see one. An hour later, I went home with two cats I never knew I wanted.

I never expected my soul mate to show up in the form of a bald, snotty-nosed, twenty-pound package at the shelter, but there she was, and I've never regretted adopting her.

~Anita Weisheit

99

The Starter Cat

There is something about the presence of a cat... that
seems to take the bite out of being alone.
~Louis J. Camuti

I had broken the news to my children a few days before. Their father and I were getting a divorce after twenty-five years of marriage. The oldest three had not been surprised, and offered their good wishes and moral support. But it had hit my youngest, then only thirteen, pretty hard.

For the next two days, he looked ashen, a sad shadow of his usual cheerful self. But on the third day, I noticed he stood a bit straighter, and there was color in his cheeks again. I asked him how he was doing.

"Better," he replied, with a hint of a smile. He was adapting to the new world order. But, he added, he was trying like heck to find a silver lining in all of this turmoil. And so came the question: "Mom, now can we get a kitten?"

I had raised a family of animal lovers. I had rarely known any time in my life that had not been accompanied by a dog or two. I got my first horse when I was sixteen. I'd had a cat for a pet as a child.

But for the quarter-century I'd been married, a cat had been impossible. My husband was deathly allergic to them. But that was then. Faced with the dissolution of the family unit, the wheels in my honor-student son's head had started to turn.

"You know, honey," I replied. "I think so!" I reined in his enthusiasm almost immediately. We would certainly have to wait until his father was no longer under the same roof, I cautioned. My son took the qualifier in stride. But that didn't mean we couldn't start looking!

I called around to local shelters, inquiring about kitten availability. Nobody seemed to have any. They suggested that I call back in a month or two.

As the formalities of marriage unraveled and my husband moved into an apartment nearby, my son's enthusiasm for a kitten only grew. I finally handed him the newspaper and suggested that he start looking at the classifieds.

He took the advice to heart, and soon afterward ambushed me in the middle of a painting project. A small ad was circled in red. "Mom, would you call this lady about this kitten?" I put the paintbrush aside, pulled off my rubber gloves, and made the call. The woman lived twenty miles away. She had just one kitten left, but another person had already asked for it. If that buyer didn't show, we would be welcome to drive over and take a look.

A few hours later, my husband arrived to pick up the kids to take them out for dinner. My son stayed home with me, ostensibly to keep me company. In fact, he had his eyes on a bigger prize. Twenty minutes after they left, the cat lady called — the other buyer had not shown up. My son could not stop grinning at his good luck.

"I really thought that she might call tonight," he explained, "so I wanted to stay just in case." As we drove, a plastic carrier for the family rabbit in his lap, he was nearly quivering with excitement. I tried to dampen his anticipation. We were "only going to look," and there was no guarantee that we'd bring this kitten home.

Inside, of course, I was praying hard that this kitten would turn out to be a good one.

The kitten was perfect: tiny, friendly, and inquisitive. He was a dynamic, eight-week-old, shorthaired fluffy ball of black with white accents. He had long white whiskers, a white tuxedo front, and white front paws that looked like they'd been dipped in cream. Mottled black and white fur on his hind feet made him look like he was wearing "footsie" pajamas.

We paid for him and raced back to the house, stopping to buy a litter box, some food, and a few cat toys. Then we whisked it all inside and hid the evidence.

Dad dropped off the kids and left, none the wiser. It took him two weeks to catch on. The rest of us, however, were enchanted. We spent the next two days passing the kitten, who we named Smokey, from lap to lap. We watched him leap and pounce, chasing a cat toy with a bell and feathers. Immediately, I hid the Easter tree, festooned with fragile eggs I had blown and hand-painted myself, that traditionally sat in the bay window.

After Easter, the girls returned to college. My older son was occupied with tennis practice and a job, and I went back to the office. I had worried about how my youngest would cope with the loneliness of an empty house during spring break. In fact, he couldn't wait to have the house to himself. It meant that he could play with Smokey all day long without interruptions.

From being a wee, shorthaired bundle of fluff, Smokey grew... and grew... and grew. His white paws, which always seemed oversized, became enormous. The short hair grew out to be a three-dimensional coat of gossamer fluff as soft as goose down, and he shed fur balls the size of tarantulas. He turned into a very big sixteen-pound boy.

When my younger son finally left for college five years later, Smokey became my personal lap anchor. And I let my heart expand to love this perfect, miniature predator, and all the personality quirks that he brought to the table.

What I didn't know when we brought him home was that the adoption of one tiny kitten would open the floodgates for more cats to join the family. First, my younger daughter and her college roommates adopted a kitten. Then my older son brought home a rescue cat of his own. And then my younger son — the one for whom I'd bought Smokey — and his wife adopted a tiny rescue kitten. I can't complain. The kitten they named Finnigan later became the inspiration for my first children's book, *Finnigan the Circus Cat*.

And now, twelve years later, Smokey the "starter cat" is still with me — a fluffy constant through thick and thin. He has outlasted the family dog, the family rabbit, my former car, two other cats, a move from the country to the city, and the motorcycle-riding, cat-phobic boyfriend I kept company with for seven years after the divorce.

Smokey still leaves fur balls the size of tarantulas around the living room. I haven't knitted a stitch in twelve years. And those hand-painted Easter eggs are still in storage.

But at night, when the lights are out and I am about to fall asleep, Smokey leaps to the side of my pillow for one last round of purring, one last reassurance that we're still in this game together. And I think, as I smile and drift off to sleep, that for a "starter cat," he sure has proved to be a keeper.

~Mary T. Wagner

100

The Story of Greta Noelle

Blessed are those who love cats, for
they shall never be lonely.
~Author Unknown

t was Christmas 2009, and we were gathered at my mother's house. My nineteen-year-old son, Levi, and my twenty-year-old nephew, Alex, spotted her first. "Grandma, there's a cat in the snow outside your window."

My mother replied, "I'll bet it's that black cat that's been around. I think it belongs to the neighbor."

Alex shook his head and explained that what he was seeing illuminated by the kitchen light was a small, lighter-colored cat. At that, I was drawn out of my seat. By the time I had opened the door, the cat was ready to come in. I crouched down low to scoop her up in my hands and held her at face level as we stared at one another.

She was lightweight and cold, with ice hanging off her matted, longhaired calico coat. I knew almost immediately I was in trouble. There was something about her sweet face and floppy ragdoll body that spoke right to my heart.

I brought her closer to my chest for warmth. By the time I turned around with her in my arms, eight of my family members were standing in the kitchen observing. At the time, my sister was working for a local pet-treat operation, and I was temporarily fostering a cat named Precious for the Berkshire Humane Society. I had asked my sister to bring some of her company's treats with her on Christmas for me to purchase and bring back to Precious, so I quickly thought to ask someone to grab them and put a few in the palm of my hand. They disappeared so quickly it gave me a sense of how starved the little bundle in my arms was.

By now, my mother had gone into her cupboard, retrieved a bowl of cat food, and handed it to me. I knelt down with the little stray and placed her on the floor in front of it. I was surprised that my usually loud, Greek family was being so quiet and still. While she ate, I petted her and wondered, *What now?* I looked up at the faces of my family and saw my seventy-five-year-old aunt who lives alone. I thought, *Even though she's never had a pet, she lives alone, and her home would be an ideal spot for this cat to land.* Then I looked over to my sister and said to myself, *If our aunt doesn't work out, then my sister would surely take this cat since she lost hers not that long ago.* And I thought, *If that doesn't work out, then my mother will take her since her cat is fourteen years old, and she might like to have another one.* Then there was my niece, Rachel, who was already begging my brother to take the cat home to New York.

In my book, this cat had a home. Or four.

But it turned out that no one wanted the stray, so I ended up taking her home. The encounter with Precious did not go well, so I kept them separated for a few days while I figured out a game plan. I called all the area vets and shelters. I took a picture of the Christmas stray and made a poster to hang in various locations near my parents' home and in vet offices. I brought her to Allen Heights Veterinary Hospital — the only vet that offered to look her over for me — and they shaved off the mats tangled in her fur and told me she seemed sweet.

And then, because I was fostering Precious for another month or two, and I never received any calls from the ads I placed, and both cats were obviously under duress, I surrendered the stray to the same Berkshire Humane Society I was on assignment with.

Over the next few weeks, I became a frequent visitor to the Berkshire Humane Society to see how the sweet, longhaired calico was doing. I noticed things about her each time I went that I hadn't noticed the time before. For example, half of her nose was orange, and half was gray. Her back legs were pure white and looked like fluffy bloomers. And she had a shorter tail than most cats.

The volunteers there would allow me into the back room where she was being treated medically and let me take her out of her cage. She would let me hold her and rock her, loudly purring the whole time. Her disposition was very sweet.

Finally, on one of my visits, a volunteer told me that the now-healthier stray was almost ready to be moved to a cage in the viewing room in hopes that someone would adopt her. I went home sad that day. The next day, I called and asked if they would keep her in the back room for a little longer. They agreed.

Over the next day or two, I reasoned that I might not have surrendered her had she and Precious gotten along. I considered that I was all set up with a foster-cat room in my house and could easily bring her home to that room, keeping Precious in the main part of the house until she could go back to her owner. It didn't take much to convince myself that living in one room for a while would be better than being confined to a cage. And last, I remembered that for the past four months, while I had been home on medical leave from my middle-school teaching job recovering from back surgery, I wished many times that I had a cat at home to keep me company.

So I marched into the Humane Society a few days later and purchased my own Christmas kitty back for $125.

What I didn't realize then was that she would be my savior eighteen months later when I was tangled up in a bicycle accident. I sustained a traumatic brain injury that caused another eight months out of work while I found my footing again. She became the answer to one of my prayers during that time, giving me comfort, company, warmth, joy, purpose, and familiarity at a time when nothing much in my life seemed recognizable.

For a few months after she came home to live with us, she did not have a name. A perfect cat needed a perfect name, I rationalized. There were many offerings from friends and family members, with Noelle being at the top considering she was discovered on Christmas.

None seemed to work for me. Finally, my husband returned home from work one day and found her sitting on the top step waiting for him. I heard his booming, deep voice say, "Greta! What's happening?" And that was that. She is Greta Noelle.

~Stacia Giftos Bissell

101

Mission Impossible

What greater gift than the love of a cat.
~Charles Dickens

Dad's behavior changed radically after Mom, his wife of sixty-five years, died. He exhibited behaviors that were totally uncharacteristic of the man we knew. He was depressed and disoriented.

His grown children lived a thousand miles away, so my sister and I convinced him to get a cat. He had always been an animal lover. We knew with his mobility problems he would need a pet service, but that was not a problem in the retirement community where he lived.

Dad said he would name the cat Joe. Male or female, the cat would be Joe.

Since I was the semi-professional animal person of the family, I was elected to find the right cat for Dad. I had therapy dogs, so I knew what it took for a successful pet partner for an elderly man. This assignment would be a challenge since I lived far away from Dad's home in San Antonio, Texas.

Being somewhat uncoordinated, very clumsy, and sometimes a bit loud, Dad was not the ideal cat parent. I made a list of requirements: shorthaired, laid-back, not needy, very confident, friendly, adaptable, and strictly indoors. The retirement community had strict rules about pet behavior, so the cat would have to be somewhat obedient. Dad had one request: The cat needed to be big.

My challenge narrowed down to almost impossible. Being a

champion of rescue adoptions, I started contacting San Antonio area rescues and shelters in late September. My target adoption date was Thanksgiving, as I would be visiting Dad then and I could get him set up with a cat.

Responses came in immediately. My animal-professional side asked the hard questions. I did not want a cat that hid under the bed or would be easily intimidated by wheelchairs, walkers, and the like. If the cat was afraid of my father, it might be disastrous to Dad's emotional wellbeing. It would be very hard to find a shelter cat that would work.

None of the available rescue cats seemed right. They were small, a bit flighty, longhaired, too old, indoor/outdoor, and on and on. I refused to lower my standards.

Thanksgiving was quickly approaching, and I started getting worried. Surely within 200 miles of San Antonio there had to be a cat for Dad. Unfortunately, I knew the wonderful cat I wanted was not the kind of cat that would be given up to a shelter.

I was scheduled to arrive the Monday before Thanksgiving, and I was batting zero. I was very frustrated. I did not want to disappoint my dad. He had perked up at the prospect of getting a cat.

I searched shelters in my area, thinking I could transport the cat to Texas, but I still could not find the right cat.

Four days before my Thanksgiving visit, I received an e-mail from a San Antonio shelter. They said they had a cat that might work.

I called and asked, "Is he big?"

"Yes."

"Is he friendly?"

"Yes, very."

"Has he been an indoor cat?"

"Yes, he is declawed."

I am not a fan of declawing, but this was almost a sure sign the cat had lived exclusively indoors. The cat named Butterscotch had been surrendered by his owner because her elderly mother was coming to live with her, and her mother was allergic to cats.

I arrived in San Antonio late Tuesday morning and went to the shelter early that afternoon.

I walked into the shelter's large cat room, which held about fifty cats scurrying about. I was intimidated. A tall countertop sat in the center of the room, and I walked up to it to get a good view of all the cats. I could not imagine how long it would take a cat to acclimate to this situation.

A mammoth tan-and-white beast of a cat leaped up on the counter, got in my face, and demanded attention. "That's him," said the shelter lady.

"I'll take him," I responded instantly as I stroked his friendly face. There was no question. He was not intimidated in this lively place. He was very outgoing, and he was huge. I had brought a cat kennel for transport, but had to borrow one of the shelter's dog kennels, as Butterscotch's twenty-two pounds would not fit into the normal cat-sized kennel.

I took the cat to Dad's and tested my assumptions. I placed the kennel in the living room and opened the door. We sat and watched. Almost immediately, he came out of the kennel, walked a few steps, plopped down, and stretched out smack dab in the middle of the living-room floor. He took in his surroundings.

"There is Joe," I said. Outgoing was an understatement; Joe was brazen.

Dad leaned forward in his wheelchair and studied the cat.

I grabbed a cat treat and patted my leg. "Come, Joe." The cat rose and trotted over to me.

For some unknown reason, I said, "Sit." The cat sat.

"Very good," said Dad.

Unbelievable! I thought.

Dad and Joe got along famously. Joe played and entertained. He loved to watch the birds Dad fed on the patio. Best of all, Joe turned Dad around. He healed from severe depression and learned to accept life as it was for him. He became the elderly version of the dad we all knew.

When Dad moved to assisted living, Joe went too, and adapted well. He became the entertainment on Dad's hall wing. Nurses, aides, administrators, and housekeepers all knew and loved Joe. When someone knocked on Dad's door, Joe ran to welcome them. He continued to be the constant in Dad's life. Our phone calls always included Dad sharing Joe's antics.

At ninety-one, Dad's time on earth ended. My two sons, a nurse, and Joe and I were at his bedside when he peacefully passed from this world. The day after Dad died, the pet sitter snapped a photo of Joe lying in Dad's favorite chair. Joe looked disheveled, disoriented, and depressed.

The pet sitter and several of the staff expressed interest in providing Joe a new home, but Dad's grown kids could not let Joe go anywhere but to one of our homes. He was part of our family. Joe traveled north to live at my brother's house. He and his wife already had three cats, but there was plenty of room for another.

Of course, Joe adapted well. He learned to chase shadows up and down the stairs, nap on the sofa, play in the snow, and watch birds from the upper deck. Realistically, we could have left Joe in a good home in San Antonio. Emotionally, we could not. He had done so much for our dad. We not only owed Joe, we honored him.

~Gretchen Allen

Meet Our Contributors

Gretchen Allen teaches people about the wonderful natural and cultural resources of our country. In her free time, she visits the elderly with her therapy dog, plays with her two non-therapy dogs and three cats, enjoys riding her horse, and paints and draws.

Catherine Ancewicz joined a creative writing ministry at her church in 2013. Since then she has written several stories about her personal experiences, as well as working on her first novel. In addition to writing, she enjoys reading, calligraphy, and pen & ink drawings. She lives in South Florida near her daughter and family.

Janet Anderson-Murch received her Master's degree in Social Work from the University of Maine in 2010. She is a child and family therapist in central Maine and enjoys spending time with her husband and adult children, as well as taking care of sheep, horses, and chickens at their family farm.

Mary Ellen Angelscribe is an international pet columnist and author of *Expect Miracles* and *A Christmas Filled with Miracles*. Animal Planet's *Must Love Cats* features her swimming cats. Read heartwarming, inspirational and miracle pet tales with educational tips on Facebook's Pet Tips "n" Tales. E-mail her at Angelscribe@msn.com.

Kiva Arne lives in beautiful Southern Oregon. She enjoys writing, hiking, skiing, kayaking, reading, going on adventures, and talking about herself in the third person.

A mother of three (James, Evangeline and Isabelle), **Mary Fluhr Bajda** received her Bachelor's degree in education, with honors, from Marywood University. She is currently working as Director of Religious Ed and Music for St. Ann's Church in Shohola. E-mail her at marybajda@ gmail.com.

Barbara Bartocci has authored nonfiction books and magazine articles for major women's magazines. She is also a professional speaker who specializes in women's groups and church groups. She is the devoted owner of Emily the kitty cat.

Gretchen Bassier works as a home healthcare aide. She is the proud aunt of Julia, Tommy, Landon and Brady. Gretchen writes short stories and novels, and hopes to start a nonprofit to benefit feral cats. Visit her blog for writing resources, reviews, story links and more at astheheroflies.wordpress.com.

Jill Berni is an avid animal lover and history buff. In addition to her years volunteering at a cat shelter, she also volunteered with her dog, Sunny, in a therapy dog program. She continues her volunteer work to this day. Jill lives in Toronto with her husband, Fred, and their two dogs. She plans to write short stories in the future.

Stacia Giftos Bissell lives in western Massachusetts. She studied mathematics at Wells College in New York and has a Master of Education degree. She has three grown children and spent much of her career as a teacher until sustaining a brain injury from a bike accident. She is now a public speaker, consultant, advocate, and educator for brain injuries.

Jan Bono writes a cozy mystery series set on the southwest Washington coast. She's also published five humorous personal experience collections, two poetry chapbooks, nine one-act plays, a dinner theater play, and has written for magazines ranging from *Guideposts* to *Woman's World*. Learn more at JanBonoBooks.com.

Freda Bradley is a professional historian. Her research business, Bridging History, centers on historic and genealogical research in the Appalachian regions of West Virginia and Eastern Kentucky. She is currently writing a book on some of the Dutch settlers during the pre-Revolutionary settlement of West Virginia.

Josh Burnell is a screenwriter, podcaster and code monkey living in Los Angeles with his wife and disapproving cat. He can often be found writing, alphabetizing his horror movies and attending rock shows. He's a big fan of Meat Loaf, the singer and the food. E-mail him at josh@dontbeyourself.com.

Eva Carter is a freelance writer whose background includes a career in the entertainment field and then finance. Photography and traveling are a few of Eva's interests.

Tori Cleaves and her sister **Nikki** live in southwest Florida. Tori is a full-time nanny for two young girls. Nikki is currently in school to become a Physical Therapy Assistant. They both love running marathons, sports, church, and working with all types of animal rescues. Duma still remains a very important part of their lives.

M. Scott Coffman recently had a story published in *Chicken Soup for the Soul: Best Mom Ever!* He and his wife, Diana, currently have two cats, and are thinking about adding a dog to the mix. They live in Auburn, IL.

Joanne M. Copeland is a dressage trainer and riding instructor in Ontario, Canada. She lives with her husband, three cats, and a palomino horse named Silver. Joanne volunteers at the SPCA and practices the ancient Japanese martial art of Iaido. E-mail her at jcdressage@gmail.com.

C. E. DeRosier lives in Wisconsin with her boyfriend and their cat.

She loves to spend her time writing, reading, playing video games, and watching movies. She can often be found with her nose in a book or at a local thrift shop.

Sharon Rene Dick works as a legal assistant at a major corporation and teaches third grade Sunday school. She is a published author of flash fiction and children's short stories. She is currently writing a Christian young adult speculative novel.

Lisa Napell Dicksteen has been a freelance writer and editor for many years. She also teaches secondary English. A native New Yorker, Lisa lives in Colorado with her husband, son, and Bear, their Lab/Pit mix. She is happiest reading, writing, or helping others with their writing. E-mail her at LMNEditorial@msn.com.

Lissa Dobbs is an avid book junkie who loves fantasy above all else. In her spare time, she enjoys reading, writing, crochet, and making dollhouse miniatures.

Ryan Dube received his Bachelor of Science in engineering from the University of Maine in 1998. He lives with his wife and two daughters in Indiana. Ryan enjoys blogging, hiking, camping, and writing. He is working on a memoir detailing his weird and wonderful life. E-mail Ryan at rdube02@gmail.com.

Jessica Edwards fell in love with literature as a child and was always seen with her nose in a book. Her love for reading has blossomed into a passion for writing. She spends sunny days exploring the Pacific Northwest. She enjoys hiking, canoeing, and seeking out new adventures.

Meredith Engerski lives in Noblesville, IN, with her husband Kevin, daughter Victoria, and two Huskies. An avid runner and competitive triathlete, she is also a contestant for Mrs. Indiana 2017. Meredith is the Practice Manager of both Cottage Animal Hospital and Allisonville Animal Hospital, where Pete has his full-time position as Greeter.

Donna Fawcett is the former creative writing instructor for Fanshawe College in London. She is an award-winning author, singer, songwriter, freelance magazine and newspaper writer and a national conference speaker. Her novels *Rescued* and *Vengeance* won "Best Contemporary Novel" in The Word Awards. Learn more at donnafawcett.com.

Award-winning author of contemporary and fantasy romances under the nom de plume Lizzie T. Leaf, **L.M. Fillingim** has a degree from the "School of Life." She is working on non-romances with a WWII historical theme and a women's fiction novel, both under her real name. When not writing, her focus is family, cooking, and travel. E-mail her at lizzietleaf@comcast.net.

Leanne Froebel received her Associate degree in nursing in 2003. She lives in Marshfield, WI, with her cats Linus, Rider, and Vinny (who always makes her smile) and some Betta fish. She enjoyed showing her cats in the past and volunteering with Vinny in pet therapy. E-mail her at leanne.froebel@yahoo.com.

Kathleen Gemmell loves playing with written words. Currently penning for online sites and magazines, Kathy is also a storyteller, an animal welfare proponent, a psychology buff, and a connoisseur of fine pizza.

Dawn Smith Gondeck and her husband ditched pursuing the typical "American Dream" and travel the U.S. full-time in an RV. She blogs about their travels, RV life, and misadventures. She has even written a few short stories on the side. You can keep up with their travels at randombitsoftrialanderror.com.

Amie Gordon-Langbein is a mother, wife, daughter, sister and friend, who also happens to be a personal and professional development coach and physician. She is known for her big heart and vibrant spirit. She loves connecting to people and their stories, and believes we each have a story longing to be told.

Lisa Faire Graham received a Bachelor of Science degree from the University of Florida, and is married with two stepchildren. After retiring from a twenty-year career with Lockheed Martin and Northrop Grumman, she is now an award-winning fine art photographer, who enjoys writing, traveling and spoiling Mitzi, her rescued Siamese.

Heather Harshman is an estate planning attorney, law professor, writer, and mother of two little ones. In between her jobs and being a mom, she posts short stories and stories about faith and traveling on her blog at HeatherHarshman.com. She enjoys bicycling, traveling, gardening, and camping with her family.

Christy Heitger-Ewing, an award-winning writer and columnist who pens human interest stories for national, regional, and local magazines, has contributed to over a dozen anthologies and is the author of *Cabin Glory: Amusing Tales of Time Spent at the Family Retreat* (www.cabinglory. com). She lives with her husband, two sons, and two cats.

Marilyn Helmer is the award-winning author of over thirty children's books and her short stories, poetry and articles have appeared in numerous magazines and anthologies in Canada and the U.S. Her penchant for entering writing contests has resulted in success with short adult fiction as well.

Marijo Herndon's stories appear in numerous *Chicken Soup for the Soul* books as well as many other anthologies and publications. She enjoys writing from her home in New York where she lives with her husband, Dave, and two rescue cats, Lucy and Ethel.

Susan A. Hoffert is currently crafting a collection of stories, inspired by her chickens, about empty nests, rediscovering faith and starting anew. Her work has appeared in *Fall: Women's Stories and Poems for the Season of Wisdom and Gratitude, Words & Other Worthy Endeavors*, and *The Skunk River Review*.

David Hull is a retired schoolteacher who now spends his time reading, writing, gardening, watching too many reruns of *Everybody Loves Raymond* and spoiling his nieces and nephews. You can contact him at Davidhull59@aol.com.

Kristin Ingersoll is an Instructional Designer, E-Developer, and frustrated writer. Kristin grew up in Indiana stealing turtles from the local creek as pets until she finally got a hamster. She now has two cats that despise, and take every opportunity to terrorize, each other. But she loves them both EQUALLY!

Jeffree Wyn Itrich has been writing since childhood. Trained as a journalist, she works in health communications. Jeffree lives in San Diego with her husband and two feisty female felines who make her laugh. When she's not writing, she quilts by hand. E-mail her at jeffreewyn@gmail.com.

Robin Jankiewicz graduated from Whitman College in Walla Walla, WA. Eventually, she and her husband moved out of Gizmo's apartment building into a house in Los Angeles, CA, where they keep busy as they raise their two boys. Eventually, they plan to adopt a rescue cat.

Marilyn June Janson received her Master of Science degree, *cum laude*, from Long Island University in 1980. She is the author of *Recipe for Rage*, a suspense novel, and two chapter books: *The Super Cool Kids Story Collection* and *Tommy Jenkins: First Teleported Kid*. Now, she is writing a YA novel. E-mail her at janlitserv@cox.net.

Janny J. Johnson was once the mom in a Pacific Northwest household with a husband, four children, an exchange student, five cats, two dogs, fish, a bird, and a bunny. She publishes in regional parenting magazines, writing about those days. Learn more at jannyjjohnson.com or on Facebook under Janny J. Johnson.

Stephanie Jones-McKee is thirty-one and has been writing since middle school. As a stay-at-home mom, she enjoys many hobbies including homeschooling her daughter, writing, drawing and painting.

Leslee Kahler has degrees in biology and history from Eastern University and Villanova University. She is married with two children and lives on a small farm with horses, ducks, and eight rescue cats. When she was a child, her father worked for an oil company, requiring the family to live overseas.

Joyce Laird is a freelance writer living in Southern California. Her features have been published in a wide range of consumer magazines and she is a regular contributor to both *Woman's World* and the *Chicken Soup for the Soul* series. Joyce is also a member of Mystery Writers of America and Sisters in Crime.

Deborah Lean is a mixed media artist and writer living in Ontario, Canada. A retired nurse and grandmother of seven, she enjoys family and numerous creative pursuits, including reading, writing, painting and crochet.

Ashley Ledlow is an aspiring writer who dedicates most of her time to the local Humane Society where she works with the many stray cats who reside there.

Brenda Leppington works as an Information Manager within the healthcare system. Brenda enjoys travelling, and sharing stories of the many animals that have been a part of her life. Brenda is a previous contributor to the *Chicken Soup for the Soul* series.

Alex Lester is a writer from Toronto, Canada. She lives with two rescue cats and a vivid imagination.

Charlotte A. Lewis is a retired accountant and former teacher. She has nine grandchildren, five greats, and two great-great-grandsons.

Charlotte has many varied interests; she likes to read, write, knit, sing, and travel. She is a self-published author of several novels ranging from historical fiction to mysteries.

Deb Louis teaches criminal justice and women's studies courses online for Eastern Kentucky University and lives in the mountains of western North Carolina, an ideal setting and inspiration for her writing. Her current cat, Blue, supervises her work and keeps the house and grounds free of undesirable critters.

Lisa Mackinder received her Bachelor of Arts degree at Western Michigan University. A freelance writer, she lives in Portage, MI, with her husband and rescue animals. Besides writing, Lisa enjoys photography, traveling, reading, running, hiking, biking, climbing, camping, and fishing. E-mail her at mackinder.lisa@yahoo.com.

Joshua J. Mark is an editor/director and writer for the online history site "Ancient History Encyclopedia." His nonfiction has appeared in *Timeless Travels* and *History Ireland* and his short fiction in *Litro* and *Writes for All*, among others. He lives with his wife Betsy and daughter Emily in upstate New York.

Carmen Marlin, a Mississippi resident, worked twenty-three years in banking before graduating *magna cum laude* in nursing (BSN) from University of Memphis. Semi-retired, she is a board member of a Humane Society, vet tech at a spay clinic, and volunteer on the state disaster relief team. She enjoys traveling and scuba diving.

A practical joke appearance years ago led to discovery and encouragement by Minnie Pearl of the Grand Ole Opry for professor **Kathryn J. Martin** to leave college to become a full-time inspirational speaker/writer as herself and as country humorist, Miz Maudie. Author of two books, Martin lives in Ponchatoula, LA.

Tim Martin is the author of *Fast Pitch*, *Rez Rock*, *Somewhere Down the*

Line: *The Legend of Boomer Jack*, *There's Nothing Funny about Running*, *Summer with Dad*, and *Wimps Like Me*. Tim has completed nine screenplays and is a contributor to twenty-four *Chicken Soup for the Soul* books.

Evelyn Shamay Mayfield, seventy-seven, took her high school education and information from libraries and worked her way from bookkeeping to freelance writing to technical writing. Evelyn self-published *The Busy Person's Prayer Book*. These days, she focuses on inspirational, uplifting works, and enjoys crafts, cats, and volunteer work.

Keturah Mazo, a current college Communication instructor and former English teacher, holds a Master of Science in Computer Education from Florida Institute of Technology. She shares two children, two dogs, and one grand cat with her husband, Richard. She likes to garden, read, and swim as well as writing essays.

Candis Y. McDow graduated from the University of West Georgia in 2012 with a Bachelor's of Science degree. She majored in Mass Communications and minored in Creative Writing. She is twenty-eight years old and lives in Atlanta, GA. Candis enjoys writing and is currently finishing her memoir.

Angela M. Meek is a single mom, Christian, and freelance writer. She has a Bachelor's in Psychology and an interdisciplinary Master's in Writing/English/Psychology. She is the editor of *Edify Fiction* magazine and is currently working on her first contemporary Christian romance novel, *Finding Ruth*, due out later this year.

Shawndra Miller lives in Indianapolis and writes about community resilience and personal transformation for publications like *Farm Indiana*, *Acres USA*, and *Confrontation* magazine, as well as at shawndramiller.com.

Michelle Close Mills' poetry and short stories have appeared in magazines, anthologies and several volumes of the *Chicken Soup for the Soul* series. Michelle resides in Florida with her husband and is owned by two cockatiels and two rescue kitties. Michelle's work can be found at authorsden.com/michelleclosemills.

Terilynn Mitchell is a licensed veterinary nurse who has cared for animals for thirty-two years. She has an uncanny knack for finding animals in need of help or redemption, focusing on those with special needs. In 2018 Terilynn will publish a collection of short stories about the ups and downs of her animal rescue work.

Sam Moorman earned a BA in Journalism and MA in Creative Writing from San Francisco State University. Following a career in construction, in retirement he now writes and is on the board of SouthWest Writers.

Jessica L. Moran has a Bachelor's of Arts degree from Monmouth College in History, and a minor in Anthropology. She currently lives in central Illinois with her husband, her Mini-Schnauzer and a cat. Jessica enjoys writing fantasy/romance and creating complex characters.

Diane P. Morey is now retired and lives in Rhinelander, WI, as a caregiver for her mother. She has a BS degree in Dental Hygiene from the University of Louisville and an MS degree in Education. She now has a beautiful gray cat with long, soft fur named Shadow. Diane also plays flute in the Rhinelander Area Community Band.

Connie Biddle Morrison grew up near the Eastern Shore of Delaware, delighting in the smells of the salty marshes. She attended the University of Delaware and, with her husband and two children, moved to north central Florida in 1978. She has been published in e-zines, print magazines, and is working on a memoir of her younger years.

Megan Nelson is an avid reader and writer. Two English degrees, a well-used library card, and a book-buying habit back up this claim. She is married to her high school sweetheart and is the proud mom of two wonderful boys. A cat and a fish complete the household.

Connie Nice is a wife, mother, and grandmother from Washington State. Writing for thirty-plus years, she loves creating children's stories and has one adult novel currently in the final editing stage. She shares her passion for history, nature, travel, family, and faith through the written word. Read her blog at connienice.com.

Sharon F. Norton is a retired teacher. She has a Master's degree in Reading and a BA degree in Elementary Education. She lives in colorful Colorado. Sharon enjoys traveling, reading, and writing.

Connie Kaseweter Pullen lives in rural Sandy, OR, near her five children and several grandchildren. She earned her BA degree at the University of Portland in 2006, with a double major in Psychology and Sociology. Connie enjoys writing, photography, and exploring nature. E-mail her at MyGrandmaPullen@aol.com.

Karen Reeves is an aspiring writer who plans to do a series of children's books on misadventures with animals. She is the mother of two grown girls and currently writes inspiring horse stories on her blog at horsetalesnstuff.com. Karen is self-employed, doing administrative work for various clients.

Sandy A. Reid continues to live in St. Louis, MO, where she and her husband share their home with two rescued dogs and another "Mama Kitty," one who decided to stay this time and who is now spayed.

Melissa Richeson mothers four loud and lovable boys on the coast of Florida. She is a freelance writer with credits in *The Washington Post*, *Florida Today*, and *Thriving Family*, among others. For leisure, she enjoys paddle boarding, going to Disney World, and playing soccer with her kids.

Rosemarie Riley was born in Australia. In 1990 she moved to the U.S. with her American born husband and two sons. She is a member of SCBWI and The National Writers Association and has been published in anthologies and magazines. She enjoys photography, reading, and traveling. E-mail her at rosemariejriley@yahoo.com.

Marti Robards resides in scenic Colorado. Her first published story, "The Loneliest Number", appears in *Chicken Soup for the Soul: Random Acts of Kindness*. Marti's passions include church, family, reading, writing, crafts, and gardening. She and her daughter, Mary, are co-owners of an Etsy Shop: ReverieCraftsLLC.

Sue Ross, it is rumored, so enjoyed uttering her first word that she said it twice; "Author! Author!" Finding stories in everything she does, Sue revels in language that lifts and inspires. With a BA degree in English, she is completing her first novel, *Polanski's Treasures*. E-mail her at kidangel@me.com.

Stormy Corrin Russell, at twenty-five years old, is a three-time novelist. She currently lives in Pennsylvania, hard at work writing books and teaching middle-schoolers. Her award-winning novels are available from any major retailer. E-mail her at stormy.russell001@gmail.com. She loves hearing from readers!

Melanie Saxton is a writer who has raised a daughter and several adopted cats and dogs in the Lone Star State. She is contributing editor for five Houston-based magazines and edits books for emerging authors. In her spare time Melanie is slowly, but surely, pursuing a Master's degree in mass communication.

A retired Marine officer, **Dirk B. Sayers** published his first novel, *West of Tomorrow*, in 2015. His next project, *Through the Windshield, Drive-by Encounters with Life*, will be available in paperback and ebook formats in November 2017. Read Dirk's unredacted comments on 21st Century life at dirksayers.com.

Troy Seate has written everything from humor to the macabre, and is especially keen on stories that transcend genre pigeonholing. His short stories and memoirs appear in numerous magazines, anthologies, and webzines. Troy lives in Golden, CO, with the dream of enjoying the rest of his life writing and traveling.

April Serock earned an MA degree in writing from Seton Hill University. She lives with her husband and son where she can see the sun rise over the Appalachians each morning. She's published romantic short stories with *Woman's World* magazine and writes nonfiction articles for money-saving websites.

Brittany L. Stalsburg lives on the Connecticut shoreline with her husband and their starter child, Candy the cat. In addition to writing, Brittany is also a public opinion researcher and strategist and the owner of the firm BLS Research & Consulting. She holds a Ph.D. in Political Science from Rutgers University.

Laurel Standley is a scientist and author of self-help nonfiction and dystopian and historical fiction. Laurel received her Ph.D. in Chemical Oceanography from Oregon State University and her Master's in Urban Affairs and Public Policy from the University of Delaware. She lives in Portland, OR, with her beloved cat Ellen.

Diane Stark is a wife, mother of five, and freelance writer. She is a frequent contributor to the *Chicken Soup for the Soul* series. She loves to write about the important things in life: her family and her faith. E-mail her at Dianestark19@yahoo.com.

L.A. Strucke received her BA degree from Rowan University. She's a frequent contributor to the *Chicken Soup for the Soul* series, *Guideposts* magazine and other publications. Her hobbies are painting, piano, and songwriting. She dedicates Boo's story to Hermione, Jadzia and Geneviève. Follow her at lastrucke.com.

B.J. Taylor says Red was one of those soulful, head-butting, tug-at-your-heartstrings cats. B.J. is an award-winning author whose work has appeared in *Guideposts*, many *Chicken Soup for the Soul* books, and numerous magazines. Reach B.J. through her website: bjtaylor. com and check out her dog blog: bjtaylor.com/blog.

Stephen Taylor is a writer and graphic artist living in the San Francisco Bay area. He volunteers as a cat care partner with a local animal shelter, and he rents himself out as a cat-sitter to a small but loyal stable of clients. He has contributed stories to three *Chicken Soup for the Soul* books.

Miriam Van Scott is an author and photographer whose wide-ranging credits include children's books, magazine articles, television productions, website content and adult nonfiction works. Her latest series, *Shakespeare Goes Pop!*, offers a modern take on the Bard's classic works. Learn more at miriamvanscott.com.

Ann Vitale lives on 150 acres in northeast Pennsylvania. Her degree in Microbiology from the University of Michigan made her a fan of Big 10 football. Living in a farmhouse in Michigan after graduation gave her stress relief from her work and furthered her love of all animals, except woodchucks. E-mail her at ann.e.vitale74@gmail.com.

Mary T. Wagner is a former journalist who changed careers at forty by going to law school. A mother of four and a grandmother, Wagner lives in southeastern Wisconsin, where she draws creative inspiration from nearby Lake Michigan and from her pets. A family kitten inspired her new children's book, *Finnigan the Circus Cat*.

Pat Wahler is an award-winning writer and proud contributor to thirteen *Chicken Soup for the Soul* books. She draws inspiration from family, friends, and the critters who tirelessly supervise each moment she spends at the keyboard. Discover more about Pat's new projects at PatWahler.com.

Anita Weisheit is a writer, reader, librarian, and dreamer of new worlds. Books, animals, and dancing are her favorite things. She lives in Wyoming with her three obnoxious cats and neurotic German Shepherd, whose antics star in her weekly blog.

Sheri Zeck enjoys writing nonfiction stories that encourage, inspire, and entertain others. Her freelance works include stories for *Guideposts*, *Angels on Earth*, and numerous *Chicken Soup for the Soul* books. Sheri writes about her faith, family, and adventures of raising three girls at sherizeck.com.

Meet Amy Newmark

Amy Newmark is the bestselling author, editor-in-chief, and publisher of the *Chicken Soup for the Soul* book series. Since 2008, she has published 140 new books, most of them national bestsellers in the U.S. and Canada, more than doubling the number of Chicken Soup for the Soul titles in print today. She is also the author of *Simply Happy*, a crash course in Chicken Soup for the Soul advice and wisdom that is filled with easy-to-implement, practical tips for having a better life.

Amy is credited with revitalizing the Chicken Soup for the Soul brand, which has been a publishing industry phenomenon since the first book came out in 1993. By compiling inspirational and aspirational true stories curated from ordinary people who have had extraordinary experiences, Amy has kept the twenty-four-year-old Chicken Soup for the Soul brand fresh and relevant.

Amy graduated *magna cum laude* from Harvard University where she majored in Portuguese and minored in French. She then embarked on a three-decade career as a Wall Street analyst, a hedge fund manager, and a corporate executive in the technology field. She is a Chartered Financial Analyst.

Her return to literary pursuits was inevitable, as her honors thesis in college involved traveling throughout Brazil's impoverished northeast region, collecting stories from regular people. She is delighted to have come full circle in her writing career — from collecting stories "from the people" in Brazil as a twenty-year-old to, three decades later, collecting stories "from the people" for Chicken Soup for the Soul.

When Amy and her husband Bill, the CEO of Chicken Soup for the Soul, are not working, they are visiting their four grown children.

Follow Amy on Twitter @amynewmark. Listen to her free daily podcast, The Chicken Soup for the Soul Podcast, at www.chickensoup. podbean.com, or find it on iTunes, the Podcasts app on iPhone, or on your favorite podcast app on other devices.

About Robin Ganzert and American Humane

Robin Ganzert, Ph.D. is a bestselling author, radio host, television producer, animal lover and CEO of American Humane. American Humane is the country's first national humane organization committed to ensuring the safety, welfare, and wellbeing of all animals. For more than 140 years, American Humane has been first in promoting the welfare and safety of animals and strengthening the bond between animals and people. American Humane's cutting-edge initiatives are always first to serve, whenever and wherever animals are in need of rescue, shelter, protection, or security.

Under Dr. Ganzert's leadership, American Humane has been named a "Top-Rated Charity" by CharityWatch and achieved the prestigious "Gold Level" charity designation from GuideStar. Dr. Ganzert was recently awarded the Global CEO Excellence Award as the top CEO of an animal welfare organization, and she was recognized by Brava as a top female CEO in Washington, DC.

A familiar face to millions of Americans from her frequent TV appearances and the highly watched Hallmark Channel's *American Humane Hero Dog Awards*, she also hosts a new podcast, *Chicken Soup for the Soul Presents Loving Animals*, which mixes practical expert pet advice with guest appearances by some of America's best-known pet lovers from the movies, music and sports. She is also the author of

Animal Stars: Behind the Scenes with Your Favorite Animal Actors, and has two new books coming out soon. Robin has appeared on NBC's *Today Show, ABC World News Tonight, Fox & Friends, On the Record with Greta Van Susteren*, and other local and national television programs.

American Humane is first to serve animals around the world, ensuring their safety, welfare and humane treatment—from rescuing animals in crisis to ensuring that animals are humanely treated. The best known program is the "No Animals Were Harmed®" animals-in-entertainment certification, which appears during the end credits of films and TV shows, and today monitors more than 1,000 productions yearly with over 3,400 production days with an outstanding safety record. American Humane's farm animal welfare program ensures the humane treatment of over a billion farm animals, the largest animal welfare program of its kind. And recently, American Humane launched Humane Conservation, an innovative initiative ensuring the humane treatment of animals around the globe in zoos and aquariums.

Continuing its longstanding efforts on strengthening the healing power of the human-animal bond, American Humane spearheaded a groundbreaking clinical trial that provides scientific substantiation for animal-assisted therapy (AAT) in the treatment of children with cancer and their families.

To learn more about American Humane, visit americanhumane.org and follow it on Facebook and Twitter. To subscribe to the weekly podcast, *Chicken Soup Presents Loving Animals with Robin Ganzert*, visit iTunes and Google Play to have a new episode automatically downloaded every week.

Thank You

We owe huge thanks to all of our contributors and fans, and to their fascinating felines. We loved your stories about your cats and how they enrich your lives. We could only publish a small percentage of the stories that were submitted, but we read every single one and even the ones that do not appear in the book had an influence on what went into the final manuscript.

We owe special thanks to Jennifer Quasha, who read the thousands of stories submitted for this book and helped us narrow them down to a few hundred finalists. Susan Heim did a masterful job editing the first manuscript.

Associate Publisher D'ette Corona continued to be Amy's right-hand woman in creating the final manuscript and working with all our wonderful writers. Barbara LoMonaco and Kristiana Pastir, along with Elaine Kimbler, jumped in at the end to proof, proof, proof. And yes, there will always be typos anyway, so feel free to let us know about them at webmaster@chickensoupforthesoul.com and we will correct them in future printings.

The whole publishing team deserves a hand, including Maureen Peltier, Victor Cataldo, Mary Fisher, Ronelle Frankel and Daniel Zaccari, who turned our manuscript into this beautiful book.

Sharing Happiness, Inspiration, and Hope

Real people sharing real stories, every day, all over the world. In 2007, *USA Today* named *Chicken Soup for the Soul* one of the five most memorable books in the last quarter-century. With over 100 million books sold to date in the U.S. and Canada alone, more than 250 titles in print, and translations into nearly fifty languages, "chicken soup for the soul®" is one of the world's best-known phrases.

Today, twenty-four years after we first began sharing happiness, inspiration and hope through our books, we continue to delight our readers with new titles, but have also evolved beyond the bookstore with super premium pet food, television shows, podcasts, positive journalism from aplus.com, and licensed products, all revolving around true stories, as we continue "changing the world one story at a time®." Thanks for reading!

Share with Us

We all have had Chicken Soup for the Soul moments in our lives. If you would like to share your story or poem with millions of people around the world, go to chickensoup.com and click on "Submit Your Story." You may be able to help another reader and become a published author at the same time. Some of our past contributors have launched writing and speaking careers from the publication of their stories in our books!

We only accept story submissions via our website. They are no longer accepted via mail or fax.

To contact us regarding other matters, please send us an e-mail through webmaster@chickensoupforthesoul.com, or fax or write us at:

Chicken Soup for the Soul
P.O. Box 700
Cos Cob, CT 06807-0700
Fax: 203-861-7194

One more note from your friends at Chicken Soup for the Soul: Occasionally, we receive an unsolicited book manuscript from one of our readers, and we would like to respectfully inform you that we do not accept unsolicited manuscripts and we must discard the ones that appear.

Chicken Soup for the Soul.

My Very Good, Very Bad Cat

101 Heartwarming Stories about Our Happy, Heroic & Hilarious Pets

Royalties from this book go to
AMERICAN HUMANE ASSOCIATION
EST. 1877

Amy Newmark
Foreword by Robin Ganzert
President and CEO, American Humane Association

Paperback: 978-1-61159-955-8
eBook: 978-1-61159-255-9

More frisky, fun

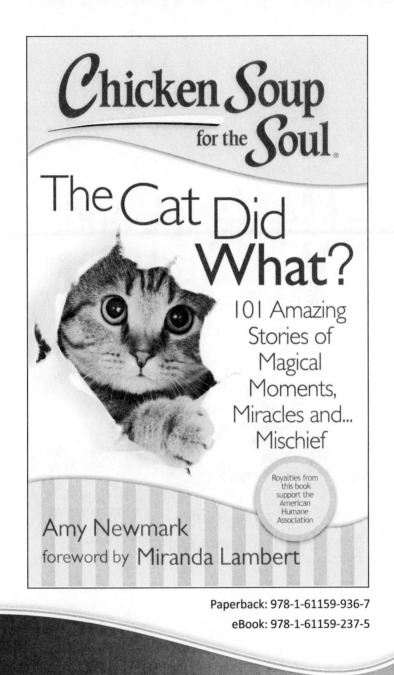

Chicken Soup for the Soul.

The Cat Did What?

101 Amazing Stories of Magical Moments, Miracles and... Mischief

Royalties from this book support the American Humane Association

Amy Newmark
foreword by Miranda Lambert

Paperback: 978-1-61159-936-7
eBook: 978-1-61159-237-5

feline friends

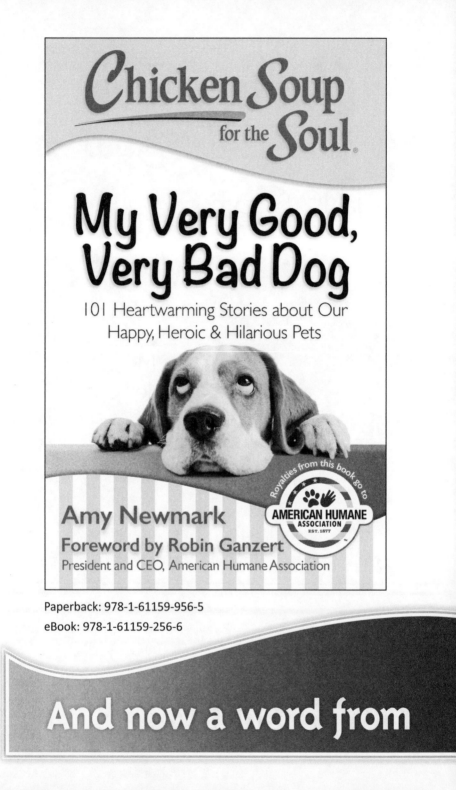

Paperback: 978-1-61159-956-5

eBook: 978-1-61159-256-6

And now a word from

Chicken Soup for the Soul

The Dog Did What?

101 Amazing Stories of Magical Moments, Miracles and... Mayhem

Royalties from this book support the American Humane Association

Amy Newmark

foreword by Miranda Lambert

Paperback: 978-1-61159-937-4
eBook: 978-1-61159-238-2

the canine companions

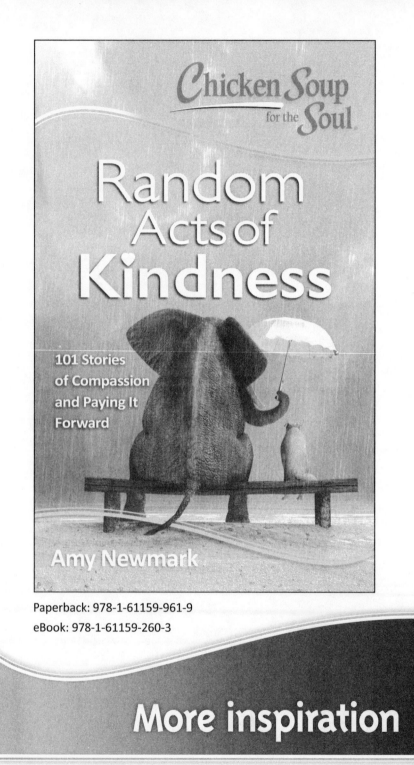

Paperback: 978-1-61159-961-9
eBook: 978-1-61159-260-3

More inspiration

Chicken Soup for the Soul®

Think Possible

101 Stories
about Using a
Positive Attitude
to Improve
Your Life

Amy Newmark
& Deborah Norville
Journalist and Host of *Inside Edition*

Paperback: 978-1-61159-952-7
eBook: 978-1-61159-253-5

and positive thinking

Chicken Soup for the Soul

Changing lives one story at a time®
www.chickensoup.com